THE
WAY
OF THE
BOUNDARY
CROSSER

www. walkingstick. org

To Sarah
with blessings for clarity,
depth, meaning, wisdom, health,
and a lotta lotta fun.

THE
WAY
OF THE
BOUNDARY
CROSSER

AN INTRODUCTION
TO JEWISH FLEXIDOXY

GERSHON WINKLER

JASON ARONSON INC.
NORTHVALE, NEW JERSEY
JERUSALEM

This book was set in 12 pt. Souvenir by Alpha Graphics of Pittsfield, N.H.

10   9   8   7   6   5   4   3   2   1

Library of Congress Cataloging-in-Publication Data
Winkler, Gershon, 1949–
    The way of the boundary crosser : an introduction to Jewish Flexidoxy / by Rabbi Gershon Winkler.
        p.   cm.
        Includes index.
        ISBN 0–7657–9986–3 (alk. paper)
        1. Judaism—Essence, genius, nature.   2. Judaism—Doctrines.
    3. Rabbinical literature—History and criticism.   4. Spiritual life—
    Judaism.   5. Jewish way of life.   I. Title.
BM565.W54   1998
296.3—dc21   97-25800
                                                                 CIP

Manufactured in the United States of America. Jason Aronson Inc. offers books and cassettes. For information and catalog write to Jason Aronson Inc., 230 Livingston Street, Northvale, NJ 07647.

If the contents of the Torah were meant to be taken literally,
you and I could have composed a much better book.
But if it is indeed inspired by the Creator,
then just as God is infinite, so is the word of God infinite,
imbued with meanings that transcend any one particular interpretation.
It is upon us to drink from the word not as from a limited chalice
but as from an eternal wellspring,
and to find ever-fresh meaning in it for each of our life situations.
Therefore, if you read scripture and it does not speak to you directly,
know that it is not the word of God.
You can then walk away from it clean and naive,
or you can stay with it, dialogue with it, wrestle with it
until it unfolds its meaning for you personally,
until it reveals its mystery.
The Torah will not carry you anywhere unless you engage it,
unless you look beyond its external narratives and internal verbiage,
unless you probe its soul, and then the soul of its soul.

Adapted from the second-century teaching of
Rabbi Shimon bar Yochai
in *Sefer HaZohar, Bamidbar* 152a

I dedicate this book to my beloved
Lakme Batya Elior,
whose enrichment of my life
knows no bounds.

Contents

1

The Boundary Crosser

For some of us, both religious teaching and practice, as they have been taught and modeled to us, seem to create a tension between our personal sense of aliveness and rightness and the relationship we seek with our Creator and our tradition. In this book, we will focus on non-"party line" lessons that preceded the more institutionalized, one-size-has-to-fit-all form of Torah we have now across the denominational board. We will also examine some radical and daring interpretations and decision-making processes that rabbis of past generations engaged out of their understanding of Torah and *halachah* as a means, not an end, to Jewish spiritual aliveness. Through these teachings, we hope to find ways in which each of us—our level of practice and learning notwithstanding—can find in Judaism both personal relevance and spiritual fulfillment without self-negation or self-compromise.

The use of the term "orthodox" in this book does not apply to Orthodox the movement, but to orthodox the mindset, which is shared by all of the denominations in Judaism, even the most "progressive." Orthodoxy is a tendency that unfolds gradually following the transformation of an inspiration into a "movement," religious, political, or otherwise. The Hasidic movement, for example, was founded by the eighteenth-century Rabbi Yisroel Baal Shem Tov, who preached spiritual openness and religious flexibility. Yet, over the past two centuries, it has evolved into a movement as rigid and as unbending as the very movements to which Hasidism had originally been a reaction. The same has occurred with the so-called liberal movements of Judaism—Reform, Conservative, and Reconstructionist. Each has gradually shifted from the fluidity that first inspired it to a rigidity of established "standards" that now define it, and the violation of which could cost a rabbi her or his pulpit. Each has, in its own way, then become orthodox.

Not that orthodoxy is wrong or bad. For a lot of people, it is right and good. For a lot of other people, however, it has been a turn-off, a significant factor in their having become alienated from their own heritage. The Jewish establishment has been blaming Jewish disinterest on intermarriage and assimilation when, in fact, these are the *consequences* of alienation. Alienation, in turn, is a consequence of ignorance, and ignorance is a consequence of disinterest, and disinterest is a consequence of our failure to teach our people the broader spectrum of Judaism that shines far beyond and above the particular party-line versions they have been fed by every denomination, respectively. Rabbi Zalman Schachter-Shalomi calls this "freeze-dried Judaism": We need to add a little water and stir it up, he says, or else it will remain inaccessible and unpalatable to many (lecture, Cong. Har Shalom, Fort Collins, Colorado, 1993).

Judaism is much bigger than the "organized religion" form in which it is known to most, the learned and the unlearned alike. Hidden away in the thickness of its forest are the individual trees and grasses that compose it but that are nonetheless swallowed up by it and, therefore, largely unnoticed by its visitors. We need, therefore, to wade through the muck of religious dogma and codes to recover a sense of what the message of Judaism is for the individual, the community, and the planet. We need to recapture the long-lost sense of what the bottom line of the Jewish spirit path is so that we can widen the openings for those who have found its passageways too narrow. What we will then discover is that Judaism offers us so much more than what it asks of us: "Open for me so much as the eye of a needle, and I shall open for you so wide that entire caravans of wagons and coaches can pass through with great ease" (*Shir HaShirim Rabbah* 5:3).

At this writing, the Jewish world is being graced with yet another infant movement, Jewish Renewal, which began with the intention of creating ever-so-broad passageways for Jewish entry and participation, and which has reinvigorated the spiritual aliveness of both affiliated and unaffiliated, touching the hearts of participants across all the denominations. It is to be hoped that Jewish Renewal will endeavor to remain just that—Jewish renewal—and not suffer the same fate as the other denominations in becoming so organized and religiously correct that it becomes just one more variation of the same theme. It is almost inevitable that when an idea becomes a movement, it stops moving; it creates boundaries for itself and etches into finite stone what had once been the fruit of an infinite spirit. Life is too short to have the standards of one age or community define the reality for another age or community. Yet, religion is set up so that we spend significant chunks of our precious lifetime fixated on its dogma, practice, and outright threats, to the sorry neglect of developing our own personal, independent takes on God and life. Why should the ancient teachers, the founders of our faith, have been allowed the thrill of achieving their own understanding of the meaning of life, while we latter-day *schmeggegs* remain stuck with their take on it all and with whatever offshoots have sprouted from their ideas over the centuries?

However, the ancient rabbis remind us that part of the fault lies with us, that we certainly should engage in nurturing the kernels of personal revelations that are seeded in each of us, meditating on our perceptions of life and wrestling with the teachings of the past that forged our mindset in the present. The third-century Rabbi Abba taught that the Torah, for instance, is called the Torah of Moses (Malachi 3:22) only because he labored over it, and that "any person who engages the Torah, in the end it gets named after them" (*Yalkot Shim'oni* on Malachi 3:22). As the thirteenth-century Rabbi Moshe ben Nachmon (Ramban) wrote about his disagreements with some of the religious legal rulings of his "superior" predecessors: "I will not be for them like a donkey, eternally hauling their books. I will explain their teachings and study their ways, but when my perception does not correspond with theirs . . . I will then decide according to what my own eyes are seeing, and will do so with legal confidence. For the Creator grants wisdom in every generation and in every period, and will not deny goodness to those who are sincere" (from his introduction to *Sefer HaMitzvot L'HaRambam*, as quoted in Rabbi Abraham Joshua Heschel's *Torah Min HaShamayim*, Vol. 2, intro., p. vi; similar sentiment expressed by Rabbi Jacob Emden, in the eighteenth century, in his introduction to *Mor U-K'tziah*). "In every generation," wrote the thirteenth-century Rabbi Meir M'iri, "permission is granted to the insightful one and to the student of Torah, to bring to the surface a whole new understanding of the teachings of the Torah, whether this new insight be applicable to him personally or to his disciples, or even for the entire generation of his time, or even for future generations of other times . . ." (*Bet Ha-B'chirah, hakdamah*, p. 24).

> In everything that one might study of nonspiritual matters there can be nothing new about it. One will then only be exploring and discovering that which already existed from the time of the creation of the world. But in studying Torah one will always be discovering new meanings, as is taught in the Talmud (*Eruvin* 54b): "It is written in Proverbs 5:19, 'Her breasts will satisfy you each time'—this means that just like a suckling child will find fresh flavor each time the child nurses at the

breast, so, too, will one who pores over the teachings of the
Torah always discover fresh meanings."
Eleventh-century Rabbi Shlomo ben Yitzchak (*Rashi*) on
Ecclesiastes 1:9

It is undoubtedly this attitude of the Jewish sages through
the ages that made Judaism unique in that, unlike most other
movements, as it expanded it also flexed, so much so that the
original textual wording of its scriptures, while revered with all
due respect, often got liberally interpreted and reinterpreted,
sometimes way out of context, in order to "support" innovative teachings that addressed more pragmatically the situational
needs of subsequent generations. The most fundamental underlying principle, in other words, remained not the *words* of the
Torah, but the *intentions* of the Torah. And those intentions,
in turn, were based on the ancient Jewish understanding that:
"Her ways are ways of pleasantness and all her paths are of
peacefulness" (Proverbs 3:17).

Therefore, when circumstances arose whereby peacefulness
or pleasantness was threatened by the status quo of a particular religious injunction or practice, or by communal or global
upset, the rabbis rose to the occasion and turned the religious
institution upside-down and inside-out. Even the scriptural verse
they employed as permission to shake traditional foundations
appears at first to be interpreted radically out of context to
imply the complete opposite of its original meaning. Taught
the second-century Rabbi Natan: "It is written, 'It is a time to
do for God because they have voided Your Torah' (Psalms
119:126)—this means that at times one needs to void the
Torah in order to do for God" (Babylonian Talmud, *Berachot*
54a). Rabbi Natan was looking for scriptural support in favor
of a decree by the sages that people ought to pronounce the
sacred name of God when greeting each other in the street
even though the Torah forbade pronouncing the holy name
יהוה haphazardly (Exodus 20:7). The promotion of peace
between people, however, took precedence over religious
injunction.

Interestingly, there was no dire need for Rabbi Natan to have twisted the psalmic verse out of its context, because the sages had already found straightforward scriptural precedence to support their view. The patriarch Boaz, for example (tenth century B.C.E.), is described as greeting a group of field workers with "יהוה be with you," and they, in turn, responded with: "May יהוה bless you" (Ruth 2:4). Did Rabbi Natan then toy with the verse "There is a time to do" and twist it out of its context unnecessarily? No, explain his contemporaries, his interpretive maneuver was necessary as a fundamental principle underlying not only the decree of the sages of his time, but also the custom of the people of Boaz's time to greet one another with the holy name (Babylonian Talmud, *Berachot* 63b). His teaching, then, was a foundation principle underlying Judaism in general—past, present, and future—and reflecting again the ancient Jewish bottom-line barometer of the rightness or wrongness of religious practice: "Her ways are ways of pleasantness and all her paths are of peacefulness." Explained Rashi: "At times we nullify the words of the Torah to act for God. So, too, for one to inquire about the well-being of another person [by greeting them with the holy name] is actually the will of God, for it is written, 'Seek out peace and pursue it' (Psalms 34:15). It is therefore permitted to dissolve Torah and do what appears to be forbidden" (on Babylonian Talmud, *Berachot* 54a).

"Appears to be forbidden," writes Rashi, because the spirit of the law supersedes the letter of the law, and the spirit of the law opts for the promotion of human harmony over religious injunction. "See how great is peace," taught Rabbi Yehudah the Prince in the second century, "that even if we worship idols but there is peace between us, then God says, 'I won't judge them for it since there is peace amongst them'" (*B'reishis Rabbah* 38:6). In this light, the "out-of-context" interpretation of Psalms 119:126 no longer seems so radical or misinterpretive. "It is written, 'It is a time to do for God because they have voided Your Torah'—this means that at times one needs to void the Torah in order to do for God." In other words, when it becomes apparent that we have neglected the spirit of the law, then it is time to "do for God," which means to override the God *word* with the God *will*. As the thirteenth-century Ramban writes: "At first, the Torah says 'You shall keep God's commandments and statutes and testimonies that God has enjoined you to do' (Deuteronomy 6:17), and then it adds, but also in matters about which God has not commanded you shall you set your heart and mind to 'do what is right and good in the eyes of God' (Deuteronomy 6:18), for the Creator loves what is right and good. This is very important" (Ramban on Deuteronomy 6:18).

Another example is what the sages did to the scriptural verse "You shall not render a false opinion during a trial in order to please the majority opinion" (Exodus 23:2), which got reinterpreted to also mean that when there is a dispute about an issue of the application of religious law, one should follow the majority opinion (Babylonian Talmud, *Hulin* 11a). Why did the teachers twist this one out of context, too? Because times were changing, disputes over the oral traditions and laws became widespread, and the people were confused and splintered. For the sake of harmony, the rabbis instituted a rule that when a bunch of teachers are arguing over a law, we establish the final ruling according to the majority opinion, with the presumption that the majority opinion will best represent that which is most pragmatic for the majority of the people. Again, the "play on words" interpretation is not that far out of place: "Do not follow the majority toward evil endeavors, but do follow the majority toward *good* endeavors" (Babylonian Talmud, *Sanhedrin* 2a).

Nonetheless, minority opinions were never discounted altogether, and they were recorded alongside the final rulings of the majority opinions. As the Talmud teaches: "Why do we record the opinions of the minority when, after all, the final rulings follow the opinions of the majority? So that in the event a rabbinic court sees the need to apply in their rulings the opinions of the minority, they will have a precedence from which to draw their verdict" (Babylonian Talmud, *Edios* 1:5 and *Tosefta Edios* 1:2). Comments the twelfth-century Rabbi Shimshon ben Avraham (*Tosefot Shants*): "And even though the opinions of the minority were not accepted by the early ones, and the majority did then not rule according to them, still, if in a future generation a majority will see the need to apply the opinions of the earlier minorities for their time and situation, the law becomes then like their ruling. For the Torah of Moses was taught with many perspectives rendering something impure and with just as many perspectives rendering it pure . . . 'and all points of view are the words of the living God'" (referring to a teaching in Babylonian Talmud, *Hagigah* 3b). There will always arise situations in which vetoed opinions find their place of application, wrote Rabbi Jacob Emden (*Siddur Rav Yaakov Emden, Hilchot Yoledet*).

> Said Rava (fourth century) to his disciples: "If a decision of mine shall ever come before you and you find yourself in disagreement with it, do not nullify it without first consulting me. If I can defend my ruling, I will do so, and if I cannot defend it, I will retract it. After I die, do not nullify any of my rulings, but neither shall you draw conclusions from them for questions arising from similar situations that may arise. Do not nullify my decisions because if I were alive I could perhaps defend them. And do not draw conclusions from them for similar situations that may arise because the individual judge should only decide based on the perceptions of his own eyes."
>
> Babylonian Talmud, *Bava Batra* 130b

The liberal flexidoxic play with which the ancient rabbis interpreted the so-called absolute word of God in the Holy Scriptures, whether for homilies or for religious legal rulings, reflects the intimate and comfortable relationship the Jewish people had always enjoyed with their Bible, with their rendition of the God word. This sort of interpretive freedom, which may seem to some like *chutzpah*, was to the Jews the next logical step in their perception of the Creator as friendly and compassionate and therefore not oblivious to the human situation, even when its needs "clashed" with the prophetically revealed God word. The *experience* of Revelation, it was understood, was but a fleeting snapshot, an intersection of human experience and the will of God as perceived in a particular moment or age by a mortal prophet or teacher. But the *content* of Revelation, Judaism reminds us, is not to be laminated in an album, void of any sense of continuity and aliveness. Rather, the God word, no matter when it is heard and no matter who hears it and transmits it, is a glimpse only of what is *starting in that moment* to pour through to us, but it is not the whole of it or the last of it in any sense. The Torah, taught the fourth-century Rabbi Avin, "is an incomplete image of Heavenly Wisdom" (*B'reishis Rabbah* 17:7). Wrote the fifteenth-century Rabbi Joseph Albo:

> It is not necessarily so that a God-ordained religion is not subject to change for a particular people, for even though the revelatory knowledge is unchanging as is its Giver [God], nonetheless it is quite possible that change would occur in the realm of the recipient [people]. For it is within the perfection of every producer to harmonize his product in correspondence with the nature of its recipient, and to adjust the product in accordance with any changes that might take place in the realm of the recipient. And this does not necessitate any change in the nature or intent of the producer. It is analogous to a physician who at first may forbid certain foods to the patient and administer a specifically designed program to which the patient must adhere with utmost strictness. But then, as the patient improves, the physician will permit that which was forbidden, and will alter the program and diet that he had originally prescribed. The physician's knowledge does not undergo any changes in this process, for he knew from the very beginning that his program of healing would undergo adjustments as the patient progressed. In a like manner, it is not out of any flaw in the divine nature that God did not prescribe at the very beginning a conduct that would suffice for

all times. For when God gave the Torah, God knew then that this particular mode of conduct would suffice for the duration of a specific period accorded by the Divine Wisdom for the preparation of its recipient and for the adjustment of their nature toward the receiving of yet *another* mode of conduct, even though these changes had not been revealed to humanity earlier. . . . And although there may then arise issues which contradict the earlier modes, this was already intended by God at the very onset. And as it would be inappropriate for a physician to prescribe rich foods such as bread, meat, and wine to those who have just recuperated as well as to small children and suckling infants alike, whose digestive tracts have not yet developed sufficiently for the absorption of such foods, likewise would it have been inadequate for the Giver of the Torah to have given a mode of conduct equally applicable to all times, for both beginners and experienced alike. Rather, it is befitting that the mode should change in accordance with any changes that might occur in the nature of the recipients.

Sefer Ha-Ikarim 3:13

The people of the book, then, always perceived the God word as fluid, as dynamic. After all, it originates in the Infinite, and is therefore more like a seed than a final product, more "like wheat from which to derive fine flour, or like flax from which to create fine garments" (*Tana D'Bei Eliyahu Zuta*, Ch. 2). It is not the final word. No one party in a relationship has the last word. And as Judaism sees the Creator as being in relationship with Creation, the final word lies in the mutual dynamics of that relationship: "Even the celestial court engages God in dispute over *halachah*" (Babylonian Talmud, *Bava Mezia* 86a).

The nature of Judaism is therefore best described in the original name for its adherents, Hebrews, or *ivrim* (e.g., Genesis 14:13, 39:14, and 41:12; Jonah 1:9), which means "those who cross boundaries," because so intrinsic in the Jewish people is the crusade for the aliveness of the human spirit that they daringly crossed spirit-hindering boundaries not only when they were imposed upon them by other religious systems, but even when they were imposed upon them by their *own* religious system. The term *chutzpah* may be popular slang these days, but to Judaism it has remained an essential backbone of its theology since its very beginnings. And it is important to examine those beginnings in order to get at the long-entombed kernel of a Judaism that was once flexidoxic and fluid.

More than 3,700 years ago, the ancestral mother and father of the Jewish people, Sarah and Abraham, lived as well-acculturated members of their country's citizenry. They lived in Ur, the homeland of their parents, in the great Valley of Shin'ar, a mighty kingdom with a mighty king named Nimrod. They appeared no different from the next woman or man in their society. They fit in, they blended well, they made no waves. They were part of the majority.

Then one day they "crossed over."

Abraham and Sarah decided to defy the status quo of a civilization and belief system that meshed less and less with who they were becoming. They dared to speak their minds and share their ideas with anyone who would listen. They dared to risk the dreaded fate of getting flung into the smoldering furnace of Kasdim, which consumed anyone who departed from the path of the mighty god-king Nimrod (*B'reishis Rabbah* 38:19). They dared to toy with the consequences of having to leave behind what had been their heritage, their ancestry, their tradition, their "proper place in the world," banished to the exile of uncertainty. They dared to penetrate the invisible barriers of a tight culture that had successfully kept its followers in line for centuries through cultic terror and physical intimidation. And, from then on, they and their descendants would remain a minority wherever they went, a living threat to those who held their way of life to be the only true and absolute way, to be uncrossable.

Abraham and Sarah were a couple of independent thinkers whose inner voices told them that the givens of life weren't all they were cracked up to be. They also professed the heretical idea that one ought to seek alternatives if one's personal aliveness was being suffocated by one's friends, family, culture, religion, or environment, and that the Creator could be related to without the intervention of lifeless idols or the mediation of celestial bodies (Rambam in *Mishnah Torah, Hilchot Avodah Zarah* 1:3). They shared their convictions openly and freely, threatening the cozy state of things as they were; as a result, they were persecuted and ultimately thrown out of the country (*Eliyahu Zuta* 25:2; Ramban on Genesis 11:28). Abraham's father, too, was exiled along with his rabble-rousing son, and though he intended to take the family all the way to Canaan, he went only as far as Harran (Genesis 11:31), the place of his ancestors, which enjoyed a close resemblance to and relationship with his hometown of Ur (Philip Biberfield, *Universal Jewish History*, Vol. 2, p. 203). Terach was not able to release himself completely from the mindset with which he had been reared. He had, after all, served as a high-ranking commander in the army of Nimrod (*Sefer HaYashar* 11:15) and had enjoyed an elite quality of life until his son and daughter-in-law started to make waves. But even in Harran, where the fugitive family had been welcomed, Abraham and Sarah resumed their public teachings about rightness, charity, and justice, and about their humanistic take on God. This time, however, rather than getting themselves kicked out, they drew a substantial following (Genesis 12:5). But just as Terach found it difficult to leave the region of his ancestry, Abraham, too, hesitated to leave his father's homeland; perhaps out of guilt, perhaps out of a sense of allegiance, of loyalty to family (*B'reishis Rabbah* 39:7). On the other hand, Sarah and Abraham yearned for some other place, yet undefined, where they could not only plant their convictions, but also nurture them to fruition. Harran was not the place; it was too much like Ur.

Then one day, out of the blue, the voice they had initially heard as their own personal yearnings was augmented by the voice of the Creator. This voice gave them the extra push they needed in order to take the frightening step of leaving behind everything that was familiar to them, to cross the boundaries established by others for their reality grid, and to embark upon a blind search for a definition of life that would be truly theirs and that would foster for them a fresh sense of the very aliveness they felt had been slowly ebbing from them in Ur as well as in Harran.

The voice they heard on that fateful day was unlike any other voice they had known in their religious upbringing. It was the voice of the Great Mystery, the mystery of every question they had ever pondered about the wonders of nature, the intrigue of beauty, the meaning of being, the origins of the universe. Ah, the Great Mystery, they had often sighed, resigned that these were questions that could not be wrestled with amid the tensions and fears that hung heavily over the Valley of Shin'ar. These were rather questions to be asked in the freedom and tranquility of the undisturbed desert to the south; in the silence of the open-ended wilderness beyond the land of the Chaldees; in the gentle, almost melodic breeze that swept through their modest home each day around twilight. This time the voice did not sing; it spoke. And it was no longer the sound of the question that they heard blowing in the wind that day; it was the sound of the answer. It was the sound of the *One Who said let there be and there was* (Psalms 33:9). And they accepted it as the authentic voice of the Creator because it identified itself not as the God of demand, but as *El Shaddai*—the God of nurturance (Exodus 6:3), literally: the Breast God.

The Great Mystery, which all along had been a silent, imaginary, but encouraging partner in their heart yearnings, now became real and spoke to them, and said exactly what they needed so much to hear: "Go to your self, away from your land, and away from your birthplace, and away from the house of your parents—to the land that I will show you" (Genesis 12:1). The eighteenth-century mystic Rabbi Zushya of Annopol intepreted the directive as follows: "First, get yourself out of your country. That means the dimness you have inflicted upon yourself. Then, get yourself out of your birthplace. This means out of the dimness that your mother inflicted upon you. After that, out of the house of your father. This means out of the dimness that your father inflicted upon you. Only then shall you be able to go to the land that I will show you" (Martin Buber, *Tales of the Hasidim: The Early Masters*).

And so they picked up their belongings, gathered their livestock, assembled those who had been inspired by their *chutzpah*, and crossed over the forboding psychic barrier that had imprisoned their spirits for seven decades, stepping boldly into the infinity of possibility. They had no idea of where they were supposed to go, of where God wanted them to go; only where *they* wanted to go. And so, with no clue from the Creator, Abraham and Sarah followed their hearts and embarked upon the first Jewish walkabout. It was a step that would be remembered by the Creator as not an act of faith, but an act of love: "I remember how open you were when you were very young; your love for me when you engaged me in relationship; how you got up and followed me deep into the wilderness, a land that had not been planted" (Jeremiah 2:2).

Ironically, they ended up in the land of Canaan, which had been Terach's original destination to begin with (Genesis 11:31). Something had moved the elder in that direction earlier, but he had instead settled in Harran, situated between Ur and Canaan along a lengthy roundabout route that circumvented a more direct but desolate course. Terach could only dream about a better place, but could not bring himself to actually make the necessary break with his past to get there. About Terach, the narrative reads: "And he went out from Ur Kasdim to go to the land of Canaan, and he came as far as Harran and settled there" (Genesis 11:31). About Sarah and Abraham, however, the narrative reads: "And they went out from [Harran] to go to the land of Canaan, and they came to the land of Canaan" (Genesis 12:5). For Sarah and Abraham, dreams and hopes were to be redeemed from the realm of the ideal and manifested in the realm of the real, no matter what it took or how long. They were, after all, in their seventies when they finally left Harran (Genesis 12:4). Of more importance is the fact that the unnamed place the Creator had alluded to turned out to be exactly where they had yearned to journey in the first place, where they had felt all along they could flourish peacefully and independently as their own clan. The Creator had said only: "to the land that I will show you," and without asking the Creator where that might be, Sarah and Abraham had followed their own personal long-time yearning: "to go to the land of Canaan."

The first *ivrim* believed, then, in a God who honored the dreams and hopes and longings of *every* person. The God of Abraham and Sarah did not impose on people agendas that ran contrary to their soul-deep aspirations. The ancient rabbis comment that the vague directive "Go to the land that I will show you" was one of the ways in which Abraham was tested by the Creator (*Midrash Tehilim* on Psalms 18:30). The conventional interpretation of this test is that it was to see whether Abraham had sufficient faith in the Creator to embark on a blind journey to "wherever." But the test may just as well have been to see whether Abraham trusted the Creator to want for us what *we* want for us when our intention is to better and enhance our lives. As Rashi comments about God's initial words to Abraham: "'Go to your self'—that is, for your own pleasure and your own good" (on Genesis 12:1). Abraham then passes the test by embarking on a journey to the place of his own dreams: Canaan, a choice that subsequently is affirmed by the Creator (Genesis 15:7).

But if, indeed, Abraham knew the Creator as a God Who looked out for what was good for him personally, why did he not then question the Creator's request that he sacrifice his son Isaac (Genesis 22)?

According to the Torah, the Creator said to Abraham: "Please take your son, your only son, the one you love, Isaac, and go to yourself to the land of Moriah and offer him up as an offering on one of the mountains there of which I shall tell

you" (Genesis 22:2). The ancient rabbis interpreted this part
of the narrative as follows:

> Said God: "Please take your son." Said Abraham: "Which
> son?" Said God: "Your only son." Said Abraham: "[Ishmael]
> is an only son to his mother and [Isaac] is an only son to his
> mother." Said God: "The one you love." Said Abraham: "But
> I love this one and I love that one." Said God: "Isaac."
>
> *Pirkei D'Rebbe Eliezer*, Ch. 31 (beginning)

Abraham sets out the following morning to fulfill the request,
but when the time comes for him to actually plunge the knife
into his son, a spirit-messenger of the Creator intervenes and
stops him in the nick of time. Then the Creator tells Abraham:
"Do not send your hand toward the young man and do not do
anything to him, for now I know that you are God-fearing in
that you did not withhold your son, your favorite one, from
Me" (Genesis 22:12).

Interestingly, when Abraham is asked to embark on this
journey to sacrifice his son, the Creator uses the term "go to
your self," the same wording employed in the initial call to
Abraham to pick up and go to the place that felt right for him
(Genesis 12:1). This highly unusual way of telling Abraham to
go somewhere meant, again, "for your own pleasure and your
own good" (Rashi on Genesis 12:1). It is clear, then, that the
Creator implied not only that Abraham should offer up his son,
but that he should also wrestle what he hears as the word of
God against what he feels inside of himself as rightness, as "for
his own good." Moreover, it ought to be noted that according
to ancient Jewish tradition (*Yalkot Shim'oni*, *Vayeira*, No.
98; *Tanchuma*, *Vayeira*, No. 23) Isaac was thirty-seven years
old at the time, not a little boy as he is commonly portrayed in
children's books and biblical legends. When Abraham and Isaac
returned from the near-sacrifice, Sarah had died. She was 127
when she died (Genesis 23:1) and had been ninety when Isaac
was born (Genesis 17:17), making the "little" Isaac old enough

for a mid-life crisis. Indeed, the ancient rabbis imagined with great creativity what went on in the mature mind of this adult man being led up the mountain by his 137-year-old father.

> The *satan* [literally, "the one who obstructs"; in Judaism, this is a spirit-messenger of the Creator whose task it is to challenge our convictions and call our bluff] appeared in the guise of a young man and walked up the mountain alongside Isaac and said to him: "Where are you going?" Replied Isaac: "To study Torah." Said the *satan*: "Dead or alive?" Said Isaac: "Can one study Torah when one is dead?" Said the *satan*: "Wretched son of a pathetic father! Do you not realize how many times your mother fasted before she was finally able to give birth to you? And now this old man has gone mad and is going to slaughter you!" Said Isaac: "Even so, I shall not dismiss the wisdom of my Creator or the will of my father."
>
> *Tanchuma, Vayeira*, No. 22

Based on the traditional Judaic premise that the Creator knows everything, it is inconsistent to presume that the Creator chose to test Abraham with the "binding of Isaac" in order to discover something about Abraham that wasn't already known to the Creator. The purpose of the test was not to make the Creator aware of anything, but to make *Abraham* aware, and thereby to make *us* aware. Notice, for example, the name given the mountain: *moriah*—literally, "God shall show." Show what? What lesson was to be presented to Abraham at this teaching mountain? That even after God has done innumerable wonders for us and acts of compassion beyond what we feel we deserve, we still have the right to express our sentiments, even if our judgment is in error; to say "no," to challenge a divine imperative when we sense a clear wrongness about it.

The test of the binding of Isaac does not occur at the onset of Abraham's relationship with the Creator, but deeply into it—*after* the Creator has helped him extricate himself from his previous paradigm (Genesis 15:7); *after* the Creator has gifted him with the land of Canaan (Genesis 12:7); *after* the Creator has saved his wife Sarah from the bedside clutches of the Pharaoh during their sojourn in Egypt for food (Genesis 12:17); *after* the Creator has made him victorious in battle against four immense armies even though Abraham's militia consisted of only 318 rookies (Genesis 14:14–15); *after* the Creator has forged a sacred and eternal covenant with him and with his descendants (Genesis 17:1–16); *after* the Creator has invited him to challenge and negotiate the divinely ordained fate of Sodom and Gomorah (Genesis 18); *after* the Creator has rescued Sarah from the bedside clutches of King Avimelech during their trip to G'rar (Genesis 20:3–4); *after* the Creator has performed a miracle for ninety-year-old Sarah by enabling her to bear her first and only child, Isaac (Genesis 21:1).

After eight major occasions of being the recipient of the Creator's kindness and mercy in incredibly large lump sums, Abraham may have felt that he had used up all his "points," that he now owed the Creator beyond repayment (*Yalkot Shim'oni, Lech Lecha*, No. 16)—so much so that the Creator had to reassure him repeatedly of the promise, mostly after a particular miracle had occurred for him (e.g., Genesis 13:14, 15:1, 17:6–8, 22:17). The Creator therefore tested Abraham for the purpose of helping him to understand that one never owes the Creator for the gifts one enjoys in life: They are gifts, not loans, and the Creator gives altruistically, not schemingly. Perhaps it was toward this lesson that the Creator asked Abraham whether he would sacrifice his own son. After all the things the Creator had done for and given to Abraham, how could he refuse? After all, the Creator had come across, in all these events, as compassionate, just, and the like. "Whatever the Creator may then ask of me," Abraham may have thought, "I am more than obligated to dish it out."

The teaching then becomes clear to Abraham that the grace and compassion of the Creator is boundless, is in no way diluted or diminished by too many good things happening in life. It also becomes clear that just as the Creator was open to Abraham challenging the divine decree to destroy Sodom and Gomorah (Genesis 18:17–32), so is the Creator open to Abraham challenging the divine request for him to sacrifice his son. Everyone has unlimited credit with the Creator, the Patriarch was taught in this test, and we never forfeit our right to react against what we feel is wrongness. Never—whether we are graced with eight earth-shaking miracles in our lifetimes or a thousand. What the Creator gives to each of us is a gift, and gifts require acknowledgment and appreciation—not compensation, and not sacrifices: "Sacrifice to God by being thankful" (Psalms 50:14). Said the second-century rabbis Hezkiah and Kohain in the name of Rabbi Abba Arecha: "In the future, every person will have to account before the Creator for all that their eyes beheld but yet they did not eat of it." The Talmud goes on to say that "Rabbi Elazar took this teaching to heart and would save up pennies in order to buy at least one brand-new exciting thing that was available if only once a year" (Jerusalem Talmud, *Kidushin* 4:12 [end]). Declining the gifts and blessings we may encounter in our lives is not considered virtuous; feeling that we do not deserve anything good is as un-Jewish as believing that God is miserly.

What, then, about the Creator's *praise* of Abraham following the interruption of the near-sacrifice: "Now I know that you are God-fearing, for you did not withhold your son from Me" (Genesis 22:12)? This depends on how we choose to understand the Hebrew for what is conventionally translated as "God-fearing": ירא אלוהים, which also may be translated as "God seeing," as in one who sees, is aware of, is in awe of, the Creator. Accordingly, Abraham names the place of this event יהוה יראה, which translates as "God will reveal" (Genesis 22:14)—that when we are about to do it wrong but our intention is to do it right, the Creator will reveal the way. As King Solomon (ninth century B.C.E.) wrote: "In all of your ways know the Creator; and the Creator shall guide you on your path"

(Proverbs 3:6). Adds the second-century Rabbi Abba Arecha: "Even if you are doing something wrong" (Babylonian Talmud, *Berachot* 63a). In this light, the praise "You did not withhold your son from Me" teaches us that even the *wrong* way in which we were about to do something before it got corrected goes neither unnoticed nor unappreciated, because "the Compassionate One looks into the heart" (Babylonian Talmud, *Sanhedrin* 106b). Sacrificing your child to God is an erroneous way to manifest your intention of honoring the Creator, even if you experience the Creator as asking you to do so, and even if your child is in his late thirties and accepts it; but the purity of your intent is not lost to the reckoning of the Creator. "Greater a wrong committed with purity of intention than a right committed with no intention at all" (Babylonian Talmud, *Horayot* 10b). No wonder that the Creator said, *"Please take your son,"* which is the literal translation from the Hebrew, not—as it is most commonly rendered—"take now your son." This was a request, not a command; as a request, it allowed Abraham room to refuse, to challenge. Nonetheless, even though Abraham may not have chosen well on this occasion, the Creator set things right for him in the end, since his heart was in a place of earnestness.

Abraham's lesson to us and the Creator's lesson to him is that God prefers a relationship with us that is based on love (Deuteronomy 6:5, 7:8, 11:1), not fear. God does not say: "I remember your fear," but "I remember your love" (Jeremiah 2:2); God does not say: "the seed of Abraham My fearful one," but "the seed of Abraham My beloved" (Isaiah 41:8).

> There are seven types of Pharisees: the Pharisee who is always looking over his shoulder to see whether anyone is watching him when he is performing a good deed; the Pharisee who announces, "Wait for me while I go and perform a good deed"; the Pharisee who [is so cautious about not looking at women that he squints his eyes and] bumps into walls until his head bleeds; the Pharisee who says, "Tell me what wrong I have

committed so that I may compensate for it with a good deed";
the Pharisee who constantly asks, "What is my duty now?";
the Pharisee who serves God out of fear; and the Pharisee
who serves God out of love. And which is the preferred Pharisee? The one who serves God out of love, like Abraham.

Jerusalem Talmud, *Berachot* 9:5 [60a] and Babylonian
Talmud, *Sotah* 22b (bracketed portion is Rashi's commentary on
Babylonian Talmud, *Sotah* 22b)

Well, then, which is it, fear or love? After all, the Jewish
scriptures and rabbinic teachings through the ages alternately
advocate each one. At one point, Moses even promotes both
in a single breath: "What does the Creator ask of you but to
fear your God and to walk in the ways of the will of your God,
and to *love* God . . ." (Deuteronomy 10:12). Elsewhere, for
example, the injunction to *love* the Creator (Deuteronomy 6:5)
is sandwiched between two injunctions to *fear* the Creator
(Deuteronomy 6:2, 6:13). English translations of the original
Hebrew scriptures are sadly disappointing. They are rendered
mostly outside of the "whole picture" of the theology in which
the scriptures flourished; they are done from a narrow view-
point that sees only *word*, but misses *meaning*. Rather, the
Hebrew word for what is translated as "fear" (יראה) is spelled
exactly the same as the Hebrew word for "seeing," therefore
connoting awe, not fear. "Awe," wrote Abraham Joshua
Heschel, "is the antithesis of fear" (*God in Search of Man*,
p. 77). Awe is responding to seeing, to really seeing and realizing the grandeur of majestic peaks, towering waterfalls, spectacular deserts, a condor in flight, another human being, yourself: the Creator mirrored in the Creation.

Awe is the trembling experience of wonderment that sends
shockwaves up and down our *shakras* the moment we realize
that what stands or flies before us is unfathomable; the moment we realize we have stepped out of the mundane and
encountered the mystery. It is in the place of awe that we begin
to know that we do not know, and therefore it is also in the

place of awe that understanding and respect and responsibility can take root in our beings. Fear is the experience of being afraid of something; awe, on the other hand, "is a sense of wonder and humility inspired by the sublime, or felt in the presence of mystery" (Abraham Joshua Heschel, *God in Search of Man*, p. 77). When we are afraid, we relinquish the sweetness and the learning that reason offers (Apocrypha, *Wisdom of Solomon* 17:12); but when we are awed, we become open to receiving the insights and wisdom that being in the universe has to offer us; which the universe itself has to offer us. This is what the ancient teachers implied when they wrote that the prerequisite to wisdom is awe of the Creator (Job 28:28; Psalms 111:10; Proverbs 1:7, 9:10, 15:33; Babylonian Talmud, *Avot* 3:21). "The beginning of awe is wonder," wrote Heschel, "and the beginning of wisdom is awe" (*God in Search of Man*, p. 74). Awe, he continues, "does not make us shrink from the awe-inspiring object, but, on the contrary, draws us near to it. This is why awe is compatible with both love and joy" (*God in Search of Man*, p. 77).

The gift of the experience of being awed by something or by someone is indeed love, that undefinable, ungraspable, yet vivid and resonating sensation that does more than make us tremble or tingle; it also makes us joyful and opens up parts of our consciousness and emotions that would otherwise remain under lock and key. Now we can understand the seemingly contradictory words of our ancient teachers: "Rejoice before God with trembling" (Psalms 2:11); or, even more elaborate: "I awed in my joy; I rejoiced in my awe; and my love prevailed over all" (*Eliyahu Rabba,* Ch. 3).

Even to those who still found it difficult to accept the definition of *yirah* as "awe" rather than "fear," the rabbis persistently taught about a quality of "fearing" God that remains inconsistent with the conventional understanding. Not that they didn't believe that one could simply and literally be afraid of God and of divine judgment and all that, but they also believed that this kind of fear is the least preferable kind.

There is the man who fears the Lord lest he be punished in his body, family, or his possessions. Another man fears the Lord because he is afraid of punishment in the life to come. Both types are considered inferior in Jewish tradition. Job, who said, "Though He slay me, yet will I trust in Him" (Job 13:15), was not motivated in his piety by fear but rather by awe, by the realization of the grandeur of His eternal love.
Abraham Joshua Heschel, *God in Search of Man*, p. 77

The sixteenth-century mystic Rabbi Yehudah Loew (Maharal) offers the following explanation of the "God-fearing" number: "The most essential thing about fear is that it comes from the power of love, for when you love someone you intend always to fulfill their wishes the best way you possibly can so that there be no gap in the love flow between you. And because of this you will likewise be cautious about disregarding their wishes altogether, even about a minor matter, for that would appear to somewhat negate the love that exists between you. And this is the kind of fear that is written about Abraham: 'Now I know that you are God-fearing'" (*Netivot Olam*, *Netiv Yirat Hashem*, Ch. 1, par. 4).

In other words, when we love someone dearly, our love is augmented by a quality of fear that is not trepidation or terror for our well-being, but a quality of fear that is more about getting it right in our day-to-day, moment-to-moment relationship with a beloved because we treasure both the person and the relationship. This sort of fear then translates more to a sort of "seeing," "awareness," the sense of responsibility that we experience more vividly with our loved ones than with others. With God, too, writes Rabbi Loew, the fear we are taught to have of the Creator is not one of "Yikes!" but one of "Wow!"; a fear that makes up that part of our consciousness that is aware (if we so choose) of the Creator being the cause and us being the effect; a sense of awe that is more naturally an outgrowth of our awareness that our very being exists only by the moment-to-moment will of the Creator that we be here. The dictum urging us to "fear" God is therefore mentioned alongside, or in the same breath as, the dictum to "love" God, more for the purpose of placing the desirable quality of "fear" of God into its proper context, which is love. "This kind of fear," writes Rabbi Loew, "is therefore a result of love. And the kind of fear that is borne out of love is certainly much loftier [than fear without love] for it comes from Love, which is higher than anything. But the other kind of fear is the kind of fear that is not borne out of love and is just a fear of God alone out of God's magnanimity . . . like being afraid of a king of flesh and blood or of anyone in a high position" (*Netivot Olam, Netiv Yirat Hashem*, Ch. 1, par. 4). As the second-century Rabbi Shimon ben Elazar taught: "Greater is one who [performs the God will] out of love than the one who performs it out of fear" (Babylonian Talmud, *Sotah* 31a). The Creator then prefers love, writes Rabbi Loew, not fear and trepidation; while love brings about joy and goodness, fear only sows destruction and negativity in the world (*Netivot Olam, Netiv Ahavat Hashem*, Ch. 1, par. 11).

It is analogous to a king who had two servants: one who loved the king and feared him, and one who feared him only but did not love him. The king set out on a journey across the ocean. The one who loved the king and feared him busied himself in the king's absence by planting gardens and orchards and all kinds of fruits. The one who only feared the king but did not love him sat around and did absolutely nothing. When the king returned from across the ocean, he saw the gardens and all sorts of fruits and reacted accordingly. When the one who loved the king then entered and saw the king's reaction, he rejoiced because the king whom he loved was gladdened by what he had done for him. The king then went to the home of the one who feared the king but did not love him and found it in shambles and reacted accordingly. When the servant entered and saw the king's reaction, he became anxious and disoriented.

Eliyahu Rabbah, Ch. 25

Adds Rabbi Loew: "[In the above analogy] do not suppose that the king [God] becomes enraged at the one who serves out of fear and not love, because that is not likely. Rather, the one who serves out of fear *experiences* God as furious at them when they transgress. But not so with the one who serves out of love, for to them will God be experienced only in a joyful way, and they will never experience God as being angry at them" (*Netivot Olam, Netiv Ahavat Hashem*, Ch. 1, par. 11). The difference between love and fear, he adds, is that the one who loves will endeavor to do good out of their love, and the one who fears will endeavor to avoid evil out of their fear. Wrote King David: "Serve the Creator with joy; come before the Creator with singing. . . . For the Creator's love and faithfulness is eternal" (Psalms 100:2).

The ancient rabbis tried their best to get these teachings across to us down the ages, to balance the teachings about fearing God with the teachings about loving God; to take the terror out of fear and to place "fear of God" in its proper context: love. But it is we who have chosen—perhaps out of fear—to tread around God-stuff fearfully rather than lovingly. Sadly, well-meaning religious teachers have all but played on that naive fear for the purpose of keeping us in line. But to the flexidoxic teachers it was always more important that the people not be so hard on themselves by presuming that God demanded perfection of them, and flawless service: "Rather serve God like the son who serves his father, that is, with joy and ease, saying, 'Even if I do not get it just right, he will not be angry with me because he is my father.' In contrast, serving God out of fear is like a hired servant who serves his master with anxiety and confusion over possibly doing something wrong" (paraphrased from *Tanchuma* on Genesis 11:7 [or No. 19]). "Do not be fearful of God's judgment. Do you not know Him? He is your relative; He is your brother. What's more, He is your father" (*Midrash Tehilim* on Psalms 118:5).

How very precious is Your love, O Creator! And the children of humans find comfort beneath Your wings; they frolic in the abundance of Your gifts; they drink from Your rivers of pleasure and good; because You are the wellspring of life; by the dazzle of Your splendor You illuminate our lives; pour out Your love to those who know You; your goodness to those with rightness in their hearts.

Psalms 36:8–10

Indeed, as one ancient writer put it: "My help will come from nothing and nowhere; for my help comes from God, Creator of the heavens and the Earth" (Psalms 121:1–2). Conventional translation of the first line in this passage reads, "From where shall my help come?" but the word מאין for "from where" just as easily translates "from nothing, nil." In other words, I can call upon the Creator in time of need even if I feel myself to be without merit and undeserving, because God will help me even מאין, from a place of nothing; I can draw from my merits account in times of need even if there is nothing in it. "For a great many seasons the Israelites were without the true God and without a teaching priest and without Torah. Yet, when they were in trouble and they turned to seek God, they found God" (2 Chronicles 15:3–4).

Contrary to popular belief, Abraham did not introduce the idea of the one God, but that the one God was compassionate, personal, and nonexacting (*Midrash Haserot V'yeterot* 1:2). This was his teaching to us and God's teaching to him. And it was from that quality of relationship with, and understanding of, the Creator that the way of the boundary crosser unfolded and evolved into the Jewish way of life. The story of Judaism is therefore more about the dynamics of the passions and unfoldings of the human spirit than about religion; and as much about drawing near to the truth of one's personal being as it is about drawing near to the truth of God. Over centuries of global influence and national evolution, however, the boundary crossers would end up creating a socioreligious structure so complex that it would inhibit its adherents from so much as challenging the very sorts of boundaries their ancestors might have crossed outright: boundaries of social, cultural, or religious strictures that in any way threatened or thwarted the aliveness of the human spirit.

Nonetheless, even as the ways of Judah would eventually become an "ism," there remained a constant stream of *ivri* (Hebrew) consciousness amongst many of the teachers that continued to mirror the attitudes, sentiments, and spirituality of Judaism that had characterized it long before it joined the ranks of organized religion. Rather than being orthodox, these teachings were flexidox, comprising general guidelines for wholesome, dynamic ways of being on the planet rather than dogmatic do-or-die disciplines designed more for the furtherance of party-line religious politics and cultural survival than emotionally honest spirituality.

This book, then, is a modest attempt to restore to Judaism some of the almost lost spirit that once gave it life; to glean carefully from "flexidoxic" Jewish teachings spanning more than 3,500 years, in order to rediscover *the way of the boundary crosser.*

2

Flexidoxy

The Book of Judaism begins with no mention of religion. Not that there weren't any religions around back then, but it was apparently unimportant. The first Jews, the clan of Abraham and Sarah, had no particular religious rite other than circumcision for male members (Genesis 17:10). And while they experienced divine revelation, they became neither religionists nor nationalists. They did not respond to the divine promise of the land of Canaan, for example, by invading it and subduing its inhabitants, but acquired it piece by piece through land purchases, squatting, and mutual treaties with the people who already lived there (Genesis 20:15, 21:22–32, 23:3–18).

The scriptural narrative about these early Jews tells us absolutely nothing about their politics or religion, probably because they did not have any. We are told, however, about their character traits, their practices as human beings, their family problems, and how they wrestled with their fledgling relationship with, and understanding of, the Creator. It is often taught that Abraham founded monotheism, which is a strange claim to make about a man who lived in the days of Malkizedek, described in the Torah itself as "a priest to the God of the Above" (Genesis 14:18). And what of Noah, who "walked with

God" (Genesis 6:9), or Enoch, who also "walked with God" (Genesis 5:21), and, of course, Eve and Adam?

So what exactly is Jewish, or Hebraic? What was the gift to the collage of the spiritual paths of the world that was so unique to these simple sheep-herding progenitors of what was to eventually evolve into one of the most complex and immutable religions in history? What quality did these unassuming ancestors possess that would one day germinate into volumes upon volumes of comprehensive codes of religious law and practice, when they themselves possessed not so much as an iota of any kind of religious system?

It is the contention of this book that hidden away in the "genetics" of the original Hebrew life path is a wealth of lessons for what being Jewish means, beyond the layers of religious institution, politics, and dogma that have all but entombed those lessons. It is doubtful that the earliest of the Hebrews would recognize their ideology in much of the form it has taken during the past three thousand years; that Abraham would relate to the laws of Moses, or Moses to the way those laws were observed, interpreted, and expanded two thousand years later; that the great and revered teachers of the talmudic period would recognize Judaism in the form it exists today, even amongst the very Orthodox whose lives are devoted day and night to the *study* of the Talmud. As the ancient rabbis themselves admitted: "The ways of the ancestors do not resemble those of the descendants, nor do the ways of the descendants resemble those of the ancestors" (Babylonian Talmud, *Bava Batra* 120a).

What, then, was unique about Abraham? Conventional understanding is that he discovered the Creator on his own, not through some tradition or teaching. Although there did exist in Abraham's period traditions and teachers who taught about the Creator, they were not prevalent in the Valley of Shin'ar where Abraham grew up. Abraham transcended his environment and culture to ask the questions that burned fiercely in his heart, questions about the miracle of life and the meaning of life, questions that led him ultimately to the conclusion that it couldn't all have gotten here without there being a Creative Intelligence to blueprint it, form it, and breathe life into it. It was then that the Creator met him and became revealed to him, the moment he began to effect a change in his life journey that would reflect his realization.

> It is within man's power to seek [God]; it is not within his power to find Him. All Abraham had was wonder, and all he could achieve on his own was readiness to perceive. The answer was disclosed to him; it was not found by him.
> Abraham Joshua Heschel, *God in Search of Man*, p. 147

But a closer look at one of the sources of this tradition yields a unique quality to Abraham's discovery of God: "He learned to know the Creator without anyone teaching him how" (*Bamidbar Rabbah* 14:7). Why would anyone need to be taught *how* to know the Creator? Is it not sufficient to just know that there is a God? But the lesson is not about knowing that there *is* a God but *knowing God*, as in intimately knowing someone, being acquainted with them. Certainly, the Bible recounts pre-Abrahamic people who believed in and communed with the Creator, but did they know the Creator intimately, or did they know only that God existed and was bigger and better and more powerful than they and that they needed to be obedient to every divine imperative? Abraham, on the other hand, knew the Creator as one would know a friend, "without anyone teaching him how." And he arrived at his knowing in pretty much the same way that he arrived at the realization that there was a Creator altogether:

> Said Rabbi Isaac (third century): Abraham may be compared to a traveler who, upon seeing a castle burning, wondered, "Is it possible that there is no one around who cares for the castle?" Whereupon the owner of the castle looked at him and said: "I am the owner of the castle." Similarly, Abraham our father wondered, "Is it possible that the world is without a

caretaker?" Whereupon the Holy Blessed One said to him: "I
am the caretaker, the sovereign of the world."

B'reishis Rabbah 39:1

In other words, Abraham asked the same question that had
been asked by other God-discoverers before him, but with a
unique twist. The question was not merely how there could be
a world without a Creator, but how there could be a world
without a Creator *who cared about it*. Enter *El Shaddai*,
the God of nurturance and compassion; enter the personal
God. This is the message of Judaism, the innovative notion of
Abraham, that the Creator is not an impersonal, distant deity
who is too big to be bothered by such mundane trivia as the
Earth and its inhabitants, and certainly not by the individual
person or the individual ant, leaf, or sand grain. Malkizedek
acknowledged the Creator as the "God of the above who owns
the heavens and the earth" (Genesis 14:19). Abraham, on the
other hand, while he, too, acknowledged the Creator in this
way (Genesis 14:22), added his more personal knowing of the
Creator as "the one who directs justice over the whole earth"
(Genesis 18:25), as an involved deity who more than owns the
heavens and the Earth and all their creatures, but who also
cares for them, and, accordingly, wishes for each of us to do
the same: "To strive for justice on behalf of the poor and
needy—this is what knowing Me is all about" (Jeremiah 22:16).

And when Abraham visioned and looked and saw and examined and understood and carved and sculpted and combined
and imaged and [the mystery] arose in his grasp—then did the
Blessed Master of All become revealed to him, and embrace
him in the Divine Bosom and kiss him on his head and call
him "My beloved," and then forge a covenant with him and
for his seed, and he believed in the One Who is, was, will be,
and Ises, Who then thought benevolence into him and forged
with him a covenant between his ten toes—this is the covenant of circumcision—and between his ten fingers—this is the
tongue—and bound his tongue with twenty-two letters and

revealed to him their secrets, and then dipped them in water, lit them in fire, gave them voice in wind, and kindled them with the cycle of seven and set them in motion with the cycle of years as ten constellations.

Sefer Yetsirah, last *mishnah*

Accordingly, while Malkizedek is described as "priest to the God of the Above" (Genesis 14:18), Abraham is described as "father of many nations" (Genesis 17:4), because that was precisely *his* understanding of and image of the Creator: a Cosmic Parent to all of creation. This was Abraham's contribution: not monotheism, not that there is a God or that there is only one God, but that the one God cares and reaches out to Creation in search of personal relationship and response: "Shall I hide from Abraham what I am about to do?" (Genesis 18:17); that the one God accompanies us both in our falling and in our rising: "I will go down with you to מצרים [literally, 'the narrow places'], and I will go up with you to bring you out of there" (Genesis 46:4).

The [Jewish Bible] has shattered man's illusion of being alone. Sinai broke the cosmic silence that thickens our blood with despair. God does not stand aloof from our cries; He is not only a pattern but a power, and life is a response, not a soliloquy.

Abraham Joshua Heschel, *God in Search of Man*, p. 238

עד אברם חרון אף של מקום (The wrath of God existed until Abraham came along), wrote Rashi (on Genesis 11:32). Not that the Creator was wrathful up until that time; rather, that was how people projected their knowing of the Creator—as a God who, like them, would certainly become furious when disobeyed or when displeased. But then along came Abraham and revolutionized the concept of God and introduced a God who was not wrathful, but compassionate and enduring: "'I will not scowl at you,' says the Creator, 'I am merciful and do not bear eternal grudges'" (Jeremiah 3:12), "for God is gracious and compassionate, patient and abundantly loving" (Exodus

34:6, and Joel 2:13). Since time immemorial, organized religion has represented a god that is an impersonal and unchallengeable figurehead, an authoritative deity that is capable at will or whim of punishing or rewarding us; a deity that is unapproachable, non-negotiable, exacting, and impatient; a deity like some kind of fiery dragon or one-eyed cyclops that is to be feared always and whose chronic fury can be pacified only by blind obeisance, regularly scheduled sacrifices, and prescribed rites that have to be implemented just so; a deity around whom humans have treaded ever so lightly ever since they first conceived the idea of "God." Judaism's contribution was therefore revolutionary in the sense that it brought the Creator within reach of the Creation, and introduced a God who preferred personal relationship to ritual sacrifices.

> On the day when I brought your ancestors out of Egypt, I never spoke to them or commanded them regarding burnt-offerings and sacrifices. Rather, this is what I said to them: "Hear My voice, then will I be your God and you will be unto Me a people. and walk within the whole of the path about which I will instruct you so that you might enjoy yourselves."
>
> Jeremiah 7:21–23

No, Abraham did not discover monotheism. He discovered something far more novel and important than that, so much so that his descendants were an enigma wherever they went, because their take on God posed a challenge greater than most people were willing to meet. The Abrahamic concept of a compassionate God Who wanted people to enjoy the blessings of life and elevate the human spirit posed a serious threat to monarchic empires and religious institutions that thrived on depriving the masses of the blessings of life and on subjugating the human spirit. The Jewish people's idea of God was therefore repelled and held as sacrilegious by the many cultures who surrounded them when they were in their homeland and hosted them during their Exile, because it was about a God Who vied for the personal well-being of everyone, with no strings attached, and Who was put off by the widespread convention of bribes and impersonal rites.

> I hate, I detest your religious festivals, and I will not delight in your sacred celebrations. And although you bring to Me burnt-offerings and meal-offerings, I shall not want them, nor will I consider your peace-offerings from your fattened-up herds. Remove from Me the noises of your many songs, and let Me not have to listen to the music of your harps. Rather, cause justice to well up like the waters, and rightness to shoot forth like a mighty stream.
>
> Amos 5:21–24

Periodically throughout history, the descendants of Sarah and Abraham also adopted the kind of god-visualizing prevalent in the cultures around them by relating to God as a deity that repressed rather than liberated the human spirit, and by promoting static religion over fluid spirituality. After all, it was and is so much simpler to keep God securely encased in religious creed and dogma, from where we can safely presume that we are worshiping God without having to engage God in the here-and-now reality of our personal lives. Most of the ancient Judaic teachers and prophets, however, remained steadfast in the original way of the boundary crosser and would, from time to time, upset the status quo of the religious practices of their people when those practices developed calluses that desensitized the people from experiencing God as imminent and organic. "The prophets," wrote Abraham Joshua Heschel, "were those who in the name of God stood up against that which most people to this very day call religion" (*God in Search of Man*, pp. 230–231):

> What do I need with all of your many sacrifices? says the Creator. I am saturated with burnt-offerings of rams and the fat of overfed herds; and I do not want the blood of heifers or lambs or billy-goats. And when you come to see My face, who has requested all this from you? You are trampling all over

My courtyard! Do not continue to bring phony sacrifices for
they are detestable offerings. Nor can I tolerate your New
Moon and Sabbath celebrations, for though they are supposed
to be sacred assemblies, they are mixed with the wrongness
of your life path. My soul despises your New Moons and holy
days. They are an encumbrance to Me; I am tired of carrying
them. . . . Rather, learn to bring about goodness; seek justice,
relieve oppression, judge on behalf of the orphans, and stand
up for the widow.

                                                         Isaiah 11:17

I will take no heifer from your house, nor billy-goats from your
herds. For all of the wildlife of the forest are Mine, and so are
the domestic animals grazing on a thousand hills. I know every
bird in the mountains; and the wild beasts of the fields are with
Me. If I were to become hungry, I would not tell you; for the
earth is Mine, and everything upon her. Do I need to eat the
flesh of cattle, or to drink the blood of goats? Rather, sacrifice to God by being thankful; and pay the Most High by keeping promises; and call upon Me in the day of trouble. I will be
there for you; so if you wish to honor Me, honor Me for that.

                                                       Psalms 50:9–15

The teaching is clear: The kind of acknowledgment, appreciation, gift-offering that the Creator welcomes is the kind that
is stirred within us by our personal inspiration, not by the external dictates and influences of cultural dogma or religious regimen. If we wish to make an offering to the Creator, out of
appreciation or out of honoring, we should do something that
the Creator *does* take delight in, such as helping those in need:
"To do lovingkindness and to live in rightness are more desirable than ritual sacrifice" (Proverbs 21:3); "for I desire
lovingkindness, not sacrifice" (Hosea 6:6).

Rabbi Yochanan ben Zakkai and Rabbi Yehoshua (first century) were walking outside of Jerusalem from where they
observed the ruins of the Holy Temple. Cried Rabbi Yehoshua:

"Woe unto us that we no longer have a means of sacrificing unto the Creator to atone for our wrongdoings." Said Rabbi Yochanan ben Zakkai: "My son, we do indeed have such a means and it is just as effective, and that is deeds of loving-kindness, as it is written [Hosea 6:6], 'For I desire loving-kindness, not sacrifice.'"

Avot D'Rebbe Natan 1:4

This understanding of sacrificing or worshiping is clearly spelled out in the last will and testament attributed to the first-century Rabbi Eliezer the Great:

My son, be ever so careful to give unto your Creator a portion of everything of which you eat. And know that the portion due the Creator is the share that goes to the poor. Therefore, take from the most superb of the delicacies which adorn your table, and render it unto your God [by giving it to the poor].

Tzav'ot Rebbe Eliezer HaGadol, No. 27

The compassion and love of the Creator knows no bounds, has no bomb-ticking expiration date, and exacts no sacrifices, bribes, dues, or fees: "You do not want a sacrifice, or else I would give it; nor do You take any pleasure in burnt-offerings" (Psalms 51:18). The human inclination to go all-out in "paying" the Creator is psychological, not spiritual. Pschologically, we tend to accommodate those from whom we need things, or of whom we are afraid. We will go out of our way to pay them homage and attention. For too long, this very human kind of projection has painted an image of the Creator as a cosmic loan shark who will break our legs or harm our loved ones if we don't cough up some "protection money" in the form of personal sacrifices or religious observances. But the way of the boundary crosser began with an outright shattering of this kind of image, introducing instead the God of altruism, who owes us nothing and yet is always giving to us: "I owe no creature anything; yet when a person performs a positive deed I reward them gratuitously, for I owe every creature absolutely nothing" (*Tanchuma, V'etchanan*, No. 3).

The personal God of Judaism asks no price of blood or sacrifice for the privilege of divine grace, only our desire for it, and even when we have no will to be close to the Creator or to believe in the Creator altogether, the God of Abraham continues to sustain us and to love us:

> They asked Rabbi Akiva (second century): "And what about such and such who is lame and emerges from a house of idolatry healed, or such and such who is blind and emerges from a house of idolatry able to see, or so and so who is deaf and emerges from a house of idolatry able to hear?" Explained Rabbi Akiva: ". . . The Holy Blessed One says, 'Shall I withhold his healing just because his time for healing coincides with his foolish visit to the house of idolatry?'"
>
> *Midrash Asseret HaDibrot*, Ch. 2, par. 1

Flexidoxy may sound like the contrast to orthodoxy, but it is more about climbing over the rows of fences that orthodoxy has constructed over the centuries in its staunch endeavors at protecting the original path, albeit to the point that the original path has become obscured for a great many Jews whose attempts at reconnecting with their heritage is more often frustrated than furthered by overemphasis on religious regimen. For such individuals, a journey *to* rather than *from* the tradition may yield an image of original Judaic life values and spiritual lessons that differ radically from those reflected in orthodox teaching and practice today across the denominational board. They may find a way of being Jewish that is more flexible than Judaism in its conventional forms is cracked up to be. Thus, flexidoxy.

However, the way of flexidoxy is not antithetical to orthodoxy, only in contrast to it; it does not conflict with orthodoxy but mirrors it, reflecting its original intent and spirit as opposed to its otherwise superficial extremities. Flexidoxy, then, posits that you can do Jewish right by following the form of Judaism that was outlined by Moses, or by David, or by Isaiah, or by Ezra, or by the rabbis of the second century or by the rabbis of today—or you can do Jewish right by following the fledgling version of it as it was played out in the persons of the first Hebrews who preceded Moses, as well as in the form that that version took initially in the Mosaic code. Flexidoxy holds that it is no more or less sacrilegious to adopt the version of doing Jewish that was ordained by Rabbi Yisroel Salanter or the Baal Shem Tov, as it is to adopt the version of doing Jewish that was ordained by Maimonides, or Rabbi Akiva, or Moses, or Abraham. That in each of these paradigm personas there is a piece, but only a piece, of the whole picture of how to be Jewish and what that means altogether.

Torah itself, wrote Rabbi Yehudah Loew of Prague, is beyond human grasp; it is, as a whole, unattainable by mortals and pragmatically irrelevant to their being on the planet. We can glimpse but flashes of it through *mitzvah*, which in itself is not Torah, but rather a vehicle to Torah, a handle (*Sifrei Maharal, Netivot Olam, Netiv Ha-Torah*, Ch. 17). According to the fourth-century Rabbi B'rachyah, "All of the *mitzvot* put together do not compare with even an iota of Torah" (Jerusalem Talmud, *Peah* 1:1). One can then "keep the Torah," in other words, not solely through the *mitzvot*, but in spite of them, because Torah is much bigger than the components by which we know it. As the third-century Rabbi Avahu remarked: "Could Moses actually have been taught the Torah in its entirety in only forty days? Not at all. Rather, the Holy Blessed One taught him only generalities" (*Sh'mot Rabbah* 41:6).

Torah means showing, or teaching; it is the expansive cosmic consciousness; "it is higher than the heavens and deeper than the abyss, longer than the Earth and broader than the sea" (Job 11:8–9). It is what the ancient mystics called מוחין דגדלות (the infinite mind), the knowing that extends beyond all givens, as distinguished from מוחין דקטנות (the finite mind), the knowing that thrives on the limited information and experience of the physical universe. Torah is representative of the intention that went into the Creation of existence, and as such it permeates every pore and crevice of the universe. It fills existence with what it is that inspired its creation to begin with, just as a painting is filled with clues of what it is that moved the artist to paint it. It must therefore be sought after like a hidden treasure (Proverbs 2:4–5), because it is anything but conspicuous, hidden away in the variety of forms in which Creation has manifested: "If someone will tell you 'I have not sought but I have found,' do not believe them" (Babylonian Talmud, *Megilah* 6b). Therefore did the ancient rabbis teach that God looked into the Torah and created the universe (*Tanchuma, B'reishis* 1:1; *Tana D'bei Eliyahu*, Ch. 31, par. 4; *Zohar, B'reishis* 46b), that it was the blueprint, so to speak, by which the universe was brought into being. Torah, it was taught, is therefore accessible to all peoples, not only the Jews (*Sifrei Maharal, Netivot Olam, Netiv Ahavat Re'a*, Ch. 1, par. 2; *Tanchuma, B'rachah*, No. 4). "All the rulers of the earth," wrote the ninth-century B.C.E. King David, "shall give thanks unto You, O Creator, for they have heard the words of Your lips" (Psalms 138:4).

The Torah of Judaism is then but one particular take on the universal Torah that is uniquely Jewish, and that the Jewish people chose to call *Torah*, but which is by no means the whole of it or the only manifested form of that greater consciousness that is Torah. "If they will tell you there is wisdom among the nations," taught the ancient rabbis, "believe it," because—again—everyone has a primal right to the divine wisdom that fills the cosmos, to that which the Jewish people call Torah, but which to other peoples is known by other names and is manifested in other forms: "Non-Jews, too . . . can grasp the essence of Torah and love God with a complete love" (*Tana D'bei Eliyahu*, Ch. 6, par. 5). The Torah, after all, was given in the wilderness, "to teach us that just like the wilderness is accessible to everyone, so is the Torah accessible to everyone" (*Tanchuma*, *Vayak'hel*, No. 8; *Bamidbar Rabbah* 1:6; *Mechilta*, *Yitro*, בחודש, Ch. 1).

"But if they will tell you there is Torah among the nations," continues the teaching, "don't believe it" (*Eichah Rabbah* 2:17), because that particular piece of divine wisdom that the Jewish people accessed in their experience, and which they chose to call Torah, is unique to them alone and cannot be grasped or experienced by other peoples, "for it is your distinct form of wisdom and understanding and distinguishes you in the eyes of all peoples" (Deuteronomy 4:6).

Torah, the particularly Jewish version of cosmic wisdom, bears with it remnants of its broader, universal composition. It does not purport that Jews are the first people on the planet or that they are better than anyone else (*Tanchuma*, *Eikev*, No. 3), or that they have the only authentic spirit-path. Torah starts with the Creation of the universe and of the first *humans*, not the first Hebrews. And throughout, even as it focuses on the particulars of being Jewish, it does not lose sight of those who are not Jewish. Forty-eight times does the Torah stress the importance of behaving sensitively toward non-Jews (*Tanchuma*, *Vayikra*, No. 2), and when Solomon builds the First Temple, his inaugural prayer includes a welcome to those who are not Jewish (2 Chronicles 6:32). In fact, part of the sacrificial rite instructed by the Torah of the Jewish people was the offering of sacrifices on behalf of the non-Jewish peoples of the world (Babylonian Talmud, *Sukah* 55b). Judaism is therefore not a proselytizing religion, because it honors the fact that there are other authentic avenues to God besides its own, and that you don't have to be Jewish to be a *tzadik*— one who lives in a way that is beloved by the Creator: "Anyone who wants to can become a *tzadik*, whether one is Jewish or not, because it has nothing to do with one's ancestral heritage or religious station" (*Bamidbar Rabbah* 8:2; *Midrash Tehilim* on Psalms 146 [toward end]). God, after all, is nondenominational: "I favor no one person over anyone else.

Rather, whether one is a Jew or a gentile, a man or a woman, slave or handmaid—whoever performs a positive deed shall find its reward alongside it" (*Yalkot Shim'oni, Lech Lecha,* No. 76). Therefore does the Torah refer to the *ger toshav,* "the stranger who lives among you," and that he or she was to be accorded all of the same rights enjoyed by Jews when the Jewish people were sovereign in their own land: "The stranger that dwells among you shall enjoy full citizenship, and you shall love them as yourself" (Leviticus 19:34). Its particulars of *mitzvot* notwithstanding, the Torah of the Jewish people never lost its source consciousness, that of the universality of all creation; that all of us are related: "Have we not all one same father? Has not one God created us all?" (Malachi 2:10). "Therefore was the human created singular," taught the ancient rabbis, referring to Eve and Adam, "so that no one can say to another: 'My ancestor was greater than yours'" (Babylonian Talmud, *Sanhedrin* 37b [*Mishnah*]).

There is no greater practical example, however, of the Torah's honoring of "other" people and their paths than the very person through whom the Torah itself became revealed to the Jewish people: Moses. The narrative describes how his father-in-law, Jethro (Yitro), came to see him in the wilderness shortly before the Grand Revelation was to happen, and how Moses honored his non-Jewish father-in-law not only by bowing to him, but, more importantly, by listening to his advice on how to lead the Jewish people (Exodus, Ch. 18)! It is mind-blowing that the greatest of the Jewish prophets, the man who spoke "face to face" with God (Deuteronomy 34:10), the supreme teacher and spiritual guide of the Jewish nation, would pay any attention to the critique of some Midianite high priest! We can understand Moses' bowing down to Jethro and honoring him and welcoming him. After all, he was still Moses' father-in-law, Jewish or not. In fact, each time the narrative mentions Jethro, he is mentioned again and again as Moses' "father-in-law," something totally unacceptable by the standards of *halachah* as observed in the traditional Jewish community today. Since interfaith marriages are not acceptable, a non-Jewish in-law is an oxymoron. But again, since Torah emanates from a wisdom source that is cosmic, not particularistic, it does not discriminate by religious affiliation. Early Judaism knew no such degree of ethnic barrier as we have today, a degree of separation from "others" that evolved not from Torah, but from centuries of being antagonized and deprecated by "others."

Can such a wounded and self-protective mindset understand Moses' heeding the counsel of a high priest of some other religion on how to guide the Jewish people and how to deal with their problems? It is indeed incomprehensible if we perceive Torah as a particularistic spirit path that is exclusive of anyone who is not a member. But it is totally comprehensible if we perceive Torah as something more than an "ism," more than the religion known as Judaism, and that the particulars of doing things Jewishly are but *part* of Torah, not vice versa. Torah, then, looms far larger than the creed it inspired; far larger than the finite, often subjective handle that is called *mitzvah*, or religious observance.

King Solomon wrote: "For the *mitzvah* is flame, and the Torah is light" (Proverbs 6:23). *Mitzvah* and Torah are therefore not synonymous with one another; religious observances do not constitute the whole of what is Torah. Where the particular *mitzvah* or precept is but a flashlight, Torah is full daylight. The second-century Rabbi Menachem ben Yosee taught: "A sin can extinguish *mitzvah*; but a sin cannot extinguish Torah, as it is written (Song of Songs 8:7): 'Many waters cannot extinguish love' [and Torah is love]. . . . The *mitzvah* is likened to a candle and the Torah is likened to light, to teach us that just like a flame illuminates only for the moment, so does a *mitzvah* enlighten only for the moment. And just as light illuminates always, so does Torah enlighten always" (Babylonian Talmud, *Sotah* 21a):

It is analogous to a man who is walking in the middle of the night amid pitch darkness, and he is afraid of thorns and of open pits and of thistles and of predatory animals and of bandits. And he does not know in which direction he is going. He then stumbles upon a candle. Now he is spared running into thorns, open pits, and thistles, but he is still afraid of running into predatory animals and bandits, and he still does not know in which direction he is going. When the light of morning arrives he is spared the danger of predatory animals and bandits, but he still does not know in which direction he is going. He then arrives at the crossroads. Now he is spared all of the obstacles.

Babylonian Talmud, *Sotah* 21a

The obstacles that lie in the way of our life journey are those things that restrain us or intimidate us from making choices that are our own, that come from our awareness of the gift of self and of the awesome responsibility of free will. It isn't until we come to a crossroads, a point of personal decision making, that we access Torah, experience aliveness. Until then we are certainly living, but by definitions and reality structures not our own. When we find our own sense of living, of who we are and what we need in life for our fullest aliveness, then we have found Torah. "No one really acquires Torah," taught the ancient rabbis, "until they have stumbled and fallen all over it" (Babylonian Talmud, *Gitin* 43a). Taught the second-century Rabbi Akiva: "More dear to God is personal insight, for even if you have mastered the books of the Torah and of the prophets and of the sacred writings, and you have studied all the rabbinic interpretations and the oral traditions, but you lack personal insight—your Torah is worth nothing" (*Midrash Otiyot D'Rebbe Akiva* [version 2], on the letter *bet*).

Torah is then not only the great eternal light that gives us our sense of safety and our clarity of vision, it is also our spirit guide, our inspiration for our life journey; it is an inner sense that mirrors a far greater outer sense guiding us from the cosmic shadows and sending us the wind to move our sails. *Mitzvah* illuminates the everyday moment-to-moment minutiae of living; Torah illuminates *mitzvah* itself. Without the consciousness of the bigger picture called Torah, *mitzvah* is a lifeless, empty shell; a form without substance; or—as Isaiah the prophet (seventh century B.C.E.) put it—"a mortal directive that is learned by rote" (Isaiah 29:13). Indeed, without Torah consciousness, *mitzvah* ceases to be divine directive and becomes instead "mortal directive."

It is obvious, then, that the early teachers clearly distinguished between Torah and its observances, that Judaism is much bigger than the religion that goes by its name. It is a way of being, of seeing, of thinking, of doing, that is reflected in the *mitzvah* but is not the *mitzvah* itself. Torah is the vast universe of the God will that is far more expansive than the *mitzvot* that make up but a single galaxy of its precepts, its stars. Therefore, how many *mitzvot* a person observes is not important, for a single *mitzvah* is but a microcosmic form of the Tao that is Torah. Taught the fourth-century Rava bar Yosef bar Chama: "The Creator says: 'Even if you will observe so much as a smidgen of the *mitzvot*—as little as a chicken takes from a trash heap in a single peck—I will include it for great reckonings" (Babylonian Talmud, *Avodah Zarah* 4a). It is wrong, therefore, to say that a person who is not observing all or most of the *mitzvot* is not living according to "the Torah way of life." The Torah way of being in the world is not limited to the so-called "613 commandments"; rather, it is a way of being that existed long before these commandments were presented and will continue as a way of being long after they are obsolete. Indeed, according to the fourth-century Rabbi Yosef, "In the time to come, the commandments will be abolished" (Babylonian Talmud, *Nidah* 61b), or, as another ancient teacher put it: "In the time to come, the Holy Blessed One shall permit that which was [ritually] forbidden" (*Midrash Tehilim* on Psalms 146:7).

Surprisingly, when one attempts to trace the origin of the concept of 613 commandments, one discovers that the absolutization of the fact that Judaism is comprised of 613 commandments is based on the exegetical speculation of a single rabbi in the third century. More astonishingly, one also discovers that the teaching about there being 613 precepts was taken blatantly out of context of the rest of that same rabbi's lesson:

> Said Rabbi Simlai: "Six hundred and thirteen precepts were given to Moses at Sinai, three hundred and sixty-five prohibitions corresponding to the three hundred and sixty-five days of the solar cycle, and two hundred and forty-eight imperatives, corresponding to the two hundred and forty-eight organs of the human body. Then came David and narrowed them down to eleven, as it is written: 'O God, who shall merit living in Your tent? Who shall merit to dwell on Your holy mountain? The one who walks a path of simplicity and performs acts of benevolence, and whose heart resonates with truthfulness; whose speech knows no deceit, and who does not wrong fellow creatures nor shame those who are kin; who despises those who are sinister, and honors those who appreciate the gifts of the Creator; who keeps promises to others, and will not renege even at personal hardship; who does not exact interest for money loaned, nor accept bribes at the expense of the innocent' [Psalms 15]. Then came Isaiah and narrowed them down to six, as it is written: 'The one who walks with deeds of benevolence and resonates with rightness; who despises profits gained from oppressions; whose hands recoil at the offer of bribes; whose ears are muffled from hearing of destructive schemes; whose eyes are shut from gazing upon evil' [Isaiah 33:15]. Then came Micah and narrowed them down to three, as it is written: 'Perform justice, love benevolence, and humble your walking with your Creator' [Micah 6:8]. Then came Isaiah again and narrowed them down further to two, as it is written: 'Be ever so cautious to do justice, and do charity' [Isaiah 56:1]. Then came Amos and narrowed them down to one, as it is written: 'Seek [God] and live' [Amos 5:4]." Rabbi Nahmon ben Yitzchak said: "Then came Habakuk and narrowed them down to one, as it is written: 'The just person shall live by their trust [in God]'" (Habakuk 2:4).
>
> Babylonian Talmud, *Makot* 23b–24a

And lest one argue that Rabbi Simlai was only toying with theoretics, the commentator Rashi explains it as more than a mere exercise in scriptural exegesis: "In earlier times, the people were saintly and could take upon themselves the yoke of multitudes of *mitzvot*. But later generations were not so saintly, and if they were expected to observe all [of the commandments], there would be not a single person who would merit to do so. Thus did David come and narrow them down to eleven, so that if people would take it upon themselves to observe these eleven alone, they would merit the observance of Torah. And so it was with each successive age, that with each descending generation they narrowed it [the bottom line of Torah] down further" (on Babylonian Talmud, *Makot* 24a, top of page). In the Babylonian Talmud we also find the whispered teaching that "one who recites only the Shema reading (Deuteronomy 6:4–8) in the morning and in the evening has fulfilled the scriptural dictum that the Torah shall not be absent from your lips day or night (Joshua 1:8). And it is forbidden to divulge this teaching to the unlearned" (Babylonian Talmud, *Menachot* 99b). How important it is, then, for the unlearned to learn beyond what it is they are taught, and to discover the broad flexibility of the path so many find or assume to be tight and narrow.

Rabbi Simlai may not have been proposing that all the hundreds of precepts in the Torah were pruned and hacked away by David, Isaiah, and the other prophets, but that all of them can be balanced upon foundation principles that number anywhere from eleven to one. The wording in Hebrew for what we have paraphrased as "narrowed them down" is הֶעֱמִידָן, which means "erected them." In other words, the teaching is that, all of the multitudes of commandments in the Torah notwithstanding, they can be set up to stand in perfect balance upon significantly lesser numbers of basic foundation principles. Wrote the sixteenth-century Rabbi Shmuel Edels: "And one who fulfills these [narrowed-down] precepts, which include within them a great portion of the commandments of the

Torah, shall dwell in the 'lofty places,' for such a one will merit very high plateaus of [spiritual] greatness" (Mahar'sha on Babylonian Talmud, *Makot* 24a ועוצם).

Levels of observance may vary from person to person, from age to age, and from community to community. However, the Torah is based upon, and is an outgrowth of, some fundamental principles that have little to do with religion and more to do with being a *mensch*, with being someone who is authentic, honest, sensitive to the feelings of others, and fair. Ironically, the bottom-line foundations to which the Torah's many commandments are boiled down in Rabbi Simlai's teaching make hardly any mention of God altogether, and completely leave out so much as a hint of religious observances. A person who lives by these foundation principles—which are more concerned with rightness of being and ethical relationships with the planet than with religious observance—is just as precious in the eyes of God as one who is "religiously" devout (*Etz Yosef* on *Vayikra Rabbah* 9:3—אורחיה דשיים), and both are observing the same Torah, not more and not less: "Whether you do a lot or whether you do a little, what matters is that your heart is directed to the heavens" (Babylonian Talmud, *Berachot* 17a).

It happened with Rabbi Yannai (second century) that he was walking along the way when he came upon a man who appeared very distinguished and saintly. Said Rabbi Yannai: "Will the rabbi consider accepting an invitation?" Said the man to him: "Yes." Rabbi Yannai took him into his home and served him food and drink. Then he examined the man's knowledge of the written tradition, but the man knew nothing. He examined him in the oral tradition, but he knew nothing; in the exegetical tradition, but he knew nothing; in the interpretive tradition, but he knew nothing. Then he said to him: "Take up [the cup] and recite [the blessing]." Said he: "Let Yannai recite the blessing in his own home." Rabbi Yannai lifted his cup and said: "Can you at least repeat after me?" Said he: "Yes." Said Rabbi Yannai: "Then say this: 'A dog has eaten of Yannai's bread.'" The man jumped to his feet and grabbed hold of Rabbi Yannai, saying: "My inheritance is in your hands, and you dare to withhold it from me?" Asked Rabbi Yannai: "How does your inheritance come to be my responsibility?" Said he: "The tradition belongs not to you alone just because you're so religious and more learned than I, but it belongs to all of us, whether we are observant or not and whether we are learned or not." Said Rabbi Yannai: "Tell me how it is that you who know nothing and practice nothing yet appear so saintly that I took you for a distinguished rabbi." Said he: "In all my days I have never returned an insult to someone who offended me, and I never passed by two people who were quarreling without trying to make peace between them." Said Rabbi Yannai: "You have so much decency, and I called you a dog! Rather, I apply to you the verse [in Psalms 50:23], 'I will show the protectiveness of the Creator to the one who blazes a path of rightness,' for one who sets their ways in rightness is equal to someone who is religiously learned and observant."

Vayikra Rabbah 9:3

What, then, is being Jewish all about? If it all boils down to being ethical and compassionate and charitable, what is so Jewish about that? Good people abound also amid other religious persuasions, as well as amongst those professing no religious affiliation or belief in God altogether. Indeed, Judaism acknowledges with nonchalance that it has no monopoly on ethics and goodness: "[Says the Creator to the Jewish people:] The non-Jews of the world perform far more good deeds about which they were never commanded than you do, and they magnify My Name in the world far more than you do" (*Tanchuma* [Buber ed.], *Ekev* 9a, based on Malachi 1:11); "It is written [Psalms 132:9:] 'Your priests shall be garbed in righteousness'—this refers to the virtuous amongst the non-Jews, who are as priests to the Holy Blessed One" (*Eliyahu Zuta*, end of Ch. 20); "Said Rabbi Meir, 'Even a non-Jewish person who is devoted to the ways of Torah is considered like a Jewish High Priest'" (Babylonian Talmud, *Sanhedrin* 59a, *Bava Kamma* 38a, and *Avodah Zarah* 3a); "I testify before the witness of the heavens and the Earth that anyone can receive upon their self the Holy Spirit, whether they are man or woman, Jewish or not Jewish, slave or free, for all is reckoned according to one's actions" (*Eliyahu Raba*, Ch. 9). Wrote the sixteenth-century Rabbi Yitzchak HaKohain Katz: "In all truth, when non-Jews perform deeds of lovingkindness, they are ישראל ממש—actual Israelites" (on *Midrash Mishlei* on Proverbs 17:1), meaning that they are then living the path that is Jewish, again alluding to the bottom-line principles of Judaism that have less to do with religion than with social hamony and benevolence. In fact, when Rabbi Akiva was asked to expound on how far one ought to go in honoring one's parents, he employed the example of a local *non*-Jewish man named Damah ben Netinah (Babylonian Talmud, *Avodah Zarah* 23b). Not that there was a shortage of examples of *Jewish* respect for mother and father, several of which are subsequently provided in the same narrative; but to Rabbi Akiva goodness was goodness whether the individual exemplifying it was Jewish or not.

Those who belittle the Jewishness of irreligious social actions Jews or irreligious humanistic Jews, are missing the point. If their dedication to the welfare of justice and human well-being comes from a place of earnestness and altruism, then even though they may never have kept a Sabbath or cared about whether or not they were eating kosher food, they are fulfilling what is most dear to the Creator (Babylonian Talmud, *Avot* 3:3). More than anything else, taught the ancient rabbis, it is about acts on behalf of others that we will be asked when we stand before the Creator in the end (*Midrash Tehilim* on Psalms 118:19). Said the third-century Rabbi Yehudah ben Yechezkiel, "Anyone who denies the virtue of doing deeds of lovingkindness denies also the root principle of the Torah"

(*Kohelet Rabbah* 7:4). In other words, the root principle of Torah is lovingkindness.

Goodness, Judaism then teaches, is unrelated to any particular religious classification, but neither is it particularly related to religion altogether. The rabbis of ancient times acknowledged that belief in God and religious devotion are not necessarily synonymous with virtue or with what is important in the eyes of the Creator: "The generation of David were religiously devout, yet they would go to war and lose because there were slanderers among them; the generation of King Achav were idol-worshipers, yet they would go to war and win because there was no ill speech between them" (Jerusalem Talmud, *Peah* 1:1 or 4a).

> Once, during a drought, it was disclosed in a dream to Rabbi Avahu (third century) that a man called Pentakakus should pray for rain. Pentakakus prayed and rain fell accordingly. Rabbi Avahu sent for Pentakakus to appear before him. Asked Avahu: "What is your occupation?" Replied Pentakakus: "I commit five sins every day. I hire prostitutes on behalf of those who desire to be with them. And I decorate the arenas where they gather, and I dance and clap my hands in order to attract customers for them. I also bring their special garments to the wash house to clean them, and I play the tambourine at their orgies." Said Avahu: "Have you ever done so much as one single good deed?" Said Pentakakus: "Once I was decorating their arena when I came upon a woman who was weeping behind one of the pillars. When I inquired as to why she was crying, she explained that her husband had been imprisoned [by the Romans] and that she was preparing to prostitute herself in order to acquire the ransom she needed to free him. When I heard this, I immediately went and sold my valuable bed and bedding and gave her money to cover the ransom. And I said to her: 'Go now and liberate your husband and do not prostitute yourself.'" Declared Avahu: "Indeed, you truly *do* deserve to have your prayers answered."
>
> Jerusalem Talmud, *Taanit* 1:4 or 5b

Many stories like this one fill the same pages of the ancient Jewish tradition as do stories and teachings of extraordinary religious devotion. It is sad that most Jews are taught the latter category to the sore neglect of the former, and thus miss out on the broader horizons of Judaic theology that posit that religious practice is sweet, but not necessarily the end-all of what it is that is important or precious to human ideals and to the will of the Creator. At best, the Jewish ideal comprises a combination of both ritual observance and ethical interaction with the world: "How beautiful it is, and how pleasurable it is to the Creator, when one combines Torah with harmonious behavior and good deeds" (Babylonian Talmud, *Avot* 2:2 and *Bamidbar Rabbah* 13:16). Bottom line, however, it comprises ethical interaction with the world alone: "One who buys and sells in truthfulness and honesty, and whom the creations find pleasant to be around, is regarded as if they had fulfilled the entire Torah" (*Mechilta* on Exodus 15:26). Rabbi Elisha ben Avuyah (second century) taught: "One who has studied much Torah and is also involved in the performance of lovingkindness is like a horse with reins; one who has only Torah learning but does not engage in deeds of lovingkindness is like a horse with no reins who soon throws its rider over its head" (Babylonian Talmud, *Avot D'Rebbe Natan* 24: 4). "One who says 'I have only Torah' has not even got Torah" (Babylonian Talmud, *Yoma* 109b). Interestingly, when the third-century Rabbi Natan bar Abba pondered which of the two ideals would best prove that one was a descendant of Abraham, he chose the bottom-line ideal: "One who is compassionate toward the creations, it is clear that they are a descendant of Abraham our father; one who is not compassionate toward the creations, it is clear that they are not descended from Abraham" (Babylonian Talmud, *Beitzah* 32b). Of course, by "descended from Abraham" Rabbi Natan meant figuratively, as in emulation of practice; descendants, then, of Abraham the lifestyle, not Abraham the man. After all, few Jews can actually claim direct descendancy from the first Jew since the Jewish people, past and present, are a mixture of Abrahamic scions and non-Abrahamic peoples who converted to Judaism over thousands of years. Judaism is not, and never was, a race.

Clearly, the rabbis endeavored always to remind its adherents that Torah was not solely about religion, but about combining religious beliefs and observances with a way of being on the planet that is in harmony with "self" and "other." Religious devotion and ritual practices alone, however, are purposeless, are irrelevant to the Creation and inconsequential to the Creator: "What does the Holy Blessed One care whether a Jew slaughters an animal according to ritual requirements or not, or whether a Jew eats of kosher or non-kosher animals? Does [the observance of these rituals] benefit God, or [does the transgression of these observances] harm God? Rather, these laws were given only for the purpose of refining human behavior and sensitivity" (*Tanchuma* [Buber ed.]), *Sh'mini* No. 7). Jewish ritual slaughter, for example, requires the utmost meticulousness in ensuring that the animal experiences no pain or terror. And the practice of eating of animals that are prey rather than predator is, as the rabbis put it: "to teach us to rather be among the pursued than among those who pursue others" (Babylonian Talmud, *Bava Kamma* 93a). Religion, then, was validated by the rabbis only when its practice raised human consciousness toward compassion and the celebration of aliveness.

Tragically, history records that, in itself, religious devotion has wrought most of the savagery and injustice ever perpetrated against humanity. How many times have individuals and whole communities been randomly slaughtered, enslaved, or relentlessly persecuted by those professing devotion to God or to some religious belief or another? It is in the name of God and religion that both national armies and civilian mobs have ravaged and savaged those whose belief systems differed in any way, whether or not that system included belief in God. Self-righteous colonialists who rationalized their conquests (read "rape") of indigenous peoples as a necessary domestication of "savagery" failed to acknowledge the fact that what *they* did was more savage, more barbarous, than anything the natives were doing. The failure to make this acknowledgment stems not from blindness of fact, but from a tunnel vision that views as legitimate all massacring and culture-raping that is done "in the name of the Lord," or under the banner of a particular religious belief system.

As essential as the ancient rabbis considered religious observance, they never forgot how those specifically prescribed practices and rituals were intended to refine and ennoble human behavior, and that they were meaningless if they did not achieve that end (*Midrash Rebbe Akiva ben Yosef al ha-Tagin*, ot פ). Taught the second-century Rabbi Hunah: "One who engages in Torah only, and not in deeds of lovingkindness, is comparable to one who has no God" (Babylonian Talmud, *Avodah Zarah* 17b). The first-century Rabbi Chanina ben Dosa taught: "It is analogous to a man who entered a shop and asked for a pint of wine, but when the shopkeeper asked him for his flask he offered him his sack. The man then ordered some oil, but when the shopkeeper asked him for his jar he offered him the corner of his shawl. Said the shopkeeper, 'You haven't any vessel and yet you wish to buy wine and oil?' Likewise with one who seeks to observe the Torah but is lacking in deeds of lovingkindness" (Babylonian Talmud, *Avot D'Rebbe Natan* [version 2] 32:8). The rabbis, then, obviously taught and fought just as hard *against* organized religion as they did *for* it, with about as many parables and admonishments advocating ritual observance as demonstrating how ethical behavior without religion was just as high and sometimes even higher:

> Rabbi Abbaya bar Chailil (fourth century), who led the academy at Pumbedissa, would receive greetings from [the angels in heaven] once every week, on Friday. Rabbi Rava bar Yosef bar Chama, who led the academy at Mechuza, would receive greetings from [the angels in heaven] once every year, on the eve of Yom Kippur. However, Abba the blood-extractor [then a form of health maintenance] received greetings from [the

angels in heaven] every day! When Rabbi Abbaya discovered that Abba, who was only a blood-extractor, received heavenly greetings daily, he became distraught with puzzlement. It was then told him [from the heavens]: "Your actions do not come anywhere near those of Abba the blood-extractor." And what were the deeds of Abba the blood-extractor? When he performed the bleeding on his patients, he maintained a separate room for men and for women. He also had a garment with many slits in it so that when a woman patient came to him, she would don it and be treated without violation of her privacy. At the entrance to his office he kept a box where his fees could be deposited anonymously, so that someone who could not afford the fee in full could deposit what they could afford without feeling ashamed. And whenever Abba noticed that a patient was destitute, he would give them some of his own money and say: "Go and empower yourself."

Babylonian Talmud, *Ta'anit 21b–22a*

But, again, if the bottom line of Jewish practice is just being a nice person, what is particularly Jewish about being Jewish? The answer is that there is a particularly Jewish way of being a nice person, just as there is a particularly Jewish way of relating with the Creator, as Abraham taught. There is a specifically Jewish theology about relationships; about giving charity, visiting the sick, or consoling the bereaved. To do good things in the world and to live ethically is not peculiar to Judaism, but to do all that with the particular quality delineated by the Jewish tradition is. This is why the rabbis pressed for the study of Torah as essential for knowing the how-to of the way of living and being on the planet that is uniquely Jewish, uniquely Abrahamic, uniquely the way of the boundary crosser (for a glimpse of the Jewish way of doing or not doing Jewish stuff, read *The Place Where You Are Standing Is Holy*, by Gershon Winkler and Lakme Batya Elior [Jason Aronson, 1995]). Of course, this is not to intimate that qualities of loving-kindness other than those of the Jewish tradition are lesser or in any way discounted. The purpose of this book is not to boast of the Judaic path of rightness over any other, but to focus on the particularity of Judaism's unique gift to the rainbow of life paths that abound on the planet. This gift has long gone unnoticed even among Jews themselves, concealed inadvertently beneath layers and layers of dogmatic hedge-building that evolved over the ages out of periodic needs to preserve an oft-threatened faith and foster religious identity in a people that has just as often been deprecated and persecuted.

Building fences around original principles, or rendering stringent that which was at one time lenient, was for many centuries considered an essential instrument for the preservation of the Judaic tradition, especially during times of national or communal upheaval. However, the rabbis also recognized the dangers inherent in excessive fence construction, that it could lead to the loss of the very thing it was intended to safekeep and could dilute the strength of the tradition altogether, a consequence with which the contemporary Jewish community has been grappling since the advent of the "modern era." Warned the second-century Rabbi Chiyya: "Let not the hedge become more important than the vineyard" (*B'reishis Rabbah* 19:4). Or: "Do not construct a hedge that is too tall, lest it collapse and tear up the garden" (Babylonian Talmud, *Avot D'Rebbe Natan* 1:1 [version 2]). Or: "Said Rabbi Yosee: 'Better a hedge a mere ten cubits high that will stand, than a hedge a hundred cubits high that will fall'" (Babylonian Talmud, *Avot D'Rebbe Natan* 1:1 [version 1]). It is one thing to tighten the opening of a sack of flour to prevent the flour from spilling out; it is quite another thing to tighten the opening of a sack of flour when the bottom is coming apart. The flexidoxic teachings in Judaism were, then, attempts at salvaging the spill by loosening that which had been excessively tightened.

It was the custom in Sura not to eat the meat of cow udder [since it might contain residue of milk]. In Pumbedissa, however, they did eat the meat of cow udder. Once, Rami bar Timri of Pumbedissa happened to pass through Sura on the eve of Yom Kippur. He came upon a field where all the inhabitants had discarded cow udders. He took them and ate them. They brought him before Rabbi Chisda. Asked Rabbi Chisda: "Why did you do this [violate the prohibition against eating cow udders]?" Replied Rami: "I am from the academy of Rabbi Yehudah, who permits us to eat [the udders of cows]." Said Rabbi Chisda: "And did you not know that you are supposed to observe the more stringent practices of either the place you are coming from or of the place you are visiting [whichever is stricter]?" Said Rami: "I ate the udders beyond the boundaries of your village." Asked Rabbi Chisda: "How, then, did you roast them?" Said Rami: "With [fire fueled by] the seeds of grapes." Asked Rabbi Chisda: "Perhaps they were from [forbidden] grapes that had been used for idolatrous sacrament." Said Rami: "They appeared to be more than twelve months old [so the laws about impure grapes would not have applied]." Said Rabbi Chisda: "Perhaps they belonged to someone and you were thus stealing." Said Rami: "Any owner must certainly have given up on them by now, for they had sprouted shoots." He noticed that Rami was not wearing *tefilin* [ritual phylacteries]. He asked him: "Why did you not put on *tefilin?*" Said he: "I have some problems with my digestion, and Rabbi Yehudah taught that whoever suffers from digestive problems is exempt from wearing *tefilin.*" He noticed he was not wearing *tzitzit* (ritual fringes) [on the corners of his garment]. He asked him: "Why are you not wearing *tzitzit?*" Replied Rami: "My mantle is borrowed, and Rabbi Yehudah taught that borrowed garb is exempt from *tzitzit* for thirty days [biblically, however, it is exempt forever (Babylonian Talmud, *Hulin* 137a)]." Later, a man was brought in for behaving disrespectfully toward his father and mother. They tied him [to a post in order to flog him]. Said Rami: "Release him! For it is taught that every precept in the Torah whose reward for observance is spelled out [as is the case with the commandment to honor one's parents] is outside the jurisdiction of any mortal court." [The man was freed.] Said Rabbi Chisda: "I concede to you that you are a man with acute perceptivity." Said he: "Were

you to study in the academy of Rabbi Yehudah ben Yechezkel
[at Pumbedissa], you, too, would acquire a sharp mind."
Babylonian Talmud, *Hulin* 110a–b

The rabbis decreed that since everyone is obligated to sound
the *shofar* on Rosh Hashanah and not everyone knows how,
it may not be sounded if the festival falls on the Sabbath, lest
the people will go about seeking teachers to coach them and
thus end up carrying [the *shofar*] in public domain on the
Sabbath, which is forbidden. . . . Once, when Rosh Hashanah
fell on the Sabbath, the surrounding communities gathered in
Yavneh. Rabbi Yochanan ben Zakkai then said to the sons of
B'teirah: "Let us blow the *shofar* on behalf of the people."
Said they: "Let us clarify the law first to see if it is permitted."
Said he: "Let us blow the *shofar* first, and then we will clarify
the law." They blew the *shofar* all over Yavneh. Afterwards,
the sons of B'teirah came to him and said: "Now let us
clarify the law." Said he: "The sound of the horn has already
been heard across Yavneh. It is inappropriate to determine
what the law is after the fact."
Babylonian Talmud, *Rosh Hashanah* 29b

Even a thousand years *after* the brazen decision of Rabbi
Yochanan ben Zakkai concerning the sounding of the *shofar*
on the Sabbath, there remained a minority of sages who continued to defy the hedge. One such dissenting rabbi was the
eleventh-century Yitzchak al Fazi (Rif), whose commentary on
the Talmud adorns the shelves of every traditional Jewish
household (Rabbeinu Asher on Babylonian Talmud, *Rosh
Hashanah* 29a–b). Rabbi Yitzchak felt, as did Rabbi Yochanan,
that even if the masses were not proficient in the sounding of
the *shofar*, if there were people in town who *were* adept at it,
there was no reason the *shofar* could not be sounded by them
on behalf of the populace. The hedge, they obviously felt in
this case, was far too thick. Nevertheless, the custom of not
sounding the *shofar* on the Sabbath prevails to this day in the
halachic codes. Even the disciples of Rabbi Yitzchak chose to

ignore the lenient opinion of their teacher and to instead follow the more stringent ruling. This appears to be the case with most hedges or fences—that the people and the rabbis chose to follow the stricter rulings, while a select few saw no reason to do so and chose the lenient options. The fourth-century Rabbi Dimi taught: "Is it not enough for you what the Torah has already forbidden, that you need to add further prohibitions to yourself?" (Jerusalem Talmud, *Nedarim* 25a).

The ancient teachers also understood that what stringency one generation or community chose for itself was not necessarily binding upon another generation or community. This is why, they explained, the opinions of the minority, or the overruled, were recorded alongside the rulings of those who received the majority vote: "So that in the event that circumstances of a future generation will necessitate the implementation of the minority opinion, it will have a precedent [rooted in the tradition] which will support its decisions" (Babylonian Talmud, *Edios* 1:5—see *Tosefot Shantz*).

"Every *mitzvah* and every word of the Torah," wrote the sixteenth-century mystic Rabbi Moshe Cordovero, "has its age in which it can and ought to be revealed and manifested" (*Shiyur Komah*, Ch. 41), meaning that each paradigm requires a particular aspect of Torah for its birthing and fruition. All the other *mitzvot* do not then become irrelevant or outmoded, but the specific ones that are experienced as addressing most pragmatically the consciousness of a particular paradigm becomes that era's primary focus of observance, that generation's particular *mitzvah*. The first-century Rabbi Yochanan ben Zakkai recognized this when he opted not to ask the Romans to spare the Holy Temple. Ritual sacrifice, he realized, was no longer achieving its purpose in the lives and in the consciousness of the people who brought them or in the priests who offered them on their behalf. The age of serving God in space had come to an end, and it was time to let go and to move into the successive phase of serving God, which was relating to the Creator through prayer and deed. In fact, the ancient rabbis admitted that the whole idea of sacrifices to begin with, for the Jewish people, was to wean them from the contemporary global compulsion of sacrificing to the powers of nature and to gods (*Vayikra Rabbah* 22:5). As Maimonides wrote:

> During that period, the universal custom among the populace, and the way in which we were reared, was to offer up in sacrifice various life forms to icons and images erected in temples of worship. . . . To forbid such practices outright would have been tantamount to a prophet coming to us in our own time, declaring: "God has hereby given you a law forbidding you to pray to Him or to call upon Him in time of trouble. And your worship will from now on consist solely of meditating and no deeds whatsoever." Therefore did the Creator tolerate the continuation of the aforementioned types of worship, but shifted them from that which was illusory and fanciful to His own Great Name. . . . It was through this divine pretense that idol-worship was wiped from the memory of our people and in its stead was established the foundation of our faith, which is the existence and oneness of God. And this was achieved without discomforting or repelling the souls of the people by abolishing ways of worship to which they had been accustomed and which had until then been the only mode of worship they had known.
>
> *Moreh Nevuchim* 3:32:46

It took bold leaders like Yochanan ben Zakkai to finally declare the culmination of that weaning period, to coach the birthing of a long-overdue paradigm shift that had been cooking for several centuries already, and whose neglect had ultimately led to religious and political corruption in the Temple officialdom. In fact, by the year 29 c.e., some forty years before the fall of the Second Temple, the rabbis had already removed their court, known as Sanhedrin, from the Temple grounds and relocated it to Yavneh, thereby also making capital punishment impossible since such judgments were permitted only in the sacred space of the Temple (Babylonian Talmud,

Avodah Zarah 8b, *Rosh Hashanah* 31a–b, *Shabbat* 15a). The acknowledgment of the end of this paradigm was so strong that the second-century exilarch Rabbi Yehudah the Prince reportedly tried to abolish Tisha B'Av—the annual day of fasting and mourning over the Temple's destruction—or at least to disregard the day altogether whenever it coincided with the Sabbath rather than to make up for it on the following day (Jerusalem Talmud, *Taanit* 4:6 [22b] and *Yevamot* 6:6 [30b]).

The *chutzpah* of these rabbis to so much as entertain the abolition of anything instituted in the Jewish religion is hereditary, transmitted through all generations through the DNA of the way of the boundary crosser. It stems from the gall of the earliest of Hebrew ancestors, whose take on religion was that it had to work for people, and that when it didn't, it had to be circumvented. The second-century Rabbi Natan ben Yosef's teaching that "the Sabbath was given into your hands, and you were not given into the hands of the Sabbath" (Babylonian Talmud, *Yoma* 85b) is one of many such dicta in ancient Jewish teaching, but is perhaps most reflective of the flexidoxic sentiments entertained by many of the leading sages throughout history. The bottom line is that your self-respect and well-being comes first, then religious observance: "Great is the dignity of the creations, for it takes precedence over a [ritual] prohibition of the Torah" (Babylonian Talmud, *Berachot* 19b; *Shabbat* 81b, 94b).

Judaism, then, was not founded upon hierarchical authority and absoluteness. No one particular prophet among the Jewish people had the "final say" on what being Jewish entailed. The unique relationship that Judaism enjoys with its scriptures and prophets is personal, and therefore interactive. The "word" does not have the only voice; the people have one, too, collectively and individually. As Abraham Joshua Heschel put it: "The Bible is more than the word of God: it is the word of God *and* man; a record of both revelation and response" (*God in Search of Man*, pp. 260–261). Even Moses, who was considered the greatest prophet, was not considered the final mouthpiece of divine revelation. As the third-century Rabbi Yosee, the son of Rabbi Chanina, taught: "There were matters of Torah that were revealed to Rabbi Akiva that had not been revealed to Moses" (*Bamidbar Rabbah* 19:4). Wrote Maimonides: "Behold, not every interpretive teaching that the sages derived from Torah was a *halachah* that originated in the revelation to Moses at Sinai" (*Sefer HaMitzvot L'HaRambam, Shoresh Sheyni*).

> Said Rabbi Yosi bar Chanina: "Four decrees did Moses ordain upon the Israelites. Then came four [later] prophets and abolished them. Moses had said: '[When you do the will of God, you shall be called] Israel [and you] shall dwell in safety, [but if you do not do the will of God] the wellspring of Jacob shall be all alone' (Deuteronomy 33:28). But then came Amos and abolished Moses' decree and said: 'How shall Jacob withstand [such a stipulation]?' and subsequently it is written: 'And God withdrew [the decree]' (Amos 7:2–3 and 5–6). Moses had said: 'And among those nations [where you shall be exiled] you will find no respite' (Deuteronomy 28:65). But then came Jeremiah and abolished this decree and said: 'Thus says God, "To the people Israel, who have been driven by the sword, I shall go to them and grant them repose"' (Jeremiah 31:1). Moses had said: 'God collects from the children for the sins of the parents' (Exodus 34:7). But then came Ezekiel and abolished this decree and said: 'The son whose father has sinned shall not die for the wrongs of his father; he shall surely live! Only the one who committed the wrong shall die for it' (Ezekiel 18:14–20). Moses had said: 'And you shall be lost among the nations and the land of your enemy shall swallow you up' (Leviticus 26:38). But then came Isaiah and abolished this decree and said (Isaiah 27:13): 'And then shall come forth all who have been lost in the land of Ashur and who have been exiled into the land of Egypt.'"
>
> Babylonian Talmud, *Makot* 24a
> (bracketed parts based on the commentary of the seventeenth-
> century Rabbi Shmuel HaLevi Edels [Mahar'sha])

Nonetheless, the most daring account of flexidoxic rabbinics is that about a teacher we know only as "Yaakov the man of K'far Nuberius near Tyre" (third century C.E.). Two stories are told about him in the Jerusalem Talmud and in midrashic literature, and in both accounts he is described as a radical interpreter of the Torah who was repeatedly called to task for his rebellious halachic rulings. Actually, all he did was demonstrate the old adage that there are many ways to interpret the Torah, and in his rulings he challenged the absoluteness of the *halachah* of his time, the absoluteness of the interpretation of Torah as laid down by the more renowned masters. The "elite" rabbis established their halachic rulings based on exegetical extrapolation from Torah writ, and he saw no reason not to do the same and, in so doing, arrive at entirely different conclusions! For example, even though Torah writ does not spell out that birds require ritual slaughter in order for them to be kosher for consumption by a Jew (Babylonian Talmud, *Hulin* 4a), the rabbis decreed that they did, basing their ordinance on exegetical interpretation of Torah. Yaakov of K'far Nuberius, however, employed the same process of exegetical intepretation and ruled that if fowl required ritual slaughter, so did fish:

Yaakov the sage from K'far Nuberius near Tyre once ruled that fish required ritual slaughter. Rabbi Chaggi heard of this and he summoned him to his court, and he came. Said Rabbi Chaggi: "From what source do you derive your ruling?" Said he: "From the verse, 'Let the waters be filled with swarms of living beings, and let winged creatures fly over the face of the earth' [Genesis 1:20]. Just as birds require ritual slaughter, so also do fish require ritual slaughter [since both are mentioned in the same verse]." Said Rabbi Chaggi: "Prepare to be flogged." Said Rabbi Yaakov: "A man shares words of Torah, and for that he is flogged?" Said Rabbi Chaggi: "You have not ruled correctly." Said Rabbi Yaakov: "According to what sources are you informing me so?" Said Rabbi Chaggi: "From the verse, 'Sheep and cattle shall they slaughter for themselves, and all sorts of fish of the sea shall they gather for themselves' [Numbers 11:21]. These [sheep and cattle] require ritual slaughter and these [fish] could just be gathered." Said Yaakov: "Go on, then, with your flogging, for it is better that I receive it."

Bamidbar Rabbah 19:3

Another example: Established *halachah* qualifies a "born Jew" as someone born of a Jewish woman. Rabbi Yaakov of K'far Nuberius, however, ruled that a child born of a non-Jewish woman is Jewish, too, if the father is Jewish. Patrilineal descent is today a subject of great controversy between the Reform movement and the so-called "traditional" movements, and is criticized as some kind of radical innovation in Judaism the likes of which has never before been known, and therefore outside the bounds of what is authentically and historically Jewish tradition. Yet it had been proposed 1,700 years ago by a teacher of what was then authentically and historically Jewish tradition!

Yaakov the sage from K'far Nuberius near Tyre once ruled that when a Jewish man had sex with a non-Jewish woman and the couple had a son, the boy could be circumcised on the Sabbath [an allowance accorded solely to a Jewish-born child, i.e., a child born of a Jewish woman]. When Rabbi Chaggi heard of this, he summoned Rabbi Yaakov to his court, and he came. Asked Rabbi Chaggi: "From what source do you derive your ruling?" Said he: "It is written that the offspring were reckoned unto the house of their fathers (Numbers 1) [so if the father is Jewish, so is the child]." Said Rabbi Chaggi: "Prepare to be flogged." Said Rabbi Yaakov: "A man shares words of Torah, and for that he gets flogged?" Said Rabbi Chaggi: "You did not rule correctly." Said Rabbi Yaakov: "According to what sources are you informing me so?" Said Rabbi Chaggi: "If a son of the nations will come to you and say, 'I wish to become Jewish on the condition that you circumcise me on the Sabbath, or on Yom Kippur,' do we violate the Sabbath to do this for him, or not? Is it not so that we violate the Sabbath to perform ritual circumcision only for the

son of a Jewish woman?" Said Rabbi Yaakov: "And from
where do you know that?" Said Rabbi Chaggi: "For it is written, 'And now let us forge a covenant with our God to exclude
all of our non-Jewish wives and whomever was born of them'
(Ezra 10:3)." Said Rabbi Yaakov: "You wish to flog me based
on a mere narrative from our history?" Said Rabbi Chaggi:
"It is also written there, 'We shall do this according to the
instruction of the Torah'" (Ezra 10:3). Said Rabbi Yaakov:
"And according to which Torah is that?" Said Rabbi Chaggi:
"From the teaching of Rabbi Yochanan in the name of Rabbi
Shimon bar Yochai that it is written 'You shall not marry with
them [the seven nations of Canaan]' (Deuteronomy 7:3)—
why? 'For they will divert your child from [God]' (Deuteronomy
7:4). Your child who is from a Jewish woman is called your
child, but a child born of a non-Jewish woman is not your child,
but her child.'" Said Yaakov: "Go on, then, with your flogging, for it is better that I receive it."

Bamidbar Rabbah 19:3

In both accounts, our hapless rabbi is being summoned to
the "Rabbi Superior" of the region and threatened with flogging, which in Judaism required the flogger to possess "much
wisdom and little strength" (Babylonian Talmud, *Makot* 23a).
Conventional commentary on these stories plays up Rabbi
Yaakov's final statement as an indication that he conceded to
Rabbi Chaggi, and that he admitted the error of his interpretation and ruling. But it is this book's contention that Rabbi
Yaakov realized that his disputation and proofs were of no use
against established dogma; that he realized that the dialogue
was going nowhere because Rabbi Chaggi was already set in
his acceptance of established *halachah*, of "the way it is," and
failed to see how his own proofs were no less exegetical, no
less interpretive speculation, than the proofs Rabbi Yaakov had
brought. So when Rabbi Yaakov said: "Go on, then, with your
flogging, for it is better that I receive it," he probably meant:
"You may as well proceed with the flogging because I shall be

silent and not feed this dispute any further because you're not hearing me; you're playing rabbinic ping-pong and engaging in pilpulic semantics." As the second-century Rabbi Ila taught: "The world thrives only in the merit of one who remains silent in a moment of conflict" (Babylonian Talmud, *Chulin* 89b); that there are times when silence is the wisest of options (Babylonian Talmud, *Avot* 3:13). Interestingly enough, Lakme Batya Elior points out that a teaching of Yaakov of K'far Nuberius is recorded elsewhere that proves how the quality of silence held a special place in his personal discipline:

> Said Rabbi Avin (fourth century): Yaakov of K'far Nuberius near Tyre interpreted Psalms 65:2 to read, "To You, O Creator, silence is praise" [a radical translation of what contextually reads, "Praise waits for You, O Creator"]. [Yaakov further said:] "Silence is a medicine for everything. It is like a priceless jewel, and no matter how high you evaluate its worth, you will underestimate it."
>
> *Midrash Tehilim* on Psalms 19:2

It is also noteworthy that our rebel rabbi is being quoted here by Rabbi Avin, who lived almost a century later. Obviously, this Yaakov of K'far Nuberius cannot be dismissed as an insignificant nobody in Jewish theological history. We ought not, therefore, to take the stories about him for granted and write him off conveniently as an erring teacher who conceded to his mistakes and promised never to make them again. Had that been the case, it would have been highly unlikely that he would indeed have continued to render halachic conclusions that ran contrary to those established by his superiors and predecessors. On the contrary: Yaakov was a man who dared to exercise his autonomy in an age when that was considered theologically dangerous, lest there be "two Torahs in Israel" (Babylonian Talmud, *Sanhedrin* 88b). Yet he stood his ground, received his reproof, and continued ruling on halachic issues according to what he believed was authentic Torah teaching.

Moreover, he preached about the virtue of silence in situations where words only furthered conflict rather than resolved it, and he practiced it devoutly: "Go on, then, with your flogging, for it is better that I receive it" than to continue fueling a dispute that is leading nowhere positive.

There did indeed exist "two Torahs in Israel," the Talmud recounts (Babylonian Talmud, *Sanhedrin* 88b), implying two or perhaps even more interpretations of Torah, each with very different halachic ramifications. The disciples of Hillel and the disciples of Shammai, for example, were in disagreement over approximately 130 issues of Torah interpretation and 115 halachic decrees and ordinances (see Rabbi Samson Raphael Hirsch, *Collected Writings* [Feldheim, 1988], Vol. 5, p. 65). Yaakov of K'far Nuberius, however, lived two centuries later, by which time the sages had decreed that the *halachah* should follow only one of the schools, primarily that of Hillel (Babylonian Talmud, *Eruvin* 13b), "in order to avoid conflict in Israel" (Babylonian Talmud, *Sanhedrin* 88b). Yet, even so, while "generally the *halachah* is like the School of Hillel, whoever wishes to do according to the School of Shammai, may do so" (Babylonian Talmud, *Rosh Hashanah* 14b).

The interdiction against disparity in *halachah* is derived from a play on the words in Hebrew for "You shall not wound yourselves," referring to the practice of mourners in some cultures to cut themselves as part of the mourning rites [Deuteronomy 14:1]. Ironically, the same rabbinic system that employed such far-flung exegesis to proscribe halachic diversity is also the very same rabbinic system that proscribed the derivation of *halachah* from exegesis altogether (Jerusalem Talmud, *Pe'ah* 2:4 [or 9b]). But prior to that decree, halachic diversity was prevalent, was commonplace, and did not—as it does today—divide the people; it did not deter the children of the disciples of Hillel, for example, from marrying the children of the disciples of Shammai, even though some of the laws about which the two schools were in disagreement concerned marriage itself (Babylonian Talmud, *Yevamot* 13a)!

Obviously, there was room for disagreement without dis-concertment, room for opposing someone else's opinion on an issue while also honoring their right to it. This applied not only to conflicts with the rulings of contemporaries, who were usually considered as equals, but also to conflicts with the rulings of predecessors, who were deemed superior in wisdom and that much closer to the core of the tradition (Jerusalem Talmud, *Gitin* 6:7 [or 37b]). The third-century Rabbi Yochanan, for example, remarked how his own generation's capacity for wisdom was like the eye of a needle compared to that of the second-century Rabbi Oshiya's generation (Babylonian Talmud, *Eruvin* 53a). Yet he is recorded as refuting two of Rabbi Oshiya's rulings (Babylonian Talmud, *Hagigah* 9a and *Zevachim* 113a). Other examples include the second-century Rabbi Elazar ben Shamua, who disputed rulings of the first-century Rabbi Eliezer ben Hurcanus (Babylonian Talmud, *Temurah* 18b and 21a); Rabbi Meir, who disputed the ruling of the first-century Hanina Ish Ono (Babylonian Talmud, *Gitin* 67a); Rabbi Natan, who challenged a verdict of his predecessor, Rabbi Yishmael the son of Rabbi Yochanan ben B'roka (Babylonian Talmud, *Pesachim* 34a); the second-century Rabbi Shimon ben Elazar, who disagreed with his predecessor Rabbi Akiva (Babylonian Talmud, *Bava Mezia* 4b and *Mo'ed Katan* 20b); the fourth-century Rabbi Ashi, who opined an alternative interpretation of law to that of his predecessor Rava (Babylonian Talmud, *Pesachim* 6a), who had disputed the halachic rulings of *his* teachers, Rabbah and Rabbi Shmuel (Babylonian Talmud, *Gitin* 2a–b, and *Bava Batra* 7b); the fifth-century Ravina, who contested the verdict of his teacher Rabbi Poppa (Babylonian Talmud, *Bava Mezia* 7b); the fourth-century Rabbi Yosef, who refuted the ruling of his teacher Rabbi Nachman (Babylonian Talmud, *Bava Batra* 6a), who had disputed *his* teachers, Rabbah bar Avuha and Rabbi Shmuel (Babylonian Talmud, *Bava Batra* 6a–b); the third-century Rabbi Yosee, the son of Rabbi Yehudah, who disagreed with his father's ruling (Babylonian Talmud, *Nedarim* 63b).

On a lighter note, the Talmud tells of two rabbis who argued with one another even after their deaths: "When they [the funeral procession] arrived at a narrow bridge, the camels stopped in their tracks. Asked the Arabian [camel driver]: 'What is happening?' Explained the rabbis: 'Neither [of the deceased] wishes to be disrespectful to the other. This one says, You go first, and this one says, No, you go first'" (Babylonian Talmud, *Mo'ed Katan* 25b). Wrote the nineteenth-century Rabbi Mordechai Yosef of Ishbitz: "One should not serve God like those who perform out of rote; therefore do not blindly follow in the [religious] ways of your teacher or of your parents [rather, everyone must find their own path to God]" (*Mei HaShilo'ach*, Vol. 2, *Yitro* 16b).

[Biblically, grain in the land of Israel could not be eaten before it had been tithed. The rabbis decreed, however, that even outside of Israel grain needed to be tithed. Biblically, tree produce in the Holy Land did not require tithing. The rabbis decreed, however, that it did require tithing in the Holy Land, but not in lands outside of Israel. There were several places near Israel around which there was controversy about whether or not they were part of the Holy Land, as delineated in the Hebrew scriptures. One such place was Bet Sh'an:] It happened once that Rabbi Yehoshua ben Ziruz (second century), the son of the father-in-law of Rabbi Meir, testified before Rabbi Yehudah the Prince that Rabbi Meir had eaten of a leaf at Bet Sh'an [without having tithed it first]. Rabbi Yehudah the Prince then declared [that since Rabbi Meir had eaten the leaf without tithing, Bet Sh'an was not scripturally a part of the Holy Land, and therefore] all the produce of Bet Sh'an was permitted [was exempt from tithing]. When Rabbi Yehudah's brothers and members of his father's family heard of this they reproached him, saying: "A place whose produce your father and your father's fathers regarded as forbidden [without tithing, even though it was outside of the Holy Land] you regard

as permissible?" Replied Rabbi Yehudah: "Scripture records
how Hezkiah 'smashed to pieces the copper serpent that
Moses had made, for unto those days the Israelites had burnt
incense to it' (2 Kings 18:4). Is it possible that [Hezkiah's ances-
tor] Assa had come and not removed it? Or that [Hezkiah's
ancestor] Yehoshafat had come and not removed it? Is it not
so that every idol in the world had been abolished by Assa
and Yehoshafat (1 [Kings 15:12]? But just as Hezkiah's ancestors left room for Hezkiah to make a mark for himself, so,
too, have *my* predecessors left room for me to distinguish myself." From this we learn that if a scholar pronounces [an innovation in] *halachah*, we do not make him retract his opinion, we do not reject him, we do not admonish him, we do
not accuse him of haughtiness.

    Babylonian Talmud, *Hulin* 6b–7a [bracketed annotations
    based on the commentaries of Rashi and Rabbeinu Gershom]

Disagreement with, or changing the ruling of, a "superior"
predecessor was not uncommon, and was the very force behind the perpetuation of Judaic tradition. It was a process that
kept Judaism alive and prevented its stagnation. In each generation, the spiritual teachers of the boundary crossers breathed
fresh life into the ancient path by daring to cross the boundaries set by the teachers of previous generations. Wrote the
seventeenth-century Rabbi Shab'tai HaKohain [Shach]: "And
even though I am not worthy to quarrel with the greats of the
earlier sages, nevertheless the Torah was placed at a corner
junction (i.e., within everyone's reach), and proofs that are lucid
will stand on the strength of their own evidence and will be
justified. And truth will show its own way" (on *Shulchan Aruch,
Choshen Mishpat, Hilchot To'en V'nit'an* 91:33).

    Indeed, in ancient times it was considered wrongful for a
rabbi who disagreed with a ruling of the prevailing rabbinic
supreme court to nonetheless abide by it—so wrongful, in fact,
that he had to do penance for acting contrary to his gut feelings and not challenging the authorities (Babylonian Talmud,
Horayot, first *mishnah*)!

Absoluteness in Jewish religious law and practice is, then, more fiction than fact. There was always ample room for negotiation, for discussion, for disagreement and challenge. Not in vain, then, is Torah called "tree of life" (Proverbs 3:18). The Torah, after all, was believed to be not a static, unyielding doctrine, but a living dynamic that flowed *with*, not against or in spite of, the everyday reality of life circumstance.

3
Halachah

Judaism is equipped with laws about how to behave, how to conduct business, what to do with your harvest, how to visit a mourner, what blessing to recite after emptying the bowels, how to observe the Sabbath and festivals, and so on. These laws and customs are alluded to in the Written Tradition, which is the Torah, elaborated in the Oral Tradition, which is the Midrash, and interpreted for individual situations and unprecedented circumstances in the Interpretive Tradition, which is the Mishnah and Talmud. These interpretations of law remained oral for centuries, until the twelfth century, when Rabbi Moshe ibn Maimon, known as Rambam or Maimonides, codified them into practical law in his compendium *Yad HaChazakah*, also known as *Mishnah Torah*. In the fourteenth century, Maimonides' codification of Jewish law was upgraded by Rabbeinu Asher in a compendium called *Tur*, and eventually in the codes of the sixteenth-century Rabbi Yosef Karo that were popularly known as the *Shulchan Aruch*. Karo's codes remain to this day the most authoritative and most frequently used of the codes, and were annotated by Karo's contemporary, Rabbi Moshe Isserles, who often qualifies Karo's rulings with contextual application and balances his opinions with those of other authorities. The codes never became the exclusive determinant of religious legal application, but served more as guidelines for halachic—or Jewish legal—rulings. These rulings in situations brought before rabbinic authorities are known as the responsa, and they make up thousands of volumes spanning centuries. The responsa are a process that continues beyond any attempt to codify Judaism, preserving the organic nature of Jewish law, and thereby its aliveness, for generations to come.

On many situational issues dealt with or not by the codes, most devotees will consult their contemporary spiritual leaders, who, in turn, will research the original contextual talmudic discussions of the issue at hand or corresponding issues, then read up on the responsa to see how others had dealt with the question, and then weigh the sources and the peculiar problem at hand until they arrive at a personal decision. Contrary to what many people presume about halachic decision making, then, codes of Jewish law were never intended as final verdicts, but as *recorded* verdicts, based on particular opinions of particular rabbis in particular ages.

Jewish law is therefore appropriately called *halachah*, which translates as "the walking." It is dynamic, always flowing, always dancing, always walking in cadence with the individual or community that follows it. Like a responsible, caring guide, *halachah* never walks too far in front of its followers, or too fast, or over terrain that is too rugged; it always looks over its shoulder to make sure that the followers are not falling behind, are not left to stumble and struggle along the way. On the contrary, the flexidoxic nature of *halachah* is in its elasticity, in its serving the follower not merely as a guide, but as a walking stick. *Halachah* was therefore never codified in the beginning; codification was, in fact, forbidden (Babylonian Talmud, *Gitin* 60b; *Temurah* 14b: "Those who write down *halachah*, it is as if they are burning the Torah"). Rather, *halachah* remained fluid and organic, affording the follower ample space to walk around it or to leap over it whenever necessary, whenever their aliveness became hindered rather than furthered during their journey. In fact, when the medieval rabbis first codified Jewish law, their efforts were met with disdain and warnings by other rabbis, who felt that codification would further freeze the already threatened fluidity of the Jewish spirit path. They felt that people would cease to engage their tradition and wrestle with its sources, and would instead make decisions about Jewish law by letting their fingers do the walking through the codes. They saw codification as a real threat to the dynamic nature of the tradition and to the essential roles that personal experience and reasoning played in interpreting its dicta for individual circumstances. They felt that codification would deprive the people of their autonomy to examine and interpret original source material toward making their own decisions about halachic application. As the twelfth-century Rabbi Abraham ibn Daud of Posquieres wrote in reaction to Maimonides' codification of Jewish law:

> There are issues about which the sages were in disagreement with one another [about what the halachic ruling is], and this author [Maimonides] selected the opinions of some over those of others and recorded them in his composition. But why should I rely on his choice of rulings and opinions when I have not had the opportunity to examine their sources with my own eyes, nor do I know anything about whether they were disputed when they were first proposed, and by whom?
>
> *Hasagot HaRa'avad* on Maimonides'
> introduction to *Mishnah Torah*

Indeed, the codification of Jewish law marked the beginning of a way of being Jewish that would be more about following the rules than engaging the experience. To this day, there are communities where people depend on the *Shulchan Aruch* in governing their personal and religious lives. When in conflict, they will not wrestle with the sources upon which the *Shulchan Aruch* is based, perhaps to discover that there were other opinions on any given issue. Rather, they will follow the code or consult their rabbis. Judaism's age-old promotion of personal autonomy and the dignity of human reason and choice have been all but supplanted by text and by rabbinic authorities who themselves often shy away from venturing beyond the margins of the text. Wrote Rabbi Yehuda Loew of Prague (Maharal):

> People who are ignorant of the meanings and the reasonings [behind the halachah] go about rendering decisions on halachic questions straight out of the Mishnah [recorded traditions of religious law]. And it is taught: "Teachers who merely repeat traditional teachings ruin the world, said Rava, 'For they render decisions only from what they have learned from others'" [Babylonian Talmud, Sotah 22a]. Explains Rashi: "They ruin the world with erroneous rulings since they are ignorant of the reasoning and situational applications of those traditions, and they compare these traditions to situations that only seem comparative." This is because they do not engage themselves in talmud [analytical study] of what they have learned from their predecessors. . . . And not for the purpose of rendering halachic decisions was the Mishnah recorded, but for the purpose of having its meaning explained, as well as the reasoning behind its traditions, through the process of talmud, and to render halachic decisions from within talmud not from within mishnah . . . for that [ruling from mishnah] surely ruins the world, as we see with our own eyes.
>
> Derech Chaim, p. 305, on Babylonian Talmud, Avot 6:7

So important to the halachic process is the independent reasoning and grappling process of the individual rabbi that "even if by his own insight and knowledge he arrives at an erroneous conclusion, he is yet beloved by God because he developed his decision from his own mind" (Maharal, Netivot Olam, Vol. 1: Netiv HaTorah, end of Chap. 15)—as opposed to "looking it up" in the prearranged codes. Once more, independent reasoning was chosen over blind or passive obeisance to any code or tradition. "All the judge has to go on," the ancient rabbis taught, "is what his own *eyes* behold" (Babylonian Talmud, *Sanhedrin* 6b).

The Talmud recounts that the second-century Rabbi Yehudah the Prince was presented one night with a question about ritual impurity. After carefully examining the situation, he decided that it was ritually impure. The following morning, he reversed his decision and declared it ritually *pure*. An hour later, however, he examined it once more and decided that it was ritually *impure*. The whole thing confused him so much that he cried out: "Woe unto me! Have I perhaps done wrong [in deciding this way and that, back and forth]?"—to which his colleagues responded: "Yes, it was wrong to do that, because a halachic authority is not expected to judge beyond what his *eyes* see" (Babylonian Talmud, *Nidah* 20b). In other words, when situations are presented to rabbis for halachic rulings, they are not required to use a magnifying glass to clarify things to a degree of absoluteness, and if that doesn't work to then use a microscope, and if that doesn't do it to then employ an electron microscope, and so on. When ruling on a halachic question, in other words, we need go no further than how the situation presents itself to us in the moment (see gloss of Rabbeinu Gershom on Babylonian Talmud, *Bava Batra* 131a); we are not required to strain our eyes in an attempt to look at the case beyond the form in which it appears to us.

Personal autonomy in the halachic process is an entitlement not only of the halachic authorities, but of laypersons, as well. Inquirers, too, have the right to do what they can to make the *halachah* work for them and their individual situation. If they asked one rabbi for a ruling and felt that it was wrong, they are entitled to bring their query to another rabbi, as long as they share with the second rabbi the decision of the first; in fact, they may bring their question to as many rabbis as they wish "so that the rabbis [if their verdicts differed] could discuss it with one another; sometimes by so doing it turns out that the ruling of the first rabbi was indeed in error" (*Tosefot* on Babylonian Talmud, *Nidah* 20b—אגמריה, and on Babylonian Talmud, *Avodah Zarah* 7b—ונשאל).

The codes of Jewish law were intended as general reference guides, not as answerbooks for situational questions. Rather, in such instances, the rabbi was urged to treat the question as if it had never before been dealt with, so that fresh insight could be obtained that would fit the special need at hand, independent of how it may have been addressed in previous ages or in other communities. That way, the *halachah* would truly remain a walking stick for the individual person or the individual community, maintaining thereby the dignity of individual human distinction and of individual circumstantial necessity. No two situations are ever alike, just as no two people are ever alike, and though similarities may be found from which to draw comparisons, those comparisons become only *part* of the process of halachic decision making, not the whole of it. The halachic process requires that the rabbi, when confronted with a question of Jewish law, go back to the original related sources in the Bible and the Talmud and rediscover there the contextual basis of the law in question, so that any subsequent study of responsa or code will not be understood in a vacuum, and also so that the rabbi may have the fullest background information necessary to render the most lenient ruling possible on behalf of the individual who brought the question in the first place. In other words, the *halachah* is supposed to work *for*, not against or in spite of, the human situation. The ancient teachers therefore frowned upon rabbis who decided *halachah* with stringency (Babylonian Talmud, *Ketuvot* 7a). Explains Rashi:

For everyone has the option of being strict, and when [a rabbi] renders a prohibitory decision, it is then not necessarily founded upon the tradition. Because when he is in doubt, when the *halachah* is not clear to him, he will take the easy way out and forbid. But one who renders a permissible ruling relies upon the tradition and upon the reasoning of his intellect, and such is truly *hora'ah*—halachic decision making.

Rashi on Babylonian Talmud, *Ketuvot* 7a

As the nineteenth-century Rabbi Shmuel of Salant once said: "I decide questions in accordance with *halachah*. One who issues halachic rulings must study diligently and comprehend his learning. In order to be stringent, however, you don't need to be such a scholar" (Y. Rimon and Z. Wasserman, *Shmuel B'doro* [Tel Aviv, 1961], p. 125).

It is interesting to note that אסור (*asur*), which is most commonly translated as "forbidden," also means "tied up" or "imprisoned," and that מותר (*mutar*), most popularly translated as "permitted," also means "untie" or "loosen." Similarly, כשר (kosher), most popularly translated as "acceptable," or "valid," also means "prepare," whereas its opposite, טריף (*treif*), most commonly translated as "not kosher," also means "ripped." Sadly, these terms sound dogmatic to a great many Jews because of the way in which they have been almost exclusively translated, when actually they are beautiful terms that teach a great deal about the spirit behind the Torah path and its directives. For example, there are two ways of taking the life of an animal before eating it: the Torah's swift, ritually prescribed manner of *preparing* (kosher) the animal for a nontraumatic release of its spirit, or the violent *ripping* (*treif*) of the animal's spirit from its body by clubbing it, shooting it, or utilizing cruel trapping devices. The concept of kosher and *treif* meats, then, has nothing to do with the slaughtered animal being blessed by a rabbi, as is the common misconception, and is hardly confined in meaning to the detailed instructions concerning ritual slaughter, or *shechitah*. Rather, it is an injunction that bids us to prepare the animal for the swift and smooth release of its soul through a painless death and not to partake of any animal that was killed by having its soul ripped from its body through insensitive slaughter. This way of thinking of kosher and *treif* is what Rabbi Zalman Schachter-Shalomi calls "eco-kosher," a consciousness that defines what is kosher or *treif* not merely by whether the meat at the butcher store bears a tag verifying that a rabbi had supervised the *shechitah*, but by whether the animal had indeed been killed by having its soul prepared for release; by whether or not laborers employed at the farm or at the slaughterhouse are working under poor or unfair conditions; by whether the animal had been kept in humane conditions prior to the slaughter; and so on. But while the term "eco-kosher" may be innovative, the concept is not, as reflected in the literal meanings of the words kosher and *treif*.

Mutar and *asur*, too, provide us with a more authentic understanding of what has been sadly translated only as "permitted" and "forbidden." *Mutar* means "unchained" or "loosened," which connotes a lot more than simply "permitted." If your hands are tied, or *asur*, if your life is tangled and you are unable to move on in your *halachah*, in your spirit walk, then it is up to you or to the rabbi whose counsel you seek to do whatever possible to unbind you, to declare for your halachic issue: *mutar*—untied, freed. It is no wonder, then, that the teachers pushed for untying over binding, *mutar* over *asur*: "The authoritative strength of one who renders permissible rulings," taught the ancient rabbis, "is superior" to that of one who renders prohibitive ones (Babylonian Talmud, *Berachot* 60 and *Beitzah* 2b). Comments Rashi:

> It is much better [for the narrator of the Talmud] to inform us
> of the teachings of the one who ruled leniently. For such a
> one relies confidently on what he has learned and is not afraid
> to permit. But the authoritative strength of those who forbid
> is baseless, because anyone can forbid, even regarding such
> things as are permitted!
>
> Rashi, on Babylonian Talmud, *Beitzah* 2b

Halachah as an organic process, as accommodating and furthering personal and communal aliveness, is not some innovative notion of the New Age. It dates back to the very beginning of the Jewish peoplehood in the wilderness of Sinai where Torah was first translated from revelation to law. For example, when several Israelites missed out on the opportunity to offer up the paschal lamb on Passover—which had to be done within a specific time frame, according to the law—they didn't take their situation lying down, but inquired of Moses the lawgiver who in turn inquired of God. Consequently, the Creator ordained a "second Passover" to enable these people, too, to partake of the paschal rite (Numbers 9:6–12):

> And there were people who had become ritually impure by reason of their tending to the dead, and thus they were unable to participate in the Passover offering on the designated day. And so they approached and stood before Moses and before Aaron on that day. And these people said to [Moses]: "We are ritually impure by reason of our having tended to the dead. Why should we be at a disadvantage because of this, in that we cannot bring the Passover offering to the Creator in its designated time together with the rest of the children of Israel?" And Moses then said to them: "Stay put, and I will hear what it is the Creator shall advise for you." And the Creator resonated in Moses to say: "Speak unto the children of Israel and tell them that anyone who becomes ritually impure by reason of tending to the dead, or anyone who is on a distant journey far from you, whether now or in a future generation—shall make a Passover offering unto the Creator. In the second month on the fourteenth day [one month after Passover] during the time between the shifting of day into night, shall they make this offering. . . ."

When the Torah "commanded" that land be apportioned amongst the male members of the tribes only (Leviticus 25:46 and Numbers 26:54), five sisters approached Moses and challenged the fairness of the law, since their father had died and they had no brothers. Why should they not receive the land that otherwise would have been assigned to their father were he alive? In this case, too, the *halachah* was adapted instantly so that if there were no surviving sons, the inheritance was to be transferred to the daughters (Numbers 27:1–8):

> And the daughters of Tzelaphchad . . . of the tribe of Menasheh the son of Joseph approached, and these are the names of his daughters: Machlah, Nowah, and Chaglah and Milkah and Tirzah. And they stood before Moses and before Elazar the *Kohein* and before the tribal leaders and the entire assembly, at the opening to the tent of meeting, saying: "Our father died in the wilderness . . . and he had no sons. Why should our father's name be forsaken amid his family by virtue of his not having a son? Give unto us a land share amongst the brothers of our father." And Moses brought their case before the Creator. And the Creator said to Moses to say: "What the daughters of Tzelaphchad are saying is legitimate. Certainly shall you give unto them a land share amongst the brothers of their father, and whatever was to be allocated to their father shall you transfer to them. And to the children of Israel shall you speak, saying: If a man dies and he has no son, you shall transfer his allotment to his daughter."

The demonstration of the flexible nature of *halachah* abounds throughout the postbiblical traditions like the Talmud. It was not a one-time phenomenon confined to the wilderness journey, but an ongoing process that more than anything else preserved the Judaic tradition. Elasticity, not rigidity, is what has kept Judaism flourishing through thick and thin across several thousands of years. The Torah is not untouchable; in times of need, the people of the book could and did alter or abolish altogether the dictates of the book of the people (Babylonian Talmud, *Yevamot* 89b and 90b). The most famous of such instances is that of the *prusbol*, a contract designed by Hillel the Elder for the purpose of counteracting some ill effects of the observance of *shemitah*, the sabbatical year, during the first century B.C.E. The Torah commanded that every seventh year the land was to be left unworked, and that all debts be canceled. Consequently, as the *shemitah* year would approach, increasing numbers of people simply refused to loan anyone money out of fear that they would never be paid back. In response, Hillel invented the *prusbol*, a legal document that enabled the borrower to bypass the law of debt cancellation during the *shemitah* year, thereby removing the factor that discouraged lenders. Hillel saw no problem, then, in adjusting an outright biblical law for the promotion of harmony amongst his people: "For he saw that people were unwilling to lend money to one another" (Babylonian Talmud, *Gitin* 36a).

A similar problem arose during the *shemitah* year in 1888. This time, it wasn't an issue of lending and borrowing; rather, it was the part of the *shemitah* law that forbade Jews to work the soil in the Holy Land every seventh year. Attempts by Jewish pioneers to resettle their homeland in this period were frustrated by this law, as it prevented them from properly cultivating the barren land and from fostering any form of reasonable economic growth. But once more was the halachic process invoked, and again were adjustments made by the rabbis, who permitted the formal sale of Jewish-owned fields and vineyards to non-Jews for the duration of the sabbatical year. This controversial ruling did not come from so-called "progressive" or "liberal" rabbis, but from three renowned traditionalists: Rabbi Shmuel Mohliver of Bialystok, Rabbi Yisroel Yehoshua Trunk of Kutna, and Rabbi Shmuel Zanwill Klepfish of Warsaw (E. Shimoff, *Rabbi Elkhanan Spector* [Yeshiva University Press, 1959], p. 134).

The Torah states that a *mamzer* (an offspring of an incestuous or adulterous union) "shall not enter into the congregation of the Eternal One" (Deuteronomy 23:3), meaning that he or she cannot marry another Jew, unless they, too, are "illegitimate." Yet the ancient rabbis ruled that if a *mamzer* did, nonetheless, submerge into the Jewish community, we do not launch any investigations. We do not conduct inquisitions into people's personal lives for the sake of halachic correctness—even regarding an issue that could affect the collective. We do not introduce doubts and cast stigmas upon people for the sake of religious purity. It is not the way of the broader, cosmic Torah path. "In any case," wrote Rashi, "all families will be declared pure in the end" (Babylonian Talmud, *Kidushin* 71a). Or, as the second-century Rabbi Yosee taught: "In the time to come, the illegitimate will be declared legitimate" (Babylonian Talmud, *Kidushin* 72b). Rabbi Yochanan, in the third century, swore before his colleagues that he could easily prove the presence of *mamzerim* in certain families in the land of Israel, but that he wasn't going to, because: "Some of the greats of this generation are intermixed among them" (Babylonian Talmud, *Kidushin* 71a).

The "law," then, was never the sole consideration in any rabbinic ruling, for the rabbis understood that the Torah is reasonable, or it isn't Torah; that *halachah* promotes positiveness, or it isn't *halachah*. They rendered their decisions often in direct contrast to the written form of Torah because they acknowledged that Torah was far more expansive than its finite manifestation in the written law. They maintained, in other words, that the most authentic interpretation of the Torah's intention could be found not in the blind, literal readings of its writ, but in the spirit of: "Her ways are ways of pleasantness, and all her paths are of peacefulness" (Proverbs 3:17). Or, as the ancient rabbis phrased it: "The Torah in its entirety exists solely for the sake of the ways of peacefulness" (Babylonian Talmud, *Gitin* 59b).

Another example: the rabbis of the talmudic period ordained that a man who has not fulfilled the *mitzvah* of bringing children into the world should remarry if his present wife is infertile. This implied divorce where bigamy was proscribed (Babylonian Talmud, *Yevamot* 64a). Yet, throughout the ages, rabbis permitted—even obligated—husbands of infertile women to remain married to them, and those wanting to marry infertile women to go ahead and marry them in situations where either the couple were deeply in love or where the woman in question might otherwise never find a mate. How did these rabbis dare to overturn the ordinances of their predecessors, and thus also the biblical mandate to be fruitful and multiply?

Wrote the nineteenth-century Rav Aryeh Zunt of Plotzk: "Because, on the contrary! The sages would never have approved of such a thing [to force the separation of a couple deeply in love], nor would such an action be pleasing to the Creator, to whom peace is sacred" (in his responsa *M'shivat Nefesh* [Warsaw, 1849], No. 18). When Rabbi Moshe Feinstein was confronted with a similar case, he prefaced his lenient ruling with these words: "Who am I to enter into discussion concerning this issue [when great sages have already ruled on it]? However, since *iggun* is at stake (*iggun* connotes a situation where a woman is barred from the possibility of marriage or remarriage due to a legal technicality), and the sages require us to make a great effort to help her, and preserving peace between husband and wife is so important that the Torah allows the Divine Name to be erased for this purpose, I will therefore not be deterred by respect for these great men" (*Iggrot Moshe, Even ha-Ezer*, Vol. 1, No. 63; see also No. 67, and a touching yet amusing related tale in *Shir Hashirim Rabbah* 1:31).

According to Torah law, heavy-duty court cases required a minimum of two eyewitnesses, and they had to be men. Women were disqualified, and so were slaves. However, if the case involved a question of *iggun*—where a woman was in danger of spending the rest of her life unable to remarry because it wasn't known for certain whether or not her missing husband was dead—the ancient rabbis not only allowed the testimony of a single witness if one came forward, but declared that it mattered not whether the witness was a slave or a free person, a man or a woman, "because of the danger of her becoming an *agunah* [a trapped woman]" (Babylonian Talmud, *Yevamot* 87b and 88a). In tricky divorce cases, too, where a woman found herself legally powerless to dissolve a marriage, the rabbis had no scruples about retroactively annulling the marriage altogether (Babylonian Talmud, *Gitin* 33a). A more recent example can be found in the timely responsa of Rabbi Moshe Feinstein (Orthodox), where he nullified a marriage retroactively when it was discovered that the husband was psychotic and therefore halachically disqualified from implementing divorce proceedings at his wife's request. Rabbi Feinstein declared the marriage *mekach tauot* ("falsified transaction"), since the woman never would have entered the marriage to begin with had she known that her husband was psychotic (*Iggrot Moshe, Even HaEzer*, Vol. 1, Nos. 79, 80, 191, and Vol. 3, Nos. 46 and 48).

Of course, the problem of *agunah* is a cancerous outgrowth of the patriarchal double standard that recognizes only the man as being qualified to initiate or terminate a marriage. Be that as it may, these examples nonetheless demonstrate the elasticity and compassion of the halachic process in the face of situations that threaten the aliveness of the individual. Sadly, contemporary Orthodox rabbis lack the guts to render such bold decisions on behalf of Orthodox women who are prevented from remarrying because their husbands refuse to grant them a *get*, a ritual writ of divorce. What is even sadder is that these women, by virtue of their allegiance to *halachah,* remain trapped and suffocated by it, because the rabbis are too timid to annul their marriages. This is an absurdity, but more than that it is a wickedness beyond any of the abominations listed by the Torah itself. There are, of course, a select few Orthodox rabbis who are prepared and eager to do something about this very un-Jewish phenomenon hiding under the guise of Torah. In the tradition of their predecessors, they are prepared to wrestle with and alter the *halachah* in order to free these women and prevent recalcitrant husbands from exploiting *halachah* and extorting money from their wives. The problem is that most Orthodox women will not accept their offer to annul their "marriages" because the rest of the Orthodox rabbinate and movement will invalidate such actions, since the rabbis in question are not "as great" as the rabbis who did perform annulments in the past and who are no longer among us. And those rabbis today who are close to being "as great" unfortunately consider themselves "too small" for "so great" an issue, ignoring the teaching in the Talmud that "excessive humility destroyed the Holy Temple" (Babylonian Talmud, *Gitin* 56b). Taught the third-century Rabbi Abba Arecha: "The verse 'Yea, a mighty host are all her slain' (Proverbs 7:26) refers to a disciple who has attained the qualifications to decide questions of *halachah* and does not do so" (Babylonian Talmud, *Sotah* 22a).

Taught the third-century Rabbi Yochanan: "Jerusalem was destroyed because they judged strictly by the letter of the law . . . they established their rulings strictly upon the letter of the law and did not judge within the margins of the law" (Babylonian Talmud, *Bava Mezia* 30b). Comments Rabbi Judah Loew of Prague: "In other words, even though the people had erred in other ways, the destruction would not have happened. . . . But since they established their rulings strictly upon the letter of the law, destruction resulted as God reciprocated in kind by responding with strict literal judgment. . . . And if they would have ruled leniently, God in turn would have judged them with leniency. . . . The distancing of compassion brings about destruction to the world" (*Netivot Olam, Netiv Gemilut Chessed*, end of Chapter 3).

The nature and function of *halachah* has been well articulated in Rabbi Eliezer Berkovitz's masterpiece *Not in Heaven* (Ktav, 1983) and needs no repetitive treatment in this book. Suffice it to say that there is little about *halachah* that was ever intended to be etched in stone, and that if it doesn't weave gently and smoothly in and out of real-time human experience, it ceases to be *halachah* and instead becomes dogma. If it hinders our aliveness instead of nourishing it, then it is not Torah, because Torah is called "tree of life" (Proverbs 3:18), and "its gift is aliveness" (Babylonian Talmud, *Avot* 6:7), and it "was given to live by, not to die by" (Babylonian Talmud, *Yoma* 85b). Dogma and Torah are as compatible as laundry detergent and powdered milk. They may look alike, but while one nurtures, the other destroys (Babylonian Talmud, *Yoma* 72b).

> The law, stiff with formality, is *a cry* for creativity, a call for nobility concealed in the form of the commandments. It is not designed to be a yoke, a curb, a straitjacket for human action. Above all, the Torah asks for love. . . . All observance is training in the art of love. To forget that love is the purpose of all *mitzvot* is to vitiate their meaning.

> . . . It is a distortion to say that Judaism consists exclusively of performing ritual or moral deeds, and to forget that the goal of all performing is in transforming the soul.

> . . . The [Torah] consists of five books. The Code of Law [*Shulchan Aruch*] consists of only four books. Where is the missing part of the law? Answered Rabbi Israel of Rizhin (nineteenth century): the missing part is the person. Without the living participation of the person the law is incomplete.
>
> Abraham Joshua Heschel,
> *God in Search of Man*, pp. 307, 310, 311

There are those who absolutize the rulings recorded in the Talmud or in the codes by applying the deuteronomic dictum that "you shall not disregard the law that [the elders of the ancient supreme rabbinic court] declare unto you" (Deuteronomy 17:11). Yet the Talmud itself warns against rendering halachic rulings from the Talmud (Babylonian Talmud, *Niddah* 7b). According to Maimonides, the injunction "you shall not disregard the law that they declare unto you" applies to any rabbinic legislation, but other rabbis disagreed and qualified this principle as applicable only to halachic rulings that are in response to specific queries, not to general halachic legislation (Ramban on *Sefer HaMitzvot L'HaRambam*, *shoresh* I; *Sefer HaKhinukh*, No. 508; *T'shuvot Tashbatz* 1:141). The Torah was meant to be understood and applied in a variety of dimensions, and no one religious body in any one age possesses any form of one-size-fits-all authority over everyone else in another age.

> Asked the sages of France, how can the ruling of both parties be the word of God when this one permits and this one forbids? And they answered with the following midrash: When Moses ascended the mountain to receive the Torah, the Holy Blessed One demonstrated to him concerning every commandment forty-nine different angles of perception [literally, "faces"] from which a matter might be declared forbidden and forty-nine angles of perception from which a matter might be declared permitted. And he asked the Holy Blessed One about this, and God said: "This knowledge shall be transmitted to the spiritual teachers in every generation so that the decision on any matter shall be theirs."
>
> From the commentary of the thirteenth-century
> Rabbi Yom Tov ben Avraham Ishbili [Ritva]
> on Babylonian Talmud, Eruvin 13b

This is a scary teaching. If there is no single absolute truth and everything is relative and situational, what is the Torah way? If this one says it's permitted and this one says it's forbidden, and both are competent rabbinic authorities, which of the two conflicting opinions represents the one true Torah way? Replies the tradition: "All of them were given from a single shepherd, all was taught by a single leader who transmitted them from the lips of the Blessed Power, as it is written (Exodus 20:1)—'And the Creator spoke all these words'" (Babylonian Talmud, Hagigah 3b).

The ideal of a singlular absolute directive on how to live is something conjured up in the mortal mind, in what the Jewish mystics dubbed מוחין דקטנות—"the small mind," the limited consciousness that is confined to givens and principles, and that is fearful of treading beyond boundaries set by precedence. But halachah thrives on מוחין דגדלות—"the great mind," the expansive consciousness that is open to possibilities and alternatives, and that is not afraid to cross boundaries set by precedence. The human is a creature of change and transformation, and cannot flourish in confinement. Perhaps it is *because* we are subject to changes and shiftings that we *seek out* absolutes, that we yearn hopefully for the illusory "one right way of doing it." For some, living this way offers the benefits of security and stability. For others, the cost of relinquishing autonomy far outweighs the benefits of not having to constantly figure things out and wrestle with situations. But even for those who prefer to believe that there is only one authentic spirit path, the ancient rabbis made it clear that—be that as it may—there are still any number of ways to make the journey. If the Torah is divinely inspired, it follows that if two people grapple earnestly with its text and come away with two conflicting interpretations, they are each inevitably drawing their conclusions by their subjective take on what is emanating from a single divine source; and that no matter how contradictory the conclusion of one of them may be to that of the other, "Both are the words of the Living God" (Babylonian Talmud, *Eruvin* 13b). "Once a Jew accepts the Torah from Sinai," writes Dr. Eliezer Berkovits, "whatever it teaches him in his search for its meaning and message is the word of God for him" (*Not in Heaven: The Nature and Function of Halakha* [Ktav, 1983], p. 51).

> For three years the disciples of Hillel and the disciples of Shammai were in disagreement over their interpretation of the laws of the Torah, when one day a Heavenly Voice declared: "These and those [both opinions] are the words of the Living God."
>
> Babylonian Talmud, *Bava Batra* 130b

Explained Rashi:

> When two sages are arguing over a halachic question, and each is putting forth the reasoning behind their verdict, there is no issue of falsehood here [that one of them must be in the wrong], for each is drawing their own conclusion on the matter. This

one argues reasons that it ought to be permitted and this one argues reasons that it ought to be forbidden; this one compares the case to one situation and this one compares it to another. One can also explain it this way: There are times when the reasoning of one rabbi is most applicable and there are times when the reasoning of another is more applicable. Thus, there are times when the reasoning behind a halachic ruling changes with so much as the slightest shift of circumstance.

Rashi on Babylonian Talmud, *Ketuvot* 57a

Each one, then, has a right to voice what they feel is rightness for a particular situation, what the law ought to be for any given circumstance, and both opinions, no matter how contradictory they are to one another, reflect authentic Torah, one not more or less than the other. There is ample room, in other words, for variation, for diversity, for the honoring of differences, without one disputant having to dismiss the other as "less" Jewish, or as wrong, or as heretical.

It is true that in ancient times there were sects, like the Sadducees, whose theology was considered erroneous by the rabbis. But that was more politics than religion. The Sadducees did worse than not accept the existence of the oral tradition that accompanied the written tradition. They also collaborated with the Roman occupiers of Israel and, accordingly, facilitated their scheme of turning the Holy Temple into an instrument of Roman power and politics. Well-meaning scholars who see rabbinic criticism of the Sadducees as diatribes against their theology fail to take into account the turbulent political climate of the times and the danger that the Sadducees posed to the Jewish nation. There were other sects, too, whose take on Torah differed quite radically from that of the rabbis, yet they were not taken to task because they lived in harmony with the rest of the people and did not support their nation's enemies, as did the Sadducees. The Essenes were one such sect, to which belonged several of the leading rabbis of that era. The Samaritans were another. The fact that there was a dispute between the rabbis about whether it was religiously correct to partake of Samaritan foods demonstrates that there was no issue about it until later, when religious particularism and the tightening of the reins, so to speak, reached a peak. The Samaritans, after all, had been around long before the question was raised. Accordingly, the Babylonian Talmud records that the eating of their foods was forbidden (Shvi'it 8:10), and the earlier Jerusalem Talmud records the opinion that it was acceptable (Avodah Zarah 5:4), even though the Samaritan standards of keeping kosher differed from the Pharisaic standards.

The early Christians were another sect about which there is no clear evidence that the rabbis held them as heretics or "outsiders," even though their evolving theology differed radically from theirs. For decades, both Christian and Judaic scholars have nitpickingly combed the folios of talmudic literature in a feeble attempt to demonstrate that the rabbis had indeed engaged in aggressive campaigns to discredit the early Christians. Books and chapters abound in which the same poor evidence is offered: Wherever the Talmud recounts rabbinic disputations with those whom the narrative calls minim, it is referring to Christians. This is pure speculation arising out of subjective theory rather than objective history. There is absolutely no proof that there existed any discord between the rabbis and the early Christians, who were, after all, religiously observant Jews. That they may have believed Jesus to be the Messiah is hardly a concern amongst a people that has known quite a few alleged Messiahs. The second-century Rabbi Akiva, for example, was certainly not ostracized for believing that Bar Kochba, the rebel leader, was the Messiah. We truly don't know who the minim refers to, but there is certainly no reason to posit they were the early Christians any more than of the hundreds of other sects that flourished during this turbulent period in Jewish religious and national history. The assumption that these minim were Christians is probably a hindsight, a rearview-mirror vision that arose from subsequent centuries of persecution at the hands of later Christendom, which had separated completely from Judaism and turned against the Jewish people. In other words, the reasoning goes like this: Who were the rabbis always at odds with? Who else could it have been but those who have persecuted Jewry for centuries: the Christians. Theories also abound that talmudic narratives about Yeshu, or "Jesus"—censored by the Church during the Middle Ages—were about Jesus Christ. Such theories ignore the fact that the narratives about Yeshu describe him as a disciple of Rabbi Yehoshua ben Perachiah, who lived almost a century earlier than the historical Jesus claimed by Christianity. This, too, is a rear-view-mirror hypothesis. After all, the Jesus mentioned in the Talmud is spoken of derogatorily, so who else could it be but the man in whose name so much suffering was caused Jewdom? But, actually, historical fact refutes the possibility that the Jesus character alluded to in the Talmud is the Jesus of Christianity. Indeed, one out of every ten Jews back then bore the name Jesus, which was simply Greek for Yehoshua, or Joshua.

It is inconsistent to assume that there was any discord between rabbinic Judaism and early Christianity. If there did exist conflict between them, it was more akin to the conflict between the schools of Hillel and Shammai than between the Pharisees and the Sadducees. It is inconceivable that a rift existed between parties of conflicting interpretive conclusions when those parties did their exegesis of Torah from a place of earnestness and authenticity. Deviation connotes rejecting the path you're on and paving instead a whole different path with a whole different direction that bears no relationship to the root path from which it supposedly sprang—á la later Christianity. Blazing trails that run from and around or alongside the path you were on all along is far from deviation; it is, rather, extending the arteries of your original spirit path to funnel its gifts toward new and expansive territories. Every now and then, in every person, there is a primordial Big-Bang explosion that erupts out of an overwhelming, deep-down yearning to do something totally different and radical, to break through the forboding barriers of what has already been, and to storm forward in a no-holds-barred fury of chaos, the kind of chaos out of which—according to ancient Judaic tradition—the universe came into being (Genesis 1:2). The churning, turning, and burning of Creation, of radical newness, stirs magically in each of us, sometimes allowed to emerge from its suppression, sometimes not. We each have our specific quest in life, and Torah—outside of the fences and hedges that have been erected around it by overprotective spiritual teachers—encourages us to heed that quest and to pursue it unceasingly, because it is in the pursuit, even more than in the ultimate discovery, that personal growth and transformation take place. The Talmud recounts how the fourth-century Rabbi Yosef refused to eat or drink anything until God came up with the answer to a question that burned fiercely within him—not just any answer, but the one that felt right for him personally:

> He fasted for forty days, praying for assurance that Torah would always remain his legacy. A voice from heaven finally called out: "The Torah shall not ever leave your lips." Not satisfied, he fasted forty more days until a voice from heaven called out: "The Torah shall not ever leave your lips or the lips of your children." Still not satisfied, he fasted a hundred more days until a voice from heaven called out: "The Torah shall not ever leave your lips or the lips of your children or the lips of your children's children!" Whereupon he declared: "From now on, Torah does not need to return to its place of lodging [i.e., no further assurances are necessary that Torah will be sustained in the family]."
>
> Babylonian Talmud, *Bava Mezia* 85a

The directives of the Torah may come across as absolutes, as unbending principles and "commandments," but in the space between every word of the text there are hordes of "buts" and "howevers" that dance about like atomic particles, holding the form of Torah intact. Without the "buts" and "howevers," the living heartbeat of Torah becomes sluggish and eventually stops throbbing; without them, Torah ceases to be what it is, transformative and dynamic. Rather than commandments, the Torah—which means, literally, "the showing"—offers instructions. The world cannot exist on absolutes, taught the ancient rabbis, void of room for variation and diversity, void of room for everyone to cultivate their unique individual take on life:

> Said the second-century Rabbi Yannai: "Had the Torah been given already sliced [with its laws already set and absolutized and void of any process of leaning to one side of an issue or the other], no leg would have any ground to stand on [the world could not survive, because the Torah requires us to interpret her many faces this way and that, and both these and those are the words of the living God]. . . . Said Moses to the Holy Blessed One: 'Teacher of the Universe! Show me how the *halachah* is determined [so that there be no question about the application of any of the laws.' But God then said to him: 'That is impossible, because the Torah requires us to interpret her many faces this way and that, and if I disclose to you the final *halachah* the Torah would then never be interpreted based on her many faces], for there are forty-nine ways of interpreting the Torah so that a thing is rendered impure, and forty-nine ways of interpreting the Torah so that a thing is rendered pure.'"
>
> Jerusalem Talmud, *Sanhedrin* 4:2
> [with Rashi's commentary in brackets]

Opponents of halachic leniency dismiss flexidoxy as a surrender to the call of the physical, to the deceptive allurement of material gratification. After all, the motto of flexidoxy seems to be "If it isn't comfortable for you, find a way out of it." But strict *halachah*, too, can just as easily be attributed to material preoccupation simply because strictness borders on extremism, and extremism is of the material realm, whereas the spiritual realm knows only simplicity and balance. "*Halachah*," wrote Rabbi Yehudah Loew "is totally abstract and perfectly simple intellect, entirely unrelated to the physical. Therefore, it does not deviate from the perfect center toward the extremes, which are related to the material" (*Netzach Yisroel*, Ch. 70). Often, stringent leanings in halachic interpretation are entangled with the physical, either as obsessive reaction to or against physical lust, or as surrender to deeply suppressed physical passion that then erupts into fanaticism under the guise of religious zeal. If the subjective rendering of *halachah* was so wrong, Judaism would never have evolved its many customs, which are basically mutations of *halachah*, adapted to fit specific timely needs and personal as well as communal tastes. Yet, as subjective as custom may be, in a great many circumstances it overrides *halachah* (Babylonian Talmud, *Sofrim* 14:18)! In fact, custom, once adopted by the people for permanent practice, takes on the same quality as *halachah* (Babylonian Talmud, *Sofrim* 14:18).

Whether one opts for orthodoxy or flexidoxy, it is far better to do *halachah* in ways that reflect one's authentic self than to do it in ways that *deflect* one's authentic self. The ancient teachers taught that one can either slaughter one's compulsion toward self-gratification, or make peace with it. Some of us would rather dance with our shadows than box them, like Abraham, father of the boundary crossers, who "transformed his compulsion and directed it toward positiveness" (Jerusalem Talmud, *Berachot* 9:5 [or 60a]). And some of us, indeed, need to lean toward one extreme in order to distance ourselves from the other; to annihilate our compulsion toward self-gratification, like David, who "became overwhelmed by his compulsion and so he killed it" (Jerusalem Talmud, *Berachot* 9:5 [or 60a]). But David got rid of it only following extenuating circumstances, after he had had an affair with a married woman, gotten her pregnant, and sent her husband to the front lines to be killed in the hope of preventing a scandal (2 Samuel 11). Nonetheless, after David owned up to what he had done, he did not develop a whole theology in reaction to his compulsion. No new laws were ordained, like "Men are no longer allowed to socialize with the wives of other men," or "Married women may no longer be seen in public," or "Sexuality is evil and to be avoided at all costs." In fact, he ended up *marrying* Batsheva, the woman with whom he had had the affair, and from their union came Solomon and the lineage that leads directly to the Messiah! Rather, David acknowledged that what he had done was out of his own personal weakness, and that it was not a commentary on the moral strengths or weaknesses of others. At one point, the ancient rabbis sought to drive physical passion out of the world altogether, but then had a change of heart when they realized that without passion life would come to a standstill (Babylonian Talmud, *Yoma* 69b; *B'reishis Rabbah* 9:9). It was, after all, with passion that God created the universe (*Bamidbar Rabbah* 10:11). And while passion "can remove a person from the world" (Babylonian Talmud, *Avot* 4:21), it also "sustains the very existence of the world" (Babylonian Talmud, *Avot D'Rebbe Natan* [version 2], end of Ch. 4).

If one cannot stand being naked or making love in daylight or while standing; if one detests kissing genitalia, or masturbating, or the idea of sexual intimacy between unmarried people—then those feelings belong rightfully in the archives of that individual's personal tastes. They do *not* belong in codes of laws and standards. Unfortunately, many of the more stringent opinions that got codified in Jewish law reflect more the personal tastes of individual rabbis than what is or is not Torah standard. For example, the ancient rabbis ruled that any position during heterosexual lovemaking is acceptable; yet, the standard *halachah* reflects solely the teaching of Rabbi Yochanan ben D'havai, who held that any position other than man-on-top is taboo—even after the Talmud records that "the *halachah* is not like Rabbi Yochanan ben D'havai, but rather whatever one wants to do [consensually] is permitted" (Babylonian Talmud, *Nedarim* 20a–b).

Halachah was never intended as an instrument of whipping people into a desired uni-form, but as a vehicle of spiritual journeying that would guide people toward individual aliveness and collective harmony within a context of responsible behavior and personal authenticity. The Torah may instruct the Jews on which animals may be eaten and how they are to be slaughtered, but Torah does not interfere with the manner in which the meats ought to be prepared; this is left up to individual tastes. Likewise, the Torah delineates with whom Jews are permitted to have sex, but does not then follow them into the bedroom to dictate the manner in which they are to make love. Like meat brought home from the kosher butcher shop, remarked the second-century Rabbi Yehudah the Prince, sexual positions were left to individual tastes and mutual consent (Babylonian Talmud, *Nedarim* 20a–b).

The halachic codes are therefore to be used as reference texts, not as the final word. Composed by rabbinic leaders across the centuries, the codes indeed reflect Torah, but through the narrow lens of select halachic opinions chosen by the codifiers for their accord with their own personal standards of morality and takes on theology. They do not represent the broader spectrum of opinions and interpretations that make up the fuller rainbow of Torah. Fortunately, latter-day editions of the classical medieval codes include the voices of dissenting opinions, which now appear in the margins of texts such as Yoseph Karo's *Shulchan Aruch* and Maimonides' *Mishnah Torah*. Unfortunately, English renditions of these texts do not include these commentaries, leading the reader to believe that they are reading an unbending, etched-in-stone code of Jewish law.

The opinions in the margins of the text are certainly not representative of all there is to say on the subjects being treated. The process of *halachah* does not end at a *cul de sac* of any text, but continues ad infinitum through the ongoing volumes of responsa literature, the notations of individual rabbis of past and present regarding situational questions that were brought to them, their responses to the queries, and the processes by which they arrived at their conclusions. The *t'shuvot*, or responses, are taken quite seriously by the rabbis who write them, for they know that once published or shared by the inquirer with others, their ruling on any given issue will become sub-ject to the scrutiny of other rabbis. In fact, a significant amount of responsa literature is devoted to dialogues between halachic authorities on issues of disagreement, where each is called to task for a decision rendered and compelled to defend their proofs against the other's counterproof.

The responsibility of responding to a query was taken quite seriously by those bold enough to take it on, not only in regard to the proofs and processes by which they arrived at their decisions, but also in regard to the expedience with which they had to respond (*Bamidbar Rabbah* 11:7). A delay in respond-ing to a situational question can leave inquirers to sink deeper into a stuck place, or leave them wondering whether their query had been of sufficient importance to merit the attention of the sage to whom it was sent. Communal disputes, for example, only intensify with the lapse of time; food under question lasts only so long. The nineteenth-century Rabbi Elchanan Spector put it this way: "What you intend to answer tomorrow should already have been answered yesterday; at the very latest, today" (C. Karlinsky, "Two Letters of Rabbi Isaac Elchanan" [*HaDarom*, Tishrei 5731], 134).

Perhaps most emphasized in the teachings of the ancient rabbis is that when a rabbi is called upon to deal with a situ-ational halachic question, he or she should make *every* attempt to render as lenient a ruling as possible, and that it is antitheti-cal to the position and authority of the rabbi to not make that effort (Babylonian Talmud, *Ketuvot* 7a). Such teachings may sound to some like a green light to always look for the easy way out of a situation. There is a difference, however, between looking for an easy way out of *halachah* and looking for an easy way out of a problematic life situation. Where is it writ-ten that one ought to refrain from making life easier, or that one ought to make life harder than it already is? As the fourth-century Rabbi Dimmi put it: "Is it not enough for you what the Torah has already forbidden, that you need to add further prohibitions to yourself?" (Jerusalem Talmud, *Nedarim* 25a).

The age-old unease between those who will not bend from the law as it is codified and those who operate their spirituality in the open spaces between the letters of the law may very well be rooted in flexidoxic versus orthodoxic tensions that have followed Judaism since its beginnings: "[In the future,] the tribe of Ephraim will no longer begrudge the tribe of Yehudah, and the tribe of Yehudah will no longer annoy the tribe of Ephraim" (Isaiah 11:13). Comments the eighteenth-century mystic Rabbi Mordechai Yosef of Ishbitz:

> These two tribes are constantly in conflict with one another. The life objective of Ephraim, as inspired by the Creator, is to concentrate on the *halachah* regarding every matter, and not to budge from obeying its every letter. . . . And the root of the life of Yehudah is to focus on the Creator and to be connected to the Creator in every situation. And even though Yehudah perceives how the *halachah* inclines on an issue, he nevertheless looks to the Creator to show him the core of the truth behind the matter at hand. . . . [Yehudah] looks to the Creator for guidance in all matters rather than engage in the rote practice of religious observances, nor is he content to merely repeat today what he did yesterday . . . but that the Creator enlighten him anew each day as to what is the God will in the moment. This [quest for ever-fresh enlightenment] sometimes compels Yehudah to act contrary to established *halachah*. . . . But in the time to come, we have been promised that Ephraim and Yehudah will no longer be at odds with one another (Isaiah 11:13). This means that Ephraim will no longer have any complaints against Yehudah regarding his deviation from *halachah*, because the Creator will demonstrate to Ephraim the intention of Yehudah, that his intentions are for the sake of the Creator's will, and not for any selfish motif. Then will there be harmony between the two.
>
> *Mei HaShiloach*, Vol. 1, *Vayeishev* 14b–15a

The *halachah* was never considered the sole definition of Jewishness. It is a means, not an end, to Jewish spiritual devotion and aliveness. Ironically, Torah is erroneously translated by many English renditions as "the law" when it actually means "the showing" or "the teaching"; it contains very little about laws, and more about the *lives* of the Jewish ancestors. Clearly, the dynamics of the dance between real life and religious ideals were considered by the Torah a far more important theme than laws. Wrote Abraham Joshua Heschel: "The fact remains that, central as is law, only a small part of the Bible deals with the law" (*God in Search of Man*, p. 324). The Torah, then, is less about how to be religiously correct than about how to be on the planet, period. Nor were the Torah's trivia about the lives of the ancestors considered in any way mundane, even in contrast to the Torah's delineation of laws. Said the second-century Rabbi Acha: "More beautiful is the washing of the feet of the servants of the households of the ancestors, than the Torah of the descendants. . . . More beautiful are the conversations of the servants of the households of the ancestors, than the Torah of the descendants" (*B'reishis Rabbah* 60:11). In other words, the way that even the *servants* of the ancient boundary crossers conducted their lives is more precious as a teaching for us about what Torah wishes to impart than all of the later codes of Jewish law and creed.

Halachah, then, is less about how to "do" Judaism just right than about how to simply be on the planet as a human being—Jewish-style. It supposes nothing of us that is outside of our humanness. "The Torah," wrote the nineteenth-century Rabbi Samson Raphael Hirsch, "does not assume anything but the ordinary conditions of life of those who are in duty bound to observe it" (*The Pentateuch* [Judaica Press] on Deuteronomy 30:12).

4

Sacred Seasons

Three pilgrimages shall you celebrate for Me in the year: the festival of the unleavened breads [*matzot*] shall you observe; for seven days shall you eat unleavened breads as I have instructed you, during the season of the moon of spring, for it is then that you came out from the narrows. And you shall not see My face in emptiness. And the festival of the harvest of the first fruits of your labor, of that which you shall sow in the field. And the festival of the ingathering at the end of the year, when you gather in the fruits of your labor from the field. Three times in the year shall all of your males appear before the face of the Supreme Being *yhvh*.

Exodus 23:14–17

Three times during the year shall every one of your males behold the face of *yhvh*, Source of your powers, in whatever place shall be chosen: during the festival of Matzot, and the festival of Shavuot, and the festival of Sukot. And you shall not behold the face of *yhvh* Source of your powers in emptiness; rather, every man according to the gifts of his hand, according to the blessings of *yhvh* Source of your powers which have been given to you.

Deuteronomy 16:16

All of the ancient Hebrew festivals correspond in theme to the cycles of nature, which in the Judaic belief system are three: the beginning of spring, the beginning of summer, and the beginning of winter (autumn)—symbolic of potential, fruition, and transformation. Since men do not bodily experience as vivid and dramatic an encounter with the Creator as do women —during the cycles of pubertal menstruation (spring), birth (summer), and menopause (winter)—the Torah specifically directs the men, albeit not to the exclusion of women, to "see the face of the Creator" during the onset of these seasons, of these three periods of visible, external changes in Nature, experiences of Creation in process. The men were therefore instructed to engage their experience with the Creator through their experiences with the cycles of the earth mother. For men, this was a real and powerful way of connecting with their femininity and a shamanic way of promoting personal realignment and balance.

The corresponding three sacred cycles of the Hebrew calendar year are listed as Matzot (Passover), or unleavened bread; Shavuot, or weeks; and Sukot, or huts. Each of the three seasonal festivals is called *chag*, which means "cycle" or "circle," referring to the seasonal cycles of the Earth and her atmosphere. Pesach or Passover celebrates spring; Shavuot celebrates summer; and Sukot celebrates autumn, or the onset of winter.

Since the early Hebrews were an agrarian people, the festivals also highlighted the three major cycles of farming. Pesach represented both planting and growing, since spring is the season when we plant new vegetation and when that which had been planted the previous year begins its exodus from the constraints of the earth to the free and open expanses of the atmosphere. As a people, the Jews therefore also celebrate during this period the beginning of their national Exodus from the constraints of Egyptian slavery to the free and open expanses of the Sinai wilderness some three thousand years ago. In fact, the Hebrew word for Egypt—מצרים—is also the word for "constraints" or "narrows." The seeds of Judaism, then, were planted not in the experience of slavery, but in the experience of redemption; not in the hibernation of winter, but in the wakefulness of freedom, of the animated aliveness that characterizes spring. Pesach, then, commemorates not Exodus, but the beginning of Exodus, just as spring marks not the season of growing, but the beginning of growing, the season that presents the potential for planting something fresh. Spring differs from winter in that winter harbors seeds of potential that are outside the realm of personal choice making, while spring offers seeds of potential that are within one's grasp. For the random workings of nature, spring calls forth winter's brew to fruition. For the deliberate choices of humans, spring provides the experience of causing something to happen, of romancing the earth and observing the fruits of one's labor in summer. Thus does the traditional liturgy describe Pesach as a remembrance not of having come out of Egypt, but of "*coming* out of Egypt"; not of completing the Exodus, but of engaging the initial processes of *making* the Exodus.

The climax of Exodus is Shavuot, marking the season of summer and the time when the ancient Hebrews experienced their revelation at Mount Sinai during their wilderness trek out of Egyptian bondage. This is the season when all that had been seeded in spring now becomes revealed; when the Exodus that had begun becomes the Exodus that is completed. Pesach is pregnancy; Shavuot is birth. Both of these festivals are very personal to the Jewish people and its historic experience. They represent not what nature does, but what individual people do in cooperation with Nature; not the general experience of the world-at-large, but the particular experience of a particular people.

Autumn, however, is different. Autumn affects not only what the individual does with her or his garden or farm, with his or her deliberate choices and actions, but also the random functioning of nature. Everything comes to a halt. The grass yellows; the leaves turn colors and drop to the ground; the vegetation

ripens or overripens and begs for picking. Autumn leaves us
no choices, offers us no control. It is seen as death. It is experienced as the loss of youth, the onset of aging. It is a season
during which we encounter our fragility, our temporal nature,
our mortality. For many, it is menopause; for many it is retire-
ment; for many it is the beginning of the end. But for those
who still live close to the earth, the experience does not begin
and end with the sight of leaves dropping lifelessly to the ground
or with a sense of hopelessness over the earth's refusal to
yield any further vegetation. For indigenous peoples—which includes the ancient earth-conscious Hebrews as well—the autumn of one's life is a time not for dying, but for transforming.
Because the message of nature during this season is not of
dying leaves but *falling* leaves, the result is trees letting go of
what they have brought to fruition so that renewal can happen again and again. The ancient rabbis therefore instituted
Tu B'Shvat (literally, the fifteenth day of the moon of Shvat)
in the dead of winter, to celebrate the beginnings of the flow
of the sap deep within the consciousness of the tree. Autumn
is a period in our lives when we need to let go of our earlier
phases of life-journeying, prepare ourselves for fresh possibilities in our lives, and celebrate the new and different modes
of being that await us. Fortunately, in a cultural atmosphere
where aging is dreaded and death is taboo, sages like Rabbi
Zalman Schachter-Shalomi are teaching seminars on "spiritual eldering," to highlight the special gifts that lie in store for
those who are in the autumn of their lives. It is, therefore, during
this crucial season that we celebrate Rosh Hashanah, a holiday for reckoning one's actions over the past year; followed
by Yom Kippur, which is about letting go of negative ways of
being in the world; and Sukot, which celebrates the positive
achievements we have harvested from our past deeds, and the
breaking of barriers of those past voices and givens that hold
us back. The three-part process climaxes with Shemini Atzeret,
which brings closure for the past year and opens up new and

different ways of being in the year to come that further our aliveness and that of others.

Agronomically, autumn is harvest time, a time for gathering in all that has sprung to life during the previous two cycles. Personally, it is a time to harvest one's actions, to call to accounting the way one has lived, to glean the positive from the negative—to separate that which you want to celebrate and foster about yourself from that which you want to change about yourself.

During this season, we engage the possibility of fresh beginnings (Rosh Hashanah); clean out the stuff we do not want to take with us into the next cycle of our lives (the ten days of turning); release our entanglements with those factors in our lives that hold us back or bring us down (Yom Kippur); call forth the spiritual warrior within ourselves by daring to take that risky leap of faith that we can actually change for the better. We take the risk that we can thrive independent of the material givens of our lives, which we demonstrate by living in a flimsy temporal *sukah* or hut instead of a well-insulated adobe; we affirm that the Creator, not stucco, is our true shelter. Finally, we celebrate the joyfulness of being alive—of life itself— to laugh and rejoice in the face of the approaching winter months and the vanishing green of vegetation. In other words, we celebrate our conviction that we live not because of, but in spite of, life itself; that our life essence is bound up not in what happens or does not happen in the physical experience, but in the inifinite grace of the great and infinite spirit of which each of us is a lucky spark. It is Rosh Hashanah time. It is Yom Kippur time. It is Sukot time. It is Shemini Atzeret time. It is a period of four festivals that the Torah lumped into one season of successive holidays. All four are inclusive in the third cycle that the Torah lists as a period worthy of special pilgrimage to a sacred site; of "seeing the Creator" and of "being seen by the Creator" (Babylonian Talmud, *Hagigah* 7a; see *Tosefot* on Babylonian Talmud, *Shabos* 55b); of ceasing the march of

time to remember that our continuity is relative to the continuing will of the Creator that we *be*; that our macrocosmic
self is dependent upon a far greater Cosmic Self.

Unlike Pesach and Shavuot, the four-part holiday of Sukot—
like autumn—is anything but particularistic. Sukot season is
universal. When the Temple stood and sacrifices were brought
to the altar, Sukot was celebrated with the offering of sacrifices on behalf of all the peoples of the world at that time (*Shir
HaShirim Rabbah* on Song of Songs 1:15). It is a period
during which the liturgy directs worshipers to beseech the
Creator on behalf of the planet, not just Israel; on behalf of all
people, not just Jews; on behalf of all of creation, not just
humans. Where Pesach celebrates the beginning of the months,
Rosh Hashanah celebrates the beginning of the year. Where
the months symbolize particulars, the year represents uni-
versals; a month is a component, a year is a whole. Where
Pesach and Shavuot commemorate one particular people's
physical redemption and spiritual experience, the holidays of
Sukot commemorate the creation of all life, the physical
redemption and spiritual experience of all creatures. Pregnancy
and birth are personal; eldering is universal. We parent our
children; we elder our communities. Pesach and Shavuot are
symbolic of the youth in us; Sukot is symbolic of the elder in
us. Autumn is when we let go of that which is ripe in us to
create space for the beginnings of that which awaits rebirth in
us—transformation.

It is unfortunate that the earth-conscious elements of these
three cyclic rites have become lost to a great many Jews in
this era. For many centuries, Jews of the western world have
been disconnected from the more imminent relationship with
the earth that they once enjoyed and that had at one time been
an integral component of their religious practice and theology.
Driven from its land by conquering nations and deprived of
land in its Exile, the Jewish peoplehood has tragically lost also
the rich, nurturing quality of being in relationship with nature.
Festivals intended for an agrarian mindset naturally take on a

whole different quality of relevance in an urban consciousness. Certainly there were Jews who continued to live close to the land here and there, now and then, but as a people—and consequently as a spirit path—the latter-day Hebrews were forced into an urban lifestyle that over the generations severed them not only from their familial ties with the earth, but also from the quality of spiritual consciousness that goes along with that. Interestingly enough, those few spiritual teachers who, through the centuries, rejuvenated Jewish spirituality when it was all but fading away into the abyss of lifeless dogma were individuals who had been nurtured and inspired not by books and academies, but by caves and mountains, deserts and forests.

> Our ancestors chose to become shepherds and nothing else, only because they found it more conducive to their meditative practices to be in the meadows and in places far from urgency. . . .
>
> Thirteenth-century Rabbi Avraham ibn Maimon,
> *HaMaspik L'Ovdei HaShem*, chapter on *Hitbod'dut*

More than two hundred of the Torah's directives depended upon a relationship with the land (*Megilat Nistar; P'ri M'gadim, Hakdamah L'Shulchan Aruch, Orach Chayim*). And so the three cyclic rites are a powerful reminder to the Jewish people not only of the closeness they once enjoyed with nature, but also of how they can recapture that quality of consciousness even today, even as urban dwellers, by reexamining the cosmology of these festivals beyond their synagogue and in-house observances. It is noteworthy that, over the past several decades, thousands of disenfranchised Jews have left the big cities for the rural life almost simultaneously with their having left religious institutional affiliation. Many of them are engaged in farming and ranching; many more simply live in the wilds and enjoy their newfound connection with the planet in remote regions from Vermont to Wyoming, from Montana to West

Virginia. It is not unlikely that their move has been inspired deep within them by their ancient genes, their ingrained yearning to live where they can most vividly experience the dynamic presence of Creator in Creation, even if it means living hundreds of miles from a synagogue or kosher deli.

Because of the Jewish people's severance from earth-consciousness, the Torah's narratives concerning earth celebration have become instead doctrines of religious particularism. Rather than earth festivals, they became "Jewish" festivals. Rather than celebrating the gifts of the Creator and the wonders of Creation, the resulting theology and liturgy turned the focus to religious worship, devoid of the downhome experiences that originally inspired such worship. David's psalms are recited, are *davvened*, when they should be sung and shouted with the joyfulness and exuberance of one who is zapped by the seductive aromas and colors of spring, summer, or autumn; with at least some of the joyfulness and exuberance that inspired those psalms. This cannot happen inside of synagogue walls, just as it did not happen inside of the walls of the Great Temple of antiquity. Rather, the people danced and sang and played musical instruments and rejoiced amid the scenic hills that surrounded them. They stirred up the dust of the earth, which, in turn, danced with them, raising their prayer and thanksgiving higher than could any organized religious service and neatly bound prayerbook. There were no rabbis and no cantors, only *kohanim*, the shamans who performed the sacred rites related to the symbolism of the respective festivals, and the *levi'im*, whose role it was to play musical instruments and sing for the people, moving them to dance and to ecstasy. As the ancient rabbis put it: "Anyone who has not experienced the rejoicing that took place during the Celebration of the House of the Water Drawing, has never witnessed true rejoicing in their entire lifetime" (*Mishnah, Sukah* 5:1). The Celebration of the House of the Water Drawing was a festive procession to fetch water for the altar from Jerusalem's fresh-water spring:

The spiritual teachers and men of noble deeds would dance before the people and juggle flaming torches in their hands while singing songs and praises. The *levi'im* would play harps, lyres, cymbals, trumpets, and instruments without number. This they did as they descended the fifteen steps that led from the court of Israelites [i.e., the court of men who were not *kohanim* or *levi'im*] to the Court of Women—corresponding to the fifteen songs of ascent [Psalms 120–134]—upon which the *levi'im* would be stationed, playing their instruments and singing songs. And two *kohanim* were posted at the uppermost entrance, which led down from the court of Israelites to the court of women, and two trumpets were in their hands. When the rooster crowed [announcing the crack of dawn], they would blow their trumpets *tekiah, teruah, tekiah* [one long blast, a series of short blasts, and one long blast]. When they reached the tenth step, they blew *tekiah, teruah, tekiah*. When they reached the court [of women], they blew *tekiah, teruah, tekiah*. They would continue to blow until they arrived at the gate leading to the east. When they arrived at the gate leading to the east, they would turn to face the west and proclaim: "Our ancestors who stood at one time in this place would turn their backs to the [west] and face the east and bow to the sun in the east (Ezekiel 8:16). But as for us— our eyes are directed to our Creator!" . . . When they reached the gate of the water, they blew *tekiah, teruah, tekiah*. . . . And they carried a golden vessel that could hold three *lugim* (1½ liters), and filled it with water from the spring [and rejoiced, as it is written: "And you shall draw the waters in joy" (Isaiah 12:3)].

Mishnah, Sukah 5:4, 4:9

What might all this rejoicing have been about? What might have moved the people to gladness and celebration, besides the festive sounds of instruments and song? Perhaps it was the experience of coming to "*see* the face of the Creator" (Deuteronomy 16:16) and ending up feeling "*seen* by the Creator"; they came to see, and ended up feeling seen. As the ancient teachers point out, both "see" and "seen" share the same

Hebraic word יראה, and so when the Torah instructs the people to make the pilgrimage three times during the year, what is classically translated as "to see the face of the Creator" can just as easily be translated as "to be *seen* by the Creator," about which the rabbis commented: "A person went up to both 'see' God and be 'seen' by God" (Babylonian Talmud, *Hagigah* 7a; see also *Tosefot* on Babylonian Talmud, *Shabat* 55b). We feel "seen" by God when we experience the gifts of life, of sustenance, of blessing, of health and serenity. It is in such moments that we can access, if we choose to, the vivid experience of being cared for by the Creator, of being "seen." It is akin to the experience of Hagar, the Egyptian sister-companion of the Hebrew Matriarch Sarah, who gives God the name *El Rowee* (literally, "the God who sees me") (Genesis 16:13). Hagar's inspiration for so naming God comes about when she feels unseen, invisible, and worthless. The Creator then speaks to her and consoles her, assuring her that she is great and that the child in her womb is destined to father many nations. She is restored to her sense of self and the precious gift that self is. She feels visible, cared about, seen; and so she appropriately names God *El Rowee*, "the God who sees me."

For an agrarian people, the harvest season, the season of the first fruits, and the season of ripeness, the end of the dry season, were all periods of natural phenomena that dramatized the Creator's real-time involvement in the process and perpetuity of Creation; periods during which they were encouraged to "see" God and witness how God, in turn, sees *them*, as evidenced by the land yielding sustenance, color, fragrance, and wonder—all gifts of the Creator. To see and to be seen then became an incredible inspiration that nurtured and enriched the body, mind, and spirit of everyone who made the connection between the festivals and their implications.

My sense of "seeing God" arises from the experience of witnessing the unfolding of the fruits of my labors; my sense of "God seeing me" arises in the experience of reaping the fruition of my labors, either during the harvest or during each miraculous phase of growth, whether that growth is happening in my field or in my life process. Therefore, during these three cycles of the year when vivid transformation occurs in the natural world around us, we were to engage the experience as an opportunity of seeing the Creator and feeling seen in return. And we were to include in this ritual the act of acknowledging the particular gifts of the Creator highlighted by that particular season. It was not to be some kind of unconscious, rote observance: "And you shall not behold the face of *yhvh* in emptiness; rather, every man according to the gifts of his hand, according to the blessings of *yhvh,* Source of your power, which have been given to you" (Deuteronomy 16:16).

THE PARTICULARS: SUKOT CYCLE— AUTUMN, OR BEGINNING OF WINTER

Rosh Hashanah

Probably what is most remembered—and dreaded—about Rosh Hashanah and Yom Kippur is the incredibly lengthy chain of liturgy that crowds the prayerbook and fills hours upon hours of sitting in the synagogue. Flexidoxic Judaism posits that not every single prayer ever composed before the Middle Ages needs to be recited, nor did their authors ever dream that their work would be piled atop seemingly endless layers of structured prayer. The further back one goes in Jewish liturgical history, the less prayers composed what is today called the prayerbook, or *sidur*—literally, "the order"—as in the order of service. Rabbi Zalman Schachter-Shalomi accordingly calls the *sidur*'s piles of compiled prayers "bulk," and encourages people to wade through the selections of the *sidur* to discover the essentials of the kind of prayer one needs in the moment.

Prayer needs to come from the heart, not a text. If the words aren't there in our hearts, then we can turn to the text to help us warm up, to prime us, to stir our own prayer expressions through the inspiration of the prayers of others. But to render the prayerbook the sole medium of prayer is thievery of the spirit. It is counterproductive to keep people pasted onto wooden pews or folding chairs for hours on end while a cantor elongates already elongated prayers. The bottom-line question is: How much of the meaning and relevance of the so-called "High Holy Days" gets through to us if half of the holiday is spent *kvetching* through hours of grueling services and the other half is spent recuperating in bed or on the sofa? It is more important that the services be narrowed down to the prayers that are selected by each community as words that best address who they are and what they are wrestling with. Nowhere in the Torah does it state that Rosh Hashanah, for instance, is a day of heavy-duty prayer. It *does* say, however, that it is a day of remembering, and a day of blowing the *shofar* or horn (Leviticus 23:24). It is therefore antithetical to the spirit of the High Holy Days to spend so much time at services that one all but forgets what one was supposed to have remembered. It is not as important to go to services on these major holy days as it is to integrate their meaning into one's personal life-journeying. The Torah is simple about this: "Three times during the year shall you see the face of *yhvh*" and "not in emptiness." Can you see God at any point during six hours of services? If so, fine. But if after six hours you still can't see God, or if the image of God starts fading away from your mind and is gradually replaced by the image of a pizza, then perhaps you need to do it differently. Perhaps you need to spend two hours at services and then go for a hike in the national forest or sit at home in solitude for a while, meditating on what has happened in your life until this moment, what it is you need to change about your life rhythm and direction, and how you intend to effect necessary or hoped-for changes. Friends may castigate you for not having attended services, but more likely you experienced Rosh Hashanah more qualitatively than they did. For them, it was a day of services; for you, it was what the Torah intended: "a day of remembrance"—a time to look inside and remember your forgotten self, your forgotten partner, your forgotten children, your forgotten parents, your forgotten friends, your forgotten community, your forgotten planet, your forgotten God.

How misunderstood, then, is the term often used to describe the High Holy Days of Rosh Hashanah and Yom Kippur: *yamim noraim*, or "Days of Awe." People take this to imply a holy day of fear and anxiety. They are, after all, days of judgment, and the liturgy reinforces this with pleas that God judge us compassionately and sentence us to a good year. For we are judged on Rosh Hashanah concerning our fate for the coming new year: who will live, and who will die; who in their time and who before their time; who by fire, who by water, who by the sword, who by famine, who by thirst, who by plague, and so on. The liturgy harps on the judgment and evokes in many a sense of worry about the verdict that will determine their fate for the new year. This sort of attitude about the Days of Awe is radically different from that reflected in some of the more flexidoxic of the ancient teachings: "Do not be afraid of God's judgment. . . . Do you not know Him? He is your kinsman! He is your brother! And, what's more, He is your Father" (*Midrash Tehilim* on Psalms 118:5).

> Customarily, when people appear before a mortal court for judgment, they approach in a morbid state of solemn countenance and with great trepidation of the outcome of their judgment. . . . Not so, however, when the day of [divine] judgment begins [Rosh Hashanah], for the Jews are then clad in white and gird themselves in festiveness and eat and drink and rejoice in the conviction that God will do wonders for them.
> Jerusalem Talmud, *Rosh Hashanah* 57b

In ancient times, the day of Rosh Hashanah is described as having been more a day of blowing a ram's horn than a day of prayer services: "In the seventh cycle of the moon's renewal, in the first day of its renewal, shall be for you a sacred calling; you shall perform no manner of labor, it is a day of sounding for you" (Numbers 29:1). What kind of sounding? Words? Routine prayers and supplications? Not at all. Simply sound— as in the sound of a ram's horn. The day calls for a simple raw sounding that does not originate in our throats, but in the whisper of our breath. This is the teaching of the *shofar*: Blow into the narrowest place, and you shall create a sound that is powerful and resonate; reach deeper than your guttural place, deep inside of you where there are no words, only feelings, and from there set free your *ruach*, your wind, your spirit, from the finite places—the parts of you that hold you back from unfolding—so that it may flow forth through the wide opening of your intention, to the expanses of the infinite. Sound the *shofar*. Specifically, the Torah instructs, sound the particular notes of the *shofar* called *t'ruah*, the call of the warrior.

The *shofar* is a vehicle of journeying to the spiritual realm, of joining your deepest sense of selfhood with the ultimate selfhood; of touching your molecular essence to the cosmic essence; of transcending your finite self to access your infinite self. In the inner space of the *shofar* between the narrow mouthpiece and the broad opening is the sacred space of transformation. There, breath becomes sound; feeling becomes expression; yearning becomes prayer. There is no prayer as powerful as the sounding of the *shofar*. It is the prayer of Chanah, whose prayer for a child was answered when she ultimately gave up on conventional prayer and instead tunneled deep into the narrowest place within her to free up the fullness of her soul-yearning. What resulted was not the most eloquent prayer ever composed. What resulted was the sound of her inner *shofar*, the inaudible quest of her self-essence:

> And Eilee the *kohen* observed her lips. And Chanah was speaking on her heart; only her lips moved, but no sound was heard, and Eilee suspected that she was intoxicated. And he said to her: "For how long will you go about with your drunkenness? Remove from yourself your addiction to wine." And Chanah replied: "It is not so, my master. I am a woman of burdened

spirit. Neither wine nor beer have I drunk. Rather, I am pouring out my soul before *yhvh*. Do not take your daughter for a licentious woman, for it is out of my intense meditation and frustration that I speak to *yhvh* in this manner." And Eilee answered: "Go then toward peacefulness, and the God of Israel shall give to you what you have asked for." And she said: "May your eyes discover gracefulness in your relations," and the woman went on her way, and she ate, and her face was no longer sad.

1 Samuel 1:12–18

A year later, Chanah became the mother of the prophet Samuel, or *Sh'muel*, which means "God listened." God hears always—all prayers, in any form. But prayer is most potent when it comes from a place far deeper than the guttural; from a place of authenticity, where all pretentions fall away and we are left standing before the Creator completely bare, completely our raw, vulnerable selves. Thus the Hebraic word for prayer is תפילה—*t'filah*—which connotes "falling." If, when we pray, we can release our grip on the illusion of our own reality and allow ourselves to then lose our balance and fall, with the faith that God will catch us and lift us up, then we have begun to learn what תפילה is.

It is the quest of the spirit to harmonize one's physical reality consciousness with one's spiritual reality consciousness, one's sense of the microcosmic with one's sense of the macrocosmic —for the person to experience each as real as the other. All existence, the Jewish mystics taught, is illusion; is but a figment of the Creator's imagination, so to speak; and אין זולתו (*eyn zuloto*), "there is nothing other than God" (Deuteronomy 4:39). Our reality, in other words, exists solely in relationship to the existence of the One who created it and is therefore contingent moment-to-moment upon the Creator's constant willing and imaging our existence. Were God to cease for a moment to think of you, you would be nonextant in that moment—Poof!

When a man creates a structure of a sort from wood, the builder does not at that moment create out of his own power the wood, but rather takes from trees that have already been created and then arranges them into a structure. And after the completion of the construction, although the builder removes his power from it and walks off, the structure remains standing nevertheless. But the Holy Blessed One—just as at the onset of creation brought forth worlds into being from absolutely nothing, likewise from then on, every day and every moment, the whole cause of their existence, arrangement, and being, is dependent solely upon the fact that the Creator is willingly influencing them every single moment with the power to exist and the nurturance of ever-new divine light. And if the Creator were to withhold from them the power of the divine influence even for so much as a fraction of a moment, all would be nothing and desolate.

> Eighteenth-century Rabbi Chaim of Volozhin,
> *Nefesh HaChayyim* 1:2, par. 1

Prayer-consciousness is, then, an exercise in letting go of your sense of reality and allowing yourself to fall into the Creator's embrace, into the alternative reality that lends existence and substance to your own reality; to fall into the *t'hom*—the abyss, the cauldron of transformation, the chaotic whirl wherein the Creator dances Creation into existence (Genesis 1:2). Then you can experience God "listening" (*sh'muel*), not just hearing. But to achieve this consciousness in prayer, you need to remove the grime that gathers over time, separating your physical self-awareness from your spirit self-awareness; you need to lift the veil that every now and then clouds your body's eye from seeing what your mind's eye is seeing. This is where the sound of the *shofar* comes in as a shamanic shattering of the barriers that stand between body and soul. Writes the eighteenth-century Rabbi Nachmon of Breslav:

And this is what is meant by the verse, "From my flesh shall I see the Source of Powers" (Job 19:26)—that is, literally through the very flesh of the body shall one behold God, meaning perceptions of the divine, meaning that the human sees and envisions spiritual perceptions by way of the body, for the soul is always visioning. But if the body is in a state of resistance, then can the soul not sustain herself nor draw near to the body to inform it of her visions for she could become caught up in the aggressiveness and resistance of the body in that the body is brazen and empowered through its own yearnings. In such an instance, one needs, in turn, to respond with brazenness but from a place of holiness, and that would be with sound, as the sages taught us: "Sighing shatters a person's stuckness" [Babylonian Talmud, *Berachot* 58b]. And when one breaks down the insolence and resistance of the body, then can the soul draw herself near to the body, for she will not be overwhelmed there. And this is the context of the verse, "Because of the sound of my sighing, have my bones cleaved onto my flesh" [Psalms 102:6] [the word for "bones" is עצמי— *atzomi*—the same spelling of the Hebrew word for "my essence" or "my self"]. "My essence" refers to the soul, for she is the essence—עצם—of the human. For the primary essence of the human—what is called the "I"—is the soul, for she is the essence that prevails eternally. But because of the resistance of the body when it gets caught up in the exclusive pursuits of its yearnings, the soul—which is the essence of the human—becomes distant from the person's body and flesh. And from the sound of sighing, which, too, is from the category of resistance, but from a place of holiness, the resistance of the body will break down. And then will the essence become drawn again to the flesh, meaning the soul to the body. And that is what is meant by "Because of the sound of my sighing has my essence cleaved onto my flesh." And thus the ritual sounding of the *shofar* is synonymous with "the sound of my sighing," and like sighing it breaks down the resistance of the human body, akin to: "Shall the horn be sounded in a village and the people not shudder?" (Amos 3:6). . . . The *tekiah* [one long blast] is the sound of resistance, *sh'varim* [three short blasts] is the sound of breaking down the resistance of the body, and *teruah* (series of short blasts in rapid

succession) is from the context of "And you shall shepherd
(*te-roah*) my people" [2 Samuel 3:2]. . . .

Likutei MaHaRan 22:5–7

The *shofar* is, then, more than a striking sound that everyone rushes to the synagogue to hear. It is the Rite of the Sacred Sound. It is a shamanic ceremony of blasting away all that
stands between us and a lucid encounter with the *shechinah*,
the divine presence, that dwells within each of us. It is a sacred
sounding that invites us to bring to the surface our deepest
yearnings from the most narrow, vulnerable places within us,
and to breathe them forth through the transformative funnel
of *shofar* and out to the wide-open expanses of endless possibility; out of our finite, constrictive reality, into the realm
of the nurturing reality of the Infinite One. Thus, the prayer
recited before the sounding of the *shofar*: "From the narrow
place I called *Yah*. Answer me, O *Yah*, in the wide expanse.
Yhvh is with me, I shall not be afraid; what can a mortal do to
me, for *yhvh* is with me as my strength" (Psalms 118:5)—that
is, God is the Ultimate Reality, so what can anyone or any
situation really do to us in our own reality that is illusory in
relationship to that of God's? In this sense, the three *shofar*
notes can also be symbolic of our faith in the constant, impreg-
nable, and eternal nature of our self-essence, our soul. We begin
as soul, existing in consistency and harmony (*t'kiah*—steady
blast). Then we come into physical embodiment and encounter contradiction and conflict (*sh'varim*—short, broken blasts).
In response, we invoke our inner warrior self and sound the
battle cry (*t'ruah*—short, quick successive blasts) and wrest
ourselves out of our stupor and back to a sense of empower-
ment and smoothness (*t'kiah gedolah*—steady blast). At the
end of our lives, we return to the realm of eternal consistency
and harmony where our Spirit Self originated (*t'kiah gedolah*—
extended steady blast).

The High-Holy-Day period is, therefore, a time for letting
go and falling, drifting in the wind to the place from where

you came, whether you're a leaf, an acorn, or a person. It is a time of going inside and preparing yourself for fresh seeding, and of clearing away all the weeds that block your view of the bigger picture. The process begins with Rosh Hashanah, is followed by *aseret y'mei t'shuvah*—the ten days of turning around—and peaks with Yom Kippur, the day of letting go, of forgiveness. Where Rosh Hashanah is a day of remembrance, Yom Kippur is a day of forgetting. On Rosh Hashanah, you remember your sins; on Yom Kippur, you forget them. On Rosh Hashanah, you glean all your deeds of the past year, along with the harvest; on Yom Kippur, you recycle, or transform, the husks of your harvest so that you are left with the positive, with the most simple and bottom-line self that you are.

Yom Kippur

To most people, Yom Kippur is considered a solemn day of fasting and worship. But in earlier times, while it was indeed a day of fasting and worship, it was not so solemn:

> Said Rabbi Shimon ben Gamliel: "No days were as festive for Israel as the fifteenth of the moon of Av [end of the dry season] and Yom Kippur [day of forgiveness]. For then would the sons of Jerusalem go out dressed in borrowed white garments in order that they not embarrass those who have less . . . and the daughters of Jerusalem would go out to the orchards and play upon tambourines. And what would they sing? 'Young men! Lift up your eyes, please, and see what it is that you wish to select for yourselves. Give not your eyes to appearances alone, but give your eyes to family.'"
>
> Jerusalem Talmud, *Ta'anit* 4:7

The Yom Kippur fast was not intended to create an atmosphere of depression and severe solemnity; Yom Kippur is, after all, enumerated amongst the *festivals*, as in festive days. Rather, Yom Kippur is a time for rejoining that which has become separated, removing the obstacles that separate people from each other, from God, from the planet, from the fullness of self. By fasting, by abstaining from the yearnings of our physical self, we stand a better chance of reconnecting with our spiritual self and becoming whole again after having been split. No wonder the ancient Jews chose this day for singles gatherings. What more opportune time to pick a mate than on a day of fasting, a day filled with personal introspection and transformation, a day when one achieved a clarity of mind that reflected concord—rather than discord—between body and spirit. This was the atmosphere the Yom Kippur fast was supposed to inspire: a fast not of self-denial, but of self-enlivening; not of self-punishment, but of self-empowerment, which in turn would then motivate the people to enliven and empower each other.

> Is this the fasting that I have chosen? That it be a day for a person to torment their soul? Is it so that one will bow down their head like a bulrush, and spread sackcloth and ashes beneath themself? Will you indeed call this a fasting, and a day that is in accord with *yhvh*'s wish? Rather, the kind of fasting that I have intended—is it not the act of loosening the hold of wickedness? And to undo the bands of the yoke? And to free the oppressed and shatter all constraints? Is it not about feeding your bread to the hungry, and bringing in to your homes the oppressed poor? And that when you see the naked, you will clothe them? And that you do not hide from your own self? If you do this, then will your light burst forth like the morning, and healing shall sprout forth quickly . . . and when you call to *yhvh*, *yhvh* will answer, and when you cry, *yhvh* will respond with: "Here I am!" . . . and your light shall then shine in the darkness, and your gloom transformed into a brilliance akin to the midday light . . . and *yhvh* shall guide you with ease always. . . .
>
> Isaiah 58:5–11

The fact that Yom Kippur is a day of making amends with people and with God makes it appear to some people as a day of gloom and anxiety: gloom over past sins and anxiety over whether or not God will forgive them. The contrary is true: Yom Kippur is a festive day because of the Jewish belief that people can change their ways, and that God is tolerant and forgiving (Exodus 34:6; Numbers 14:18; Jonah 4:2; Joel 2:13; Nehemiah 9:17; Psalms 103:8). Probably, the solemnity of the day comes not from its theme, but because we're simply starving for a knish.

"Days of awesomeness" is probably a more fitting term for these Holy Days than Days of Awe, for they are not scary but spectacular, marvelous, astonishing, phenomenal—in other words, awesome. They are days that celebrate the wondrous capability of the human spirit to transform itself, to better itself, to effect change in self and in relationships with others. They are days that likewise celebrate the remarkable way in which the Creator deals with our negative choices and deeds after we have acknowledged our foibles and weaknesses and have committed ourselves to at least an *attempt* at correcting them. It is awesome that, even though another year has gone by with a lot of the same mistakes, God is still open to forgiving us; is still tolerant of our not getting it totally right; is still patient with our persistence in old habits that stand in the way of our improvement. Taught the third-century Rabbi Sh'muel bar Nachmon: "The gates of returning are never shut, and the arms of the Creator are always outstretched to receive those who choose to take that single step back to rightness" (*Devarim Rabbah* 2:7). Or: "Even if there be ninety-nine accusations against a person, and only a single merit in their favor, the Creator tips the scales of judgment toward the single merit" (*Pesikta Rabati* 38b, or Ch. 10).

> At the moment when a person commits a sin, the angels rush to the Creator and declare: "Defend your holy name! Go down upon the earth and set the mountains ablaze!" And the Creator replies: "This person is going through a difficult period right now; if they realize their wrong and return to Me, I will accept them."
>
> *Midrash Tehilim*, on Psalms 94

Sadly, these are the kinds of flexidoxic teachings that get left out of the standard repertoire of mainstream religious education about the "Days of Awesomeness," and about a God who bears with us and does not foam at the mouth. The flexidoxic side to Judaism tried in vain to provide a sense of balance to the way God was being portrayed to the people by teachers who were more concerned with scaring the people into religiously correct obeisance *to* God than with inspiring them into personally authentic relationship *with* God:

> It was asked of wisdom: "What is the fate of the sinner?" Replied wisdom: "Evil shall pursue the sinner" [Proverbs 13:21]. It was asked of prophecy: "What is the fate of the sinner?" Replied prophecy: "The soul that sins shall die" [Ezekiel 18:4]. It was asked of the Torah: "What is the fate of the sinner?" Replied the Torah: "Bring a sacrifice and be atoned" [Leviticus 1:4]. It was asked of the Creator: "What is the fate of the sinner?" Replied the Creator: "Return unto Me and I will receive you" [Jeremiah 3:1], for it is written: "Good and just is *yhvh*; therefore does *yhvh* show the way to the one who has gone astray" [Psalms 25:8].
>
> Jerusalem Talmud, *Makot* 2:6

Going astray is human, is normal. In fact, Judaism teaches that חטא (*chett*)—what is called "sin," or distancing oneself from God—is often a necessary component of the process of תשובה (*t'shuvah*), literally "returning," coming near to God. More endearing, then, is the act of making your way back across the moat that separates you from feeling close to God than being so goody-goody that you're always joined at the divine hip: "When a person turns with earnestness from their wrong ways, their proximity to God is such that even the most perfect of saints cannot approach it" (Babylonian Talmud, *Berachot* 34b).

The formula is quite simple. The Torah states that the antidote to חטא (*chett*), to distancing, is קרבן (*korban*), customar-

ily translated as "sacrifice," but literally meaning "draw near."
When there was חטא—distance—you brought a קרבן חטאת
(*korban chattas*)—usually translated as "sin offering," but
actually meaning "narrowing the distance." The sacrificial
rite of ancient Judaism had nothing to do with placating a
wrathful, bloodthirsty deity, but with encountering the God of
reconciliation.

> "With what shall I come before *yhvh*? And bow myself before
> *yhvh* on high? Shall I come before *yhvh* with burnt-offerings?
> With calves a year old? Will *yhvh* be pleased with thousands
> of rams? With tens of thousands of rivers of oil? Shall I per-
> haps give my firstborn for my transgressions? The fruit of my
> body for the sins of my soul?" It has been told you, O human,
> what is good, and what it is that *yhvh* seeks from you: Only
> that you act in fairness, love benevolence, and walk humbly
> with the Source of your powers.
>
> Micah 6:6–8

The so-called "sin" offering was no more than a symbolic
gesture of the individual's desire to draw near to God across
the gap that had been forged by her or his wrongness. These
individuals brought animals that belonged to them, that they
had spent their own livelihoods either raising or purchasing.
A deer, or any other animal of the wilds, was not permitted as
a sacrifice, because it did not represent any aspect of the
person's selfhood. It was beyond possession. It was wild and
free. You had to bring something of yours (Leviticus 1:2), and
in offering it to the Creator you expressed your earnestness
about drawing near where you have strayed far; this was done
by the gesture of offering a life that in some way represented
your own life, because it was a life that owed itself to you for
feeding it, protecting it, and sheltering it. It was, at the same
time, a recognition that distancing from God occurs a great
deal of the time when we—even momentarily—substitute God
with our self as the source of everything we are, everything
we achieve, and everything we possess. To draw near again

across this gap, we bring something we own and acknowledge its primary source by *restoring* it to its primary source.
None of this, however, was worth even the symbolism of it if
the person who brought the offering had not also acknowledged their wrong. The most important component, again,
is *t'shuvah*, turning back (Zachariah 1:3–4; Hosea 14:2–3;
Ezekiel 14:6, 18:30; Malachi 3:7).

You did not sin against God or your fellow creatures and
simply bring a sin offering. You acknowledged your deed, asked
for forgiveness, made restitution if necessary, and made a
commitment to not do it again; only then did you bring your
offering (Babylonian Talmud, *Rosh Hashanah* 17a and *Yoma*
85b). Only if your sin was unintentional did you bring a "sin"
offering (Leviticus 4:2, 13, 22, 27). Someone who erred unintentionally and was bothered by it would be more likely to
exercise caution in not doing it again. Therefore, the Torah
states: "And it became known to the person" (Leviticus 4:23
and 28), meaning that the individual realizes the wrongness
of what she or he has done—only then could they bring an
offering. No animal is worth sacrificing for someone about
whom it is not clear that their intentions are earnest, that the
death of the animal would perhaps be in vain. The blood that
flowed along the floor of the Great Temple in Jerusalem was
not to be the residue of some kind of assembly-line atonement
factory. When it became just that during the Roman occupa-
tion and Sadduccean control of the Temple rites some two
thousand years ago, the Holy Temple collapsed, along with
the entire institution of animal sacrifices in Judaism. The rabbis
of that era knew that it was forthcoming, and understood that
the paradigm of this rite was approaching its end and that a
new paradigm was to take its place, one in which the people
would dispense with the gestures of penance and be left with
no choice but action and personal transformation. Nor did an
offering have to be blood; it could also be flour or currency
(Leviticus 5:11). Contrary to popular presumption, these sacrifices did not end up in the belly of a hungry god who de-

manded to be fed every time someone "made an oops" (Psalms 50:8–15); they were eaten as a sacred meal by the *kohanim*, the shamans responsible for facilitating the process (Exodus 30:15–16; Leviticus 6:19, 22 and 7:6–8).

Judaism teaches that the most potent form of coming back to God across the moat of one's wrongness is not sacrifice, but sincere acknowledgment followed by positive change. To do this is a far greater "offering" to the Creator than any possible gesture of ritual. As David wrote: "I acknowledged to You my being distant, and my wrongfulness I did not conceal; I said, 'I will confess to God regarding my errors'—and You, You forgave the mistakes that created my distancing" (Psalms 32:5).

Judaism also teaches that "distance from God" is a purely subjective experience, that we might by deed or choice *experience* being distant from God, but that God is always at our side, waiting for us to turn around: "The Holy Blessed One follows the sinner all through the marketplace, waiting patiently for them to turn around" (*Peskita D'Rav Kahana* 163b). One of the major reasons that Christianity failed to attract the Jews is that Judaism does not perceive the journey back to God as so arduous and steep that it requires the aid of a redemptive savior. Indeed, the ancient rabbis held that Adam and Eve could have returned to the Garden of Eden after they had been thrown out, had they only believed in a God of reconciliation (*B'reishis Rabbah* 25:10). The angels at the gates to paradise, wielding their flaming swords, represented no more than the usual obstacles of discouragement that stand in the path of those contemplating turning back, whether it is to make amends with people or with God. The Talmud recounts how the second-century heretic Acher (formerly, Rabbi Elisha ben Avuyah) wished to repent of his wayward behavior, but then changed his mind. When his disciple Rabbi Meir asked him to explain, he said: "I was about to repent when I heard a heavenly voice proclaim, 'Return, O you erring children [and I will heal your wrongness]' [Jeremiah 3:22]—except for Elisha ben Avuyah" (Jerusalem Talmud, *Chagigah* 1:2 [7b])! In the end,

Elisha returned anyhow, realizing that the special exclusion implied a special invitation. The flaming-swords phenomenon is but a test of our conviction: Do we truly want to go back across the distance created by our wrongness, or are we unable to get past our image of God as vengeful and unbending? "I will not frown at you," God responds, "for I am a compassionate God; I do not bear eternal grudges. I only ask that you acknowledge your mistakes" (Jeremiah 3:12–13).

Said Rabbi Chanina bar Yitzchak (fourth century): When Cain wandered the earth [after unintentionally killing his brother Abel], he encountered Adam the First [who had been driven from the Garden of Eden for eating of "the forbidden fruit"]. Said Adam to him: "And what, pray tell, was the result of your judgment?" Replied Cain: "I acknowledged the wrongfulness of my act and was exonerated." When Adam the First heard this, he wept and said: "Woe! So great is the power of *teshuvah* [turning back], and I did not know it!"
Vayikra Rabbah 10:5 and *Peskita D'Rav Kahana* 160b

Indeed, God so cherishes our desire to turn around that God is even willing to make the first move, an acknowledgment that God, too, shares responsibility for our going astray! As the ancient rabbis put it: "Says the Holy Blessed One, 'Is it that you are embarrassed to do penance and to return to Me? Behold, I will be the first to do penance and to return to *you*" (*Pesikta Rabati* 184a , or Ch. 44)!

It is likened unto a king whose son had wronged him and fled from him on a journey of one hundred days. His friends urged him, saying: "Return to your father." But he said to them: "I am unable to." When the king heard about this, he sent a messenger to his son, saying: "Take but however many steps toward me as you are able to, and I shall meet you the rest of the way." Likewise does the Creator say to us: "Return unto Me and I shall return unto you" [Malachi 3:7].
Pesikta Rabati 184b–185a, or Ch. 44

The idea of God sharing in a person's process of "repentance" may sound sacrilegious to those who image God as an exacting deity or, more to the point, a cosmic spoiled brat who revels in one-way relationships where the only responsible party is the other. The God of Judaism, on the other hand, is portrayed as a God who seeks mutual relationship, and in every mutual relationship both parties share in what happens with the other, for better or for worse. Especially is this true in the relationship of parents with their children in that although parents may not have directly caused their kids to commit a wrong, they are nonetheless participants in their children's processes, in their children's choices and actions. Judaism describes God not only as Creator, but also as Parent (Exodus 4:22, 23; Deuteronomy 8:5; Isaiah 63:9, 16, and 64:7; Hosea 11:1; Psalms 103:13; I Chronicles 28:6). Therefore, the notion of God bearing some of the responsibility for the very choices we make that distance us from God is Judaically reasonable, logical, and scriptural: "O God, why do you cause us to stray from your ways?" (Isaiah 63:17), because the God of Judaism is a personal God. The "Days of Awesomeness" are, therefore, annual reminders to us that God is nowhere near as exacting or judgmental of us as we project from our place of feeling "distant."

> Says the Creator: "Open up to me so much as the eye of a needle, and I shall open up for you so wide that entire caravans of wagons and coaches can pass through, and with great ease."
> *Shir HaShirim Rabbah* 5:3

Turning back to God out of fear of punishment was considered by the ancient rabbis as an incomplete or handicapped process of personal transformation, not unlike the unwholesome act of making up with a friend because you're afraid that the friend may get back at you or may not loan you her boat for your planned fishing expedition next Sunday. Rather, a full transformation requires an earnest desire to follow through on one's sense of rightness that arises out of one's acknowledgment of a sense of wrongness. This quality of turning back, of *t'shuvah*, then achieves a transformation not only of where one is at present, but also of where one has come from, including all the wrongness that had been part of, and led up to, the current realization.

> Those who repent out of fear, their past sins are considered retroactively as if they were committed unintentionally; those who repent out of love, however, their past sins are retroactively transformed into merits.
>
> Babylonian Talmud, *Yoma* 86a

How incredible, then, is the High-Holy-Days season, a period whose theme is about God's compassion and love, a series of festivals intended to remind us of the God "Who forgives all your sins, Who heals all your ills, Who redeems your life from the abyss, Who adorns you with lovingkindness and compassion. . . . For *yhvh* is full of compassion and is gracious, slow to anger and full of mercy. . . . Nor has *yhvh* dealt with us according to our sins or punished us according to the intensity of our wrongness . . ." (Psalms 103:2–4 and 8–10). This, after all, is the season of harvest, of gleaning the positive from the negative, of gathering in the bounty of the Creator's gifts to us, and of experiencing thereby the Creator's constant love for us in the vivid form of the sustenance we now gather for our enjoyment and survival through the coming winter moons. It is a cosmic way of saying: "I have forgiven you as you asked me to [Numbers 14:20], so refresh and renew yourself and get on with your life."

Sukot

This is where Sukot comes in—a nine-day celebration of the brazenness of the human spirit, the dependable grace of the Creator, and the illusion of the material. For most of this period, we are instructed to live in fragile, temporary huts with branches for our roofs (Leviticus 23:42–43). During this time, we reinforce in ourselves what we have come to realize during the "Days of Awesomeness"—that the elements of our physical reality, our sturdy homes and indoor plumbing, are as vulnerable as we are and can go at any minute, leaving us bare of what we have been accustomed to perceive as the "necessities of life." During Sukot we leave our secure homes and sit inside flimsy huts that the wind can whisk from us with little effort, and celebrate the strength of spirit against any material odds. Our shelter is our Creator. Our reality is that of God. Nothing else is truly lasting. Life is fleeting. All that we have is temporal. All that we are is relative. In this reality, there are no absolutes—only pitiful second-guesses. And so we leave our narrow perception of life, the illusion of security represented by our homes and all our "things," and sit instead in the expanses of the outdoors, in view of the bigger picture, exposed to the cosmos; at the mercy of the elements, and in awe of the mystery.

Nonetheless, the laws of Sukot are also mindful of the possibility of physical discomfort to the point of distraction. As in all matters, Judaism teaches simultaneous concern for the needs of the spirit *and* the needs of the body; both are sacred and both need to be addressed, never one to the neglect of the other. Therefore, while the ancient teachers stressed the importance of dwelling in the *sukah*, they also reminded people that the comfort of the body was also important; that one cannot celebrate the spirit without the well-being of the body. Therefore, if while you are in your *sukah* it begins to pour, you are certainly permitted to forego the observance and to seek shelter and comfort indoors (Babylonian Talmud, *Sukah* 29a). Even if mosquitoes are bugging you, you do not have to discomfort yourself with dining in the *sukah* (Jerusalem Talmud, *Sukah* 2:10). If you are a married man, and your wife for whatever reason is not going to sleep in the *sukah*, you are not required to separate from her on account of *sukot*

(*Rama* [16th-century Rabbi Moshe Isserles] and *Magen Avra-ham* [17th-century Rabbi Avraham Gumbiner] on *Shulchan Aruch, Orach Chaim* 539:2). After all, the precepts of the Torah were intended for aliveness, not disconcertment (Leviticus 18:5; Ezekiel 20:11; Nehemiah 9:29).

Sukot's tie to nature goes beyond the agronomical relationship with the harvest season during which it occurs. The *sukah* itself symbolizes the human's ecological relationship to the earth. In ancient Israel the *sukah* was constructed out of palm branches—specifically the date palm, a tree that grows near water, albeit in the desert. The fruit of this tree flourishes and ripens where other vegetation is scarce and cannot survive. Not only do the umbrellalike branches of the date palm shelter the desert traveler from the sun, but its dates are a source of high-energy food, and its husks serve as forage for camels. The fibers of this tree were used also, mostly for weaving ropes and baskets. When parched wilderness travelers spotted such a tree, it meant a welcome oasis of water, shelter, and replenishment. It is clear that these trees marked the places in the Sinai Desert where the ancient Hebrews camped during their forty-year wilderness trek; thus the availability of the material that would have been necessary to construct the *sukah* during their desert wanderings.

> Also on the fifteenth day of the seventh cycle of the moon's renewal, when you gather in the produce of the land, you shall celebrate the festival of *yhvh* for seven days; the first day shall be a period of sacred repose, and the eighth day, too, shall be a period of sacred repose. And on the first day you shall take unto yourselves the fruits of the most majestic tree, and the branches of the palm trees, and the offshoots of the myrtle bushes, and the willows that grow by the creek, and you shall rejoice with these before your Creator for seven days. . . . In huts [*sukot*] shall you dwell for seven days, all citizens among the Israelites shall dwell in huts. Thereby shall all generations know that I caused the children of Israel to dwell in huts dur-

ing the process of My taking them out of the land of narrows;
I am *yhvh*, Source of your powers.

Leviticus 23:39–44

Traditionally, the fruit of the "most majestic tree" is considered to be the *etrog*, or citron. The *etrog*, a lemon-like fruit, is the only flora whose female part of the flower remains attached to the fruit even after it has fully ripened. The second species of the Sukot rite—the palm branch, or *lulav*—is the embryonic cradle of the date fruit. The third species of the rite, the myrtle twig, or *hadas*, is capable of surviving far from water and even long after it has been separated from its bush. On the other hand, the fourth species, the willow twig, or *aravah*, can survive neither separate from its tree nor far from water. The species correspond to the history of the ancient Hebrews' journey back to their ancestral homeland. The *lulav* symbolizes the oases of palm trees that sustained them and sheltered them in the desert; the *aravah*, which grows on the eastern banks of the Jordan River, symbolizes the people's vulnerability in anticipating the climactic transition from journeying to settling; the *hadas*, which grows on the western banks of the Jordan, symbolizes the sense of independence and immortality that the people experienced once they crossed the river and reached the soil of home; the *etrog* symbolizes the people's hopes for the fertility of their homeland, for the harmonious relationship of the feminine with the masculine.

In each our lives, these four species of the Earth's gifts constitute powerful shamanic means of bringing together the many diverse, and often contradictory, parts of our selves, and joining them in a consciousness of connectedness. This, after all, is the primal theme of Judaic monotheism: the awareness of the connectedness of everything, the familial unity of Creation, the interdependence or ecology of all that exists in all of the universes, cosmically and microcosmically. It is not about the oneness of the Creator; it is about the oneness of the Creation, the acknowledgment of which is essential to realizing the oneness of God. Thus we join that which has aroma (*aravah*) with that which has no fragrance at all (*hadas*); that which is potential, embryonic (*lulav*), with that which is fruition, realization (*etrog*); that which needs connectedness and subtance to stay alive (*aravah*) with that which does not (*hadas*); that which is heart, the place of the erratic and the dynamic within us (*etrog*), with that which is spine, the place of the static and the structural within us (*lulav*). Each of us is composed of the symbolic attributes of these species, and when we combine them in our grasp as a single bundle we honor the paradox and the contradiction, the very distinct and often opposite feelings, tastes, idiosyncracies, qualities, opinions, and perspectives that each of us has not only in relationship to others, but also in relationship to our selves as we continue to grow and transform.

During the Sukot prayer service, we hold the four species all together, touching one another, directly opposite our hearts —our center. And from our center we then reach out, waving them in unison in the four directions, then up to the sky, then down to the earth, then back to our hearts. It is a prayer without words, a prayer empowered by gesture alone. In essence, the prayer that our hearts yearn for all of Creation, whether spirit or matter, is to be blessed with the symbology of the four species: respite and nurturance (*lulav*); the balance of the feminine and the masculine (*etrog*); the well-being of the physical (*aravah*)—that all living things have access to their sources of sustenance and nourishment; and the well-being of the spiritual (*hadas*)—that whatever within us and without us thrives independent of the material universe will continue to flourish even after it is separated from its physical manifestation. The fulfillment of all these hopes requires the help of the Creator, and therefore the mantra chanted over and over again as we parade around the prayer space on Sukot is "*Hosha-na,*" which, literally, means: "Help, please!"

The four directions in which we wave these earth beings correspond to the four sacred winds described by Isaiah the prophet: "The wind of the Creator, the wind of wisdom and insight, the wind of counsel and balance, the wind of knowing and being aware of the Creator" (Isaiah 11:2). The power in the four winds or directions is to bring to us aliveness and renewal when we are feeling stuck and stagnant: "Call forth the spirit of all the four winds and say to her, 'Come and breathe life into those who have been nullified'" (Ezekiel 37:9).

Shemini Atzeret

The Sukot triad culminates with Simchat Torah, the rejoicing over the Torah, over the sacred guide, the gift that all these observances and their underlying teachings represent. Until now, we have been practicing the symbology of these festivals and absorbing their meanings into our personal and planetary experiences. Now that the period is reaching its conclusion, it is time to express our gratitude for these lessons as the gift that they are: "For a wonderful acquisition have I given unto you; do not shove aside My Torah" (Proverbs 4:2). In the Torah itself, this final day of the sacred triad of Rosh Hashanah, Yom Kippur, and Sukot is called Atzeret, or "the closing": "And on the eighth day shall be a closing for you" (Numbers 29:35). Known more popularly as Shemini Atzeret, this concluding festival is celebrated indoors. Slowly, we wean ourselves from the symbolic practices, from waving the palm branches, from eating in the *sukah*, and we return to the space where we will be spending the coming winter moons. Shemini Atzeret is a sacred time all its own, during which we allow all that we had practiced symbolically to become integrated into our life experience. It is a festival of winding down the long day of the harvest period, of the festival season, of personal and environmental transformation, and allowing it all to gel as we enter the sleep of winter. Winter, then, is like night. It is a time when all that has happened in the day cycle has the opportunity to settle in, to germinate in the kernels of our soul-being. In fact, the ancient Hebraic word for evening is *erev*, which also means "merging," and the word for morning is *boker*, which means "discernment." Night is for everything to come together. Night is when all distinction fades away and all merges into a single cauldron to be churned and stirred until the coming of light when all is given back to form, to distinction, to discernment and clarity.

Probably the most essential lesson of the Atzeret festival is the sacredness of closing, whether it is closing a holy day or period, or closing a relationship context that isn't working, or closing a business transaction, or a weekend retreat. It is about the importance of doing some kind of sacred closing ceremony for any event or experience that has arrived at the edge of a shift or transition, such as from the Sabbath to the rest of the workday week, or from being single to being married, and so on. Judaism is replete with rites for closings as well as for beginnings, though most closings inevitably also mean new beginnings. It is sad that there are some life-transition cycles that have no prefabricated ceremonials in the tradition, such as menopause, stillbirths, "coming out." What is perhaps sadder, however, is that people complain about the absence of such ceremonies, assuming that whatever has been handed down until now represents everything that Judaism has to say—period. In truth, the lifecycle ceremonies of Judaism did not all come down to us from Moses on Mount Sinai, but from people no different from those who are complaining that there are no ceremonies to address their specific life shifts. The Torah describes not a single *personal* lifecycle ritual, and for good reason. Personal life shifts are just that: personal. The rites facilitating such transitions belong, therefore, not in the domain of the body of the religion, but in the domain of the *people* of the religion. No ritual has come down through the ages for what you are going through? Then *mazel tov!* You have been chosen to innovate one! *Nu?* We're waiting! The marriage ceremony, for instance, was invented by the rabbis; so was the divorce ceremony. And even though the rabbis ordained the rites of conversion, they left it pretty much open for creative play, requiring solely immersion in a living body of water, plus circumcision for a male convert. Other than that, the ceremony itself was left up to the individual and the community effecting the conversion. Few people are aware that Judaism does not require one to procure a rabbi to facilitate any of these lifecycle events, not even marriage, divorce, or conversion. To become married, for instance, the most orthodox *halachah* requires only that the couple declare their intention of being married to one another in front of two Jewish male witnesses who are practitioners of the path of Torah.

PESACH CYCLE

Passover, or Pesach, means just that: "to skip," "leap," or "pass over," as in the story of how the Creator "skipped over" the homes of the Israelites during the tenth plague that befell the ancient Egyptians for their refusal to release the Israelites from bondage (Exodus 12:13). The Torah refers to this festival as the "festival of *matzot*," the festival of the unleavened bread (Exodus 23:14, Leviticus 23:6, and Deutoronomy 16:16), and refers to the rite of the festival as the *pesach*, or Passover, "unto the Creator" (Exodus 12:11).

The lesson of Passover belongs not only to the Jewish people, but to all peoples. After all, the Torah teaches that other peoples, too, left Egypt along with the Exodus of the Jews (Exodus 12:38). Nor does "Egypt" imply only the ancient North African kingdom. In Hebrew, the word for Egypt is *mitzrayim*, which literally means "the narrows," the places in our lives that constrict us, intimidate us, and prevent us from taking chances or making choices that are our own—in other words, that keep us out of reach of God's gift of personal aliveness.

The festival of Passover commemorates the miraculous Exodus of the Jewish people from 210 years of slavery in the land of Egypt. The festival is described in the twelfth chapter of the Book of Exodus, where the people were instructed about how to prepare for their freedom. They were to slaughter a lamb and roast it in fire. The blood of the animal was then painted, using a sage-like bundle, on both sides of the entrances to their homes and also on the crossbeam over the top of the doorway.

The blood on the doorposts was to remind the people that the journey through the passageway to freedom was flanked by both life and death. The blood on top of the passageway was symbolic of how these opposite experiences, life and death, are in the same red blood that flows through all of us, and that comes from and goes back to the One Creator of all, in whose hands are life and death. Going from a bad place to a better place, from slavery to freedom, can be an experience of new aliveness, but the death of the past also needs to be respected. After all, we are who we are today because of who we were yesterday, for better or for worse. When you change, you change to someone else, but also *from* someone else. And the mystery of your personal transformation, of your rebirth, is represented by the blood overlooking your journey, the blood on top of your doorway to freedom: the One God in whose power it is to give life, to take back life, to transform life.

The lamb, the Torah continues, was to be eaten at twilight, the time of merging, when light fades into darkness, when day merges into night, when the time of wakefulness transforms into the time of dream, the time of spirit. Our freeing happens in the dream place, for there we are safe from the critic within who is always denigrating our hopes and visions; there we are far from the inhibitions that often stand in the way of our life walk. Night, or darkness, is the womb within which our tomorrows are nurtured, and where our deepest soul yearnings are impregnated.

Lamb is symbolic of innocence and vulnerability. When we experience a miracle, we can easily lose our sense of mortality, our sense of how fragile we really are and how much we need God's partnership in our lives. A miracle can trick us into thinking that we are infallible, untouchable; after all, God just performed a miracle for us, so nothing can touch us. Miracles, which are supposed to remind us that God is alway taking care of us even in less dramatic ways, therefore can have the opposite effect on us and make our heads swell until we see ourselves as "holier than thou" (Isaiah 65:5). And so God instructed the people that during this incredible miracle of freeing them from Egypt with all sorts of wondrous acts, they were to eat a lamb; they were to integrate into their beings the fact that though all these miracles were being performed on their behalf, they were to remember always how fragile and vulnerable they are, and that this is why God is intervening for them. And to prevent them from developing a holier-than-thou attitude toward their oppressors during this time of victory, God adds: "And I will pass over the land of Egypt during that night, and I shall take back the life I gave to the firstborn in all of Egypt" (Exodus 12:12–13)—in other words, it could just as easily be *you*. No one is beyond wrong choices. As the first-century rabbi Hillel the elder taught: "Do not be too sure of yourself until the day you die" (Babylonian Talmud, *Avot* 2:4).

Even to this day, therefore, when Jewish people celebrate their *seder*, their Passover feast, they do not sing all of the psalmic praises usually sung on festivals, and they remove a drop of wine from their goblets for each of the ten plagues that befell the Egyptians during their Exodus. This is in accordance with the teaching in the Book of Proverbs: "When your enemy falls, do not rejoice" (Proverbs 24:17). Judaism believes that God's concern is for all creatures and all peoples, not for any one religion or nation, and that drowning the Egyptian army in the Red Sea was not something that the Creator took delight in: "Do I delight in the death of the wrongdoers? Rather,

I prefer that they return from their wrong way and live" (Ezekiel 18:23). There is a *midrash*, an ancient rabbinic exegetical teaching, that when the Israelites and their friends made it to the other side of the Sea of Reeds, the angels were about to join them in their song of thanksgiving (Exodus 15:1–18 and 21) when the Creator silenced them and said: "The works of My hands are drowning, and you want to sing?" (Babylonian Talmud, *Megilah* 10b). The rabbis of two thousand years ago also explained this sensitivity for the death of the Egyptians as the reason that Passover is the only festival for which the Torah does not instruct us to rejoice, and also the reason why the prayer of praise, or *Hallel*, is not recited in full during this holiday (*Pesikta D'Rav Kahana* 189a).

On the night of the fourteenth day of the moon of Nisan, the firstborn of Egypt died, which compelled the Pharaoh to finally free the Jewish people. Yet it was not a time for celebration for the Jews, but a time for awe. The Passover meal was not some kind of sit-down dinner. The people were instructed to eat this meal with their coats on, with their sandals on their feet, and their walking sticks in their hands (Exodus 12:11). It was a sacred rite of passage for a people about to be led out of constriction, out of slavery, by the very hand of God. It was a celebration of rebirth, of new life, but also an awareness of death. There is always a cost, a shadow side, to the new choices we make in life, even when those choices are for our betterment. Every mother knows that in order to bring forth new life, for instance, she had at some point to push very hard against the fine line between life and death.

What exactly was this *pesach*? It was an offering of a lamb— either goat or sheep (Exodus 12:5)—that was roasted and eaten whole with not even so much as a broken bone (Exodus 12:8–10, 46). Moreover, only a Jewish person was allowed to eat this *pesach*, and non-Jews could join in the *pesach* feast only if they first converted (Exodus 12: 45, 48). All this was to be done only on the first night of the festival. And before the Israelites departed Egypt, the blood of this feast-offering was to be painted on the doorposts of all the homes in which the feast was being observed, as well as on the crossbeams over the doorways (Exodus 12:7):

> For I will pass across the land of Egypt during that night and will take back life from all of the firstborn males in the land of Egypt, both human and animal; and I will also execute judgment upon all the gods of Egypt, for I am the One Who Is'es everything. And the blood [of the lambs] shall be for you as a sign upon the houses where you are; and when I see the blood, I will pass over you, and no plague shall befall you to destroy you while I disturb the land of Egypt.
>
> Exodus 12:12–13

One can easily change the vowels of the word פסח so that it reads *pise'ach* rather than *pesach*, while still maintaining its same spelling of פסח. *Pise'ach* means "lame," as in the physical impairment of that part of the body whose fullness of functioning is required for unrestricted walking. One does not walk smoothly from woundedness; rather, one limps, as did the Patriarch Jacob (Yaakov) following his overnight struggle with a spirit being (Genesis 32:32). Jacob, too, was engaged in an exodus, a frightening journey from a place of woundedness and conflict to a place of peacefulness and healing by way of a path of uncertainty and fear (Genesis 32:8). More than two centuries later, his descendants embarked on a similar journey—leaving behind them generations of conflict and hurt—toward a destination of promise and hope, across a moat of chaos and unknowing. The lameness that comes with such an Exodus relates to the hesitation to take the bold first steps necessary to liberate oneself from constrictiveness; to leave that which is known and dependable, albeit strenuous and disempowering, for that which is unknown and challenging, albeit healing and empowering; to tear oneself from the securities of the givens of life in order to create sacred space for newness to happen. The prophet Yeshayahu (Isaiah) alludes to this when he dares the people to prepare for personal and national transformation: "Clear a path in the wilderness for the One Who Is'es" (Isaiah 40:3).

Pesach, then, is not only about remembering how the Jews were once slaves and how God made miracles and delivered them. There have been, between then and now, far greater miracles of redemption, physically and spiritually, for Jews and for other peoples who were saved not only from bondage, but from certain death and outright annihilation. Pesach, the Torah specifies, is about how God "passed over" our space when we were caught up in a whirlwind of life and death, of bondage and freedom. We were then instructed to eat lamb—then a symbol of innocence and vulnerability—in its entirety, meaning that we were not to cover up how scared and mortal and limited we were feeling when our journey forward was about to begin. The lamb was to be consumed whole, with not so much as a broken bone, and anything remaining had to be burned. This was a sign that we were ready for making the Exodus, for becoming alive, for moving from deathness to aliveness, for taking whole steps—not ambivalent ones, not one step backward for every step forward.

Egypt was in chaos, the One Who empowers was stirring the stagnation of the land of the narrows, taking back life-energy that had been misused toward deathness. And the choice was ours—to either remain stuck, thus welcoming the death-energy, or to declare our vulnerability and ready ourselves for life, in which case the death-energy would pass us by and not cause us any harm. Therefore, when we partook of this shamanic meal, we also had to be dressed and packed and ready to go with hiking stick in hand (Exodus 12:11). The original *pesach* meal was not a celebration; it was a shamanic rite of getting you to acknowledge your deepest, purest, most innocent and vulnerable self—your lamb—and then, from that place, to muster your faith in life in the very face of death. All around you the firstborn of Egypt were dying. But your first-born was spared, because blood was painted on both sides of your exit place, the fresh blood of both life *and* death, symbolic of your vulnerable and ambivalent straddling of the choices in your life: aliveness versus stagnation.

"Firstborn" means more than the oldest in the family; "Firstborn" means the vivid experience you have of your self-power, of your immortality. Therefore, all firstborn of your herd, or of your orchard and field, or of your own womb, had to be "offered" to God, to the Creator who gave it to you (Exodus 13:2), even the first of your baking dough when you are baking bread (Numbers 15:20–21). It is always the *first* of our personal accomplishments that is the most difficult for us to relinquish, and is the most difficult for us to attribute to source-powers other than our own. It is with firstborn stuff and beings that we most easily forget the wellspring of all that exists and of all that comes into existence. It is the firstborn, therefore, that we have to bring to the Creator as an "offering," meaning an acknowledgment of whom it really came from before we fashioned or facilitated its earthly manifestation, and of whom it is that now grants it continued existence. We bake the bread, we plant the appleseeds, we get pregnant with our children; but bread, trees, and babies remain a mystery to the very people who bring them about.

Of course, God has no need for the firstborn offering or any other offering (Psalms 50:9–15), and so these offerings were made toward the sacred service and to the *kohain*, the shamanic facilitator who administered it (Deuteronomy 18:4). Firstborn humans were naturally not "offered," nor were non-kosher animals; but instead were offered in proxy by a set monetary amount, a practice known today as *pidyon ha-ben*, or "the redemption of the [firstborn] son." Only firstborn males require this rite, probably because of the patriarchal misconception that there is a greater sense of "honor" in giving birth to a boy than to a girl.

The death of the firstborn humans and animals in Egypt was the climactic stirring-up of the mired reality structure of a people who had mistaken themselves for gods and had forgotten their own mortality and that there was a higher Power than their

Pharaohs, a consciousness that had turned them into a nation of slavemasters and at one point had resulted in the systematic extermination of newborn Jewish boys (Exodus 1:15–22). Their evil was in their stagnation, and their stagnation was rooted in their firstbornness, their sense that everything came solely from their own power and that therefore they were masters over all. The Israelites were, therefore, instructed to eat the lamb of *pesach*, of lameness—of vulnerability and mortality—and to place the blood thereof around the passageways of their dwellings as an expression of their acknowledgment that life and death are in the hands of the One who gives it and takes it. All of this was going on during a long, dark night of the soul, when life was indeed being given and taken: given anew to those who acknowledged its source, and taken from those who claimed it as their own, and who consequently claimed also the power to lord life and death over others.

The Hebrews were further instructed to eat the *pesach* offering together with bitter herbs (Exodus 12:8). The bitter herb is a shamanic vehicle for preserving the experience of woundedness even as we begin our journey toward healing. An integral part of resolution is being vividly in touch with the conflict. Otherwise, the hurt lingers on and the scars never fade. The Torah, however, is more concerned with the *lesson* that one can extricate from bitter experiences than with the bitterness of the experience itself. And the lesson Judaism took from the Egyptian experience was about sensitivity to the needs and welfare of the stranger, of someone who is not of one's heritage or culture, not of one's country or community. It is the most repeated directive in the Torah, mentioned no less than thirty-six times (Babylonian Talmud, *Bava Mezia* 59b), the gist being: "And you shall love the stranger as yourself for you were once strangers in the land of Egypt" (Leviticus 19:34, Deuteronomy 10:19).

The people were also instructed to bake their bread differently (Exodus 12:18–20). It was to be a bread of simplicity—just flour and water, no leavening ingredients that would cause it to rise. The road to personal freedom requires a return to basics, to the sacredness of the very simple gifts of life that often get buried beneath layers and layers of fluff. Fluff can mean voices in our heads that aren't our own, that don't address the reality of where we are in the moment, that hold us back from moving forward, from daring to be alive in the sense of what that means to us. Fluff is the extra weight we put on over the course of our lives that prevents us from experiencing the lightness of being, that keeps us so bogged down in *doing* life that we miss out on the everyday gift of *living* life. Thus, the meaning of the word *pesach*: "leaping," as in becoming so light, so freed-up that we skip about as opposed to *schlep*, or "drag." Getting into this consciousness, Passover teaches us, is necessary for newness to unfold in our lives. First we need to clean our selves of *chometz*—the leavening, the fluff, the weightiness of our lives, and restore ourselves to simplicity and lightness. As Rabbi Yehudah Loew of Prague put it:

> *Matzoh* is called *lechem oni* [bread of poverty] because freedom requires us to become as the poor in the sense that they are not in bondage to *things*, to property, and are thus more free to re-situate themselves at will than those who are attached to much property and belongings.
> *Hagadah Shel Pesach l'Maharal M'Prague*
> [*Ha Lachma An'ya*]

The Torah's instruction around *matzoh,* however, included more than the proscription against leavened products. It included also the act of *ridding* your place of leavening, of fluff, as a ritual in its own right (Exodus 12:15). Newness does not happen as a fresh layer simply slopped over that which once was; newness happens when we clear a space for it to happen, when we clean out the leavening from our lives, the bulk that is preoccupying our time and energy and thereby preventing meaningfulness from coming into our being and nurturing us with fresh aliveness. Leavening is also the stuff that is always puffing up and rising every time we attempt to bake something different, something that is reflective of who we are by our own definitions as opposed to the definitions established for us by others, by the Pharaohs in our lives. To do this process, it becomes necessary for us to ritually—that is, conscientiously— sweep out and burn completely all that hinders us and intimidates us, all that enslaves us by keeping us back from the journey into the Wildness, into the chaotic moat that stands between where we are now and where we feel we want to go. Leavening, then, represents the gap between our excitement about going and our fear of getting there.

The ancient Israelites are recorded in the Hebrew scriptures as having left Egypt for a forty-year walkabout through the מדבר—*midbar*—"wilderness." But the Hebrew word מדבר means more than a place of Wildness. The word also implies that which "resonates," that which "expresses," or that which "sounds." The metaphor of the wilderness journey is about going into the void place to be able to experience what is resonating deep inside of us, what is sounding, what is speaking to us. It is only then that the chaos of journeying away from stagnation and toward aliveness bears its intended results and brings us to the place of clarity, or the promised land. But the Torah clearly places greater, if not exclusive, emphasis on this journey than on the destination itself. It is the journey that moves the process of our growing from the static to the dynamic. Arriving at our destination means only that we are at the next place of leverage for the next step or steps. Passover is never finished. It comes around again every year. Leavening is rich and delicious, but once a year we burn it and return to the simplicity of *matzoh*, of flour and water baked to its minimum substance; once a year we call the bluff of the fluff and examine how much of it is really who we have become or are ready to become, and how much of it is bulk, old stuff that is weighing us down in our journey. By year's end, we have to wonder whether our sense of our self is truly ours, or whether it but parrots other people's expectations of who we ought to be. And so, in the nick of time, *pesach* comes around and we spend some time cleaning out the leavening from our physical homes, or, shamanically, cleaning out the fluff from our spiritual selves in readiness for new growth waiting to happen. And while we are doing this as a spiritual discipline, the earth is doing it as a simple, natural next step, clearing the way for the renewal of flora, for bringing forth potential to fruition. It is spring.

But the initial stage for this process is engaging the void, the emptiness of wilderness. Of course, one finds in the wilderness an abundance of fauna and flora, rocks and mountains. The wilderness is not empty of "things"; it is, however, empty of the leavening that crowds our lives, that fogs our vision, that clouds our consciousness. There is no religion in the wilderness; no culture, no reality map other than our own, and no voices other than our own. It was in the wilderness that the primary inspirers of the Judaic spirit path exercised their quests, and found voice for their visions (see the 12th-century Rabbi Avraham Ibn Maimon's chapter on *Hitbod'dut* ["meditation"] in his classic *HaMaspik L'Ovdei HaShem*). The wilderness showed them the bigger picture that went beyond the narrowness of their personal life situation, of their communal life situation, of their religious life situation. There they discovered and rediscovered God a thousand times over. There it was so quiet that they could no longer hear their critic. For the critic is heard only in the garrulousness of leavened confusion, not in the silence of pristine chaos where the disarray of rock piles, fallen tree limbs, and decaying leaves draw forth the desire to paint or to sculpt, or to just meditate and marvel.

> Ask now the beasts and they shall teach you, and the birds of the skies and they shall tell you; or speak to the Earth and she shall teach you; and the fishes of the sea shall declare to you.
> Job 12:7–8

In contemporary times, we reenact the richly symbolic and shamanic ceremony of *pesach* with a learning-teaching-telling feast called the *seder* or "arrangement," a format for the cele-bration of *pesach* established by the ancient rabbis following the fall of the house of sacredness and, with it, the Second Commonwealth of the Jewish people. The *seder* and its guide-book *hagadah*, or "the telling," have since undergone repeated revisions over the succeeding centuries, but continue to this day to maintain their original content and intent.

OMER *CYCLE*

Beginning with the second evening of Passover, the Jewish people are engaged in a sacred counting known as *sefirat ha-omer*, or "the counting of the *omer*." This fifty-day period connects the festival of Passover—the time of freedom from Egyptian bondage—to the festival of *Shavuot*, the time of collective spiritual experience in the Sinai wilderness. Since Judaism is very much an earth-based spirit path, this sacred counting is associated with the *omer*, or sheaf of the first fruits (Leviticus 23:10–17), reflective of the step-by-step phases of the earth's unfolding during spring and early summer. This daily awareness of the gradual unfolding of nature helps us to be-come aware of our own gradual growing processes, of mov-ing from potential to fruition alongside the sprouting earth and budding trees.

More importantly, however, the ritual of counting each day during this period is intended to remind us how every moment is a special and unique gift in itself. Often we chainlink one day to the next, holding one day's experience contingent on what happened yesterday or what we hope will happen tomorrow. The counting of the *omer*, then, reminds us how sacred each day is, regardless of the past or the future, and how we need to make the best of it and not get caught up in the anxiety of tomorrow or the guilt of yesterday, to the neglect of today.

The Sacred Counting also teaches us how each phase of our personal growth is precious in the eyes of the Creator, even when it appears to human judgment as insufficient or too slow. On the contrary, this daily ritual teaches us that every stage of the process, every new step we take toward improving our lives, is sacred and wondrous. It isn't easy to change, to consciously grow ourselves toward new places in our lives, toward fresh potentials, but if we so much as try, the Creator helps us and celebrates our every move forward. As an Apache elder is quoted as having said every morning before starting his day: "There isn't a thing on earth that the Creator and I can't accomplish together" (heard from Dennis Many Dreams, Apache medicine man). Or, as a first-century rabbi put it: "The Ancient One says to us, 'Open for Me so much as the eye of a needle, and I shall open for you wide enough for horses and wagons to pass through'" (*Shir HaShirim Rabbah* 5:3).

The period of the Sacred Counting is for each of us an opportunity to reach for our betterment and for the betterment of others, receiving each day as a gift for personal and global renewal, and each phase of our spirit-journey as the greatest accomplishment in our lives.

SHAVUOT CYCLE

The final seasonal cycle in the Torah is the season of the blossoming, the cycle of the ingathering, when the fruits of spring have become ripe for picking. This festival commemorates the climax of the Passover experience, the receiving of the Torah by Moshe on Mount Sinai on the fiftieth day of the wilderness journey.

Also known as the "festival of weeks," Shavuot commemorates the revelation in the wilderness of Sinai, when the Great Mystery spoke to an entire people, numbering well over two million women, men, and children, made up of twelve Jewish tribes and multitudes of other peoples who joined them in their dramatic Exodus from enslavement (Exodus 12:38). Occurring seven weeks following Passover, Shavuot is the climax of the experience of freedom from bondage and of the beginning of the Jewish people's forty-year journey through the wilderness to the land of their ancestors.

This revelation of the Creator to these nomads occurred not in the Promised Land of their destination, but in the middle of nowhere. The ancient rabbis taught that this was to make it clear to the people that divine revelation belongs to no particular nation or individual. Like the wilderness, it belongs to everyone.

> God does not discriminate between any of the creations, but receives all. The gates are open at all times, and all who wish to enter may enter.
>
> *Midrash Sh'mot Rabbah*, No. 19

The revelation of Torah to the Jewish people, the rabbis taught, was no different:

> And why was the Torah given in the desert? For just as the desert is open to all and belongs to no one, so is the Torah freely accessible to all who wish to study her. And also so that a Jewish person shall not proclaim to a convert: "I am a child of Torah for it was given unto me and my ancestors, whereas you and your ancestors were not children of Torah but were strangers."
>
> *Midrash Tanchuma, VaYak'hel*, No. 8

The revelation in the wilderness of Sinai took the physical form of what we today know as the Ten Commandments—or, more accurately, the Ten Sayings—as well as the Five Books of Moses. Judaism calls this the Torah, which is Hebrew for "the showing." Many people erroneously think that Torah means "the Law." The Torah doesn't tell you what to do, it *shows* you. It is a guide, not a code (see the chapter on

"*Halachah*"). It's not about law, but about life. Judaism has a great number of laws, but is not a religion of law. All these laws were intended to promote harmony in the world, between people and each other, people and the planet, people and the Creator. Therefore, when Hillel the Elder was approached by a Roman who wanted to be taught the entire Torah, the rabbi's response was: "Don't do to others that which is distasteful to yourself. This is the whole of Torah. The rest is commentary. Go and study it" (Babylonian Talmud, *Shabat* 31a).

It is customary for Shavuot to decorate prayer space with flowers and other colorful and fragrant representations of the earth's summer yield. Most people assume that this is to decorate the synagogue, but it is to remind worshipers of the gifts of summer for which they are celebrating Shavuot to begin with. The Torah mentions this festival not as a commemoration of the revelation at Sinai, but as a celebration of the first fruits. That it happens to coincide with the fiftieth day following the Exodus, and therefore the time of the Great Revelation, seems to make no difference to the Torah narrative, which makes mention of only the summer blossoms. The teaching in all this is clear: Divine revelation is not confined to a text, to some momentous "word of God" oration. Divine revelation is a phenomenon that is recurring in each moment that this universe is alive. As the third-century Rabbi Tanchum bar Chiyya taught:

> A much greater event is rainfall than the giving of the Torah, for the giving of the Torah brought joy to the Israelites alone, but rainfall brings joy to all peoples and to all animals, both wild and domestic, and to the birds.
>
> *Midrash Tehilim* 1:17

Shavuot teaches us to see Divine Revelation not solely in the supernatural events of spiritual mindblowing proportions, but also in the natural day-to-day mundane stuff like flowers blossoming in late May and hummingbirds whirling in mid-air and bees buzzing in the orchard, and the moments when you *don't* have an ache anywhere on your body. When you celebrate the receiving of the Torah, celebrate *all* of creation, for we are all the word of God, as it is written: "And God spoke *all* these words" (Exodus 20:1), and it is also written: "By the Word of God were the heavens made, and by the wind of God's breath all of their beings came to be" (Psalms 33:6). And it is written: "For God spoke, and [creation] came to be; God commanded, and it was established" (Psalms 33:9).

Every breath you take is the word of God. Life is Torah. Torah is life (Proverbs 3:18). Shavuot is about the celebration of aliveness during the season when the earth, one of your major teachers in life, demonstrates aliveness most vividly in colors, in aromas, and in abundance of that which nourishes you. You've waited for this moment eagerly and conscientiously for seven weeks. And now the day has come: Shavuot, the festival of weeks, the festival of the climax of the wait, the climax of the anticipation of the fruition of the gifts of the earth and the potentials of your own personal liberation and renewal processes, all of which began in the season of spring during the sacred cycle of Pesach.

CYCLE OF SHABBAT

Once every seven days, the Torah instructs us, we are to step back and have a seat in the waiting room while the world bounces about without us, in spite of us, notwithstanding us. This is *Shabbat*. Literally, the word connotes rest, as in sitting or idling. It also means "to remove." This is a day when we remove ourselves from the spin cycle of the week, pull ourselves off the track of urgency, and instead seek respite. The importance of having at least one such day every week cannot be overemphasized. Going nonstop may feed our bank accounts, but it starves our souls, our consciousness of self and other. If you're always on the go, you may never get anywhere.

Your achievements will, your money will, your fame will, but your self will be left behind, stranded at some remote bus stop somewhere along the journey of life.

Shabbat is deemed so important that the Torah describes it as the only "commandment" that God ever observed: "And the Source of powers blessed the seventh day and made it sacred, and withdrew in that day from the act of Creation which the Source of powers had created to unfold" (Genesis 2:3); "For the One Who was, is, will be created the heavens and the Earth, the ocean and all that is within it during six days, and laid it all down on the seventh day. Therefore did the One Who was, is, will be bless the *Shabbat* day and make it sacred" (Exodus 20:11); "For the One Who was, is, will be created the heavens and the Earth during six days, and on the seventh day withdrew and settled in" (Exodus 31:17).

Shabbat does not stand outside of this process called Creation. It is rather an integral component of the creative process. *Shabbat* is the gelling time, the coalescing time, the being-pregnant time. During this period of *not* doing, a great deal gets done, our work and ideas have the space to breathe and to evolve. Dough rises only after we have ceased kneading and have stepped back to leave it alone. Response comes to us only after we have stopped talking. Healing happens only after we have let go. Every process has its *Shabbat* component. Every day has its night, its time for withdrawal from doing, its time for simply being.

Shabbat is a time for remembering, for recapitulating. The Torah instructs us to "*Remember* the *Shabbat* to make it sacred" (Exodus 20:8), which implies that in order to make it sacred, special, you need to consciously commemorate it. It is the act of remembering, of acknowledging this one day during the week as an oasis in the ordinary flow of time, that makes it holy. How this is marked in ritual observance has varied from age to age, from community to community, and from individual to individual. But the most universal marking of this day is the ritual of combining wheat, grape, and oil (Leviticus 23:13) as in *challah* (wheat), wine (grape), and flame (oil). These three elements are symbolic of the three planes of soul manifestation in the physical experience: *nefesh*, the craving/appetitive self, *ruach*, the expressive/emotive self, and *neshamah*, the reasoning/transcendent self. *Challah*, being earthy, is symbolic of *nefesh*; wine, being stimulating, is symbolic of *ruach*; and flame, being combustive energy, is symbolic of *neshamah*.

Shabbat is therefore more than a "day of rest." It is a day of bringing together all the personalities of our being that had gotten fragmented during the tumult and chaos of daily living. The *challah*, the wine, the burning candles, remind us that we are composed of these three basic personas, or soul manifestations, and that each of them is sacred, that they are not separate realities, that they are not just mood swings, but together form the wholeness of our selfhood, one not any more important than the other. The *Shabbat* table therefore demands the presence of all three elements, all three attributes. Your craving self is no less an important manifestation of your soul than your emotive self, and your enlightened guru self is no more important than your bladder self. Not unlike the Three Musketeers, your slogan on *Shabbat* is: "All for one and one for all!" During the week, you split up your personas and send each in a different direction: one to work for what you crave, another to play out what you feel, and a third to meditate or space out. On *Shabbat*, however, all three personas merge as one, and all of them accompany you everywhere you go and in *every* encounter you have. You treat yourself to a feast of *extra*-special delicacies, allow yourself to feel the love you have for and from those joining you at the table, and are left with little choice but to glimpse your essential self.

For those with family, *Shabbat* is a magical time to come together for once-a-week delicacies, for once-a-week kinds of play and interactions. In an era when we are spending so little quality time with our children and lovers, this is an important opportunity to nurture and appreciate our families. Likewise, for those who are living alone, *Shabbat* is a time to step outside the lone place and invite a friend for a *Shabbat* meal. In Orthodox Jewish communities there exists, to this day, the heartwarming practice married folk have of inviting single women and men to their homes for *Shabbat* meals. Of course, if being alone is what you prefer, then that becomes your *Shabbat* pleasure, or *oneg*. Basically, then, this is a day when you celebrate the gift that you are, the gift that others are, the gift of being alive, and the fact that the world continues spinning even when you're not turning the wheel. Six days a week is for Doing. The seventh day is for Being.

The ancient rabbis taught that one of the meanings behind the God name *Shadai* is *sh'amar dai*, or "the One Who said enough" (*Yalkot Shim'oni, Lech Lecha*, 17:1). In other words, the Creator could certainly have continued creating *ad infinitum*, but consciously chose to call it a day and step back to allow Creation to unfold through Creation itself: "And the Source of Powers blessed the seventh day and made it sacred, and withdrew in that day from the act of Creation which the Source of Powers had created to unfold" (Genesis 2:3). The teaching is simply this: Don't strive to achieve *every*thing; let someone else have a crack at it, too. And at least once a week cry out the mantra "Enough," and step off the merry-go-round. We know that you are perfectly capable of continuing your creation, your accomplishments, your perfecting. You don't have to prove it to anyone. But when inside you cries "Enough!" it's time to stop the world and get off. Often, however, we are so busy *doing* that we can't hear our inner voices. That's where *Shabbat* comes in. You're smack in the middle of a heap of doing, when all of a sudden it's Friday and the sun is slowly slip-sliding away. What an incredible feeling of power you now feel as you turn off your computer or tractor or telephone. What a revelation that you are, after all, not a robot, but are capable of stopping dead in your tracks and shifting gears at whim. *Shabbat* is therefore a lot more than an observance of some nice Jewish ritual. It is an exercise in self-empowerment and self-worth. Indeed, without a *Shabbat* to remind us that we exist *in spite* of all that we do, not *because* of all that we do, our sense of the value of life itself either ebbs or numbs.

As crucial and as sacred as is *Shabbat*, Jewish law bids us to "transgress" or forego its observance altogether in situations that are threatening to one's life or health, "and the more zealous one is about this, the more praised are they" (Babylonian Talmud, *Yoma* 85b). As the first-century Rabbi Yaakov taught: "The *Shabbat* is given into your hands; you are not given into her hands" (Babylonian Talmud, *Yoma* 85b).

CYCLES OF SHEMITTAH AND YOVEL

It is a fundamental Jewish belief that the Earth does not belong to us, but that we belong to the Earth (Genesis 2:7). We are, after all, called אדם (*adahm*), from the word אדמה (*adamah*), which means "earth." The Hebrew word for "human" then translates as "earth being" (Genesis 5:2; *Pesikta D'Rav Kahana* 34b). In the Torah, we are told that all of the Earth belongs to the Creator, and that we are but strangers and settlers on the Earth, not its owners (Exodus 19:5; Leviticus 25:23). To remind us of this and to divert us from a consciousness of possessiveness and dominance, the Torah instructs us that every seven years we ought to step back and allow the land to rest for an entire year. This observance is known as *shemittah*, literally, "letting go." Not only is *shemittah* a time for letting go of our exploitation of the Earth, but it is also a time for letting go of debts, of all the I.O.U.'s people have left with us in times of need (Leviticus 25:4; Deuteronomy 15:1–2).

Shemittah, then, not unlike *Shabbat*, is a period of recapitulation, of returning to center collectively as a people. Nor does it end there. Every seven times seven *years*, the cycle spirals to *yovel*, or the Jubilee year. Again, the land is not worked, and all land is returned to those who lived on it before they were forced to sell it owing to financial difficulties (Leviticus 25:28). Like the *shemittah* cycle, the *yovel* cycle, too, is a reminder that we don't own the land: "You shall not make any permanent sales of the land, for the land is Mine and you are but squatters and settlers upon her" (Leviticus 25:23).

CYCLE OF THE MOON: ROSH CHODESH

The most influential of the sky beings in the ancient Hebrew spirit path is the moon. The Hebraic calendar, therefore, is lunar, and all sacred festivals are determined by the varying phases of the moon. Accordingly, the Hebrew word for "month" is *chodesh*, which means "renewal," because in the eyes of the human on the Earth, the moon is constantly renewing, never static, never stuck. Every evening the moon appears differently, waxing and then waning, growing and then shrinking, hidden and then visible, even varying its times of appearances from night to night. The moon is therefore considered a powerful guide and influence for the ever-dynamic life journey and personal unfoldings of the human. Every moment involves us in change or with the potential for change. Every day brings us up against choices that shift our lives, that have us waxing or waning, growing or shrinking, hidden or seen, and changing our pace, our relationship with time.

Reckoning time and influence by the moon is possibly one of several remnants in the Hebrew tradition of ancient feminine spirituality. Unlike conventional astrological science, which tends to reflect patriarchal qualities of absoluteness and staticity, lunar astrology is more reflective of the feminine quality of flexibility and process. The sun, like the man, is direct and linear, fixed and piercing, while the moon, like the woman, is fluid and reflective, powerful but not overwhelming, brilliant yet easy on the eyes. Solar is more definitive, moon more process, more experiential; therefore, you won't get as clear an answer from lunar astrology as from solar astrology, because lunar astrology is more personal and relative to your life flow in the moment, while solar astrology is charted. The sun is therefore symbolic of the etched-in-stone written tradition, and the moon is symbolic of the more flexible oral tradition.

The sun is not without its role in all this, of course, being after all the source of the light that is reflected by the moon. Nonetheless, the moon is considered most immediately relevant to human personal life journeying. The shifts we experience in our lives, like the lunar phases, are determined by reflections, by our orbit around people and circumstances and how we inflect those encounters.

The initial sighting of that very thin sliver of the first-moon phase is therefore a sacred event and celebration in Judaism. On the one hand, it may symbolize possession of very little God light, or of being distant from the Creator, of being far from spiritual. On the other hand—the way the Hebrew tradition sees it—if someone is in the spiritual blink and manages to open his or her self up to so much as even a very thin sliver of the God light, it is more dear to the Creator and more holy than someone who has already achieved full inflection of the light. As the first-century Rabbi Ben Heyhey put it: "Life's rewards are reckoned according to one's efforts, not one's achievements" (Babylonian Talmud, Avot 5:23). A second-century sage quotes the Creator as saying: "Open up for Me but so much as the eye of a needle and I in turn will open up for you so wide that entire caravans can pass through" (Shir HaShirim Rabbah 5:3). Or: "The Creator says to us, 'Take but one step toward Me, and I shall meet you the rest of the way'" (Midrash Pesikta d'Rav Kahana, 184b–185a [Ch. 44]).

Judaism understands the human process as an ever-dynamic journey that is in constant motion in spite of our well-intentioned attempts at stopping it, at "settling down." No one is all good or all bad, in other words, because one can always change for better or for worse. This led Hillel the Elder to say: "Do not be so sure of yourself until the day you die" (Babylonian Talmud, Avot 2:4). The phasing of the moon, therefore, symbolizes the human cyclic tendency to reach crescendos of enlightenment or inspiration or spiritual awareness, only to then plummet into the abyss of confusion, alienation, or frustration. We all experience highs and lows, our moments of faith and our moments of doubt, our moments of hope and our moments of disappointment, our moments of motivation and our moments of stagnation. The lesson of the moon is that phases are okay and are part of our life process, and that the same forces that phase us into the shadow will in turn phase us gradually into the light, and that when we wane and drop and get low and uninspired, this, too, is part of our growing, of our aliveness. It is the exhalation before the inhalation. It is the predawn dimness before the daylight brightness, the chaos and emptiness that often precedes the emergence of personal renewal. Judaism therefore honors the gift of moon both when it is with least light and when it is with most light. When it reflects its first light, it is celebrated as Rosh Chodesh, or "beginning of renewal," while the seasonal festivals of the cycles of nature and of corresponding spiritual commemorations are celebrated when the moon is in its fullness. Both newness and fullness, then, have their respective sacredness and celebrations, as does fullness in our lives and the seeming dimness than preempts newness in our lives.

Originally, Rosh Chodesh was predominantly a feminine celebration, a sacred time given into the hands of women. One of the reasons given for this in the ancient writ is "because they were not involved in the Golden Calf incident" (*Pirkei D'Rebbe Eliezer,* Ch. 45), or any other incident of rebellion in the wilderness journey (*Bamidbar Rabbah* 25). A more likely reason is, again, the corresponding dynamics of feminine nature and our experience of the phases of the moon, such as the relationship between the periods of women's menstrual and birth cycles with the varying stages of lunar shadow and illumination. Also, whereas the moon is the smaller of the two Great Lights described in the Book of Genesis (1:16), Judaic tradition holds it as equal to the sun at the beginning of time (Genesis 1:14) and, again, at the end of time (Isaiah 30:26).

Woman, too, is held to be the cause of redemption at the beginning of time and at the end of time (Babylonian Talmud, *Sotah* 11b).

CYCLES OF FASTING AND MOURNING

The Hebrew calendar picked up commemorative observances as the journey through history continued beyond the initial Torah revelation that spelled out only the seasonal cycles discussed until now. With the fall of the House of Sacredness, or *Beit HaMikdash*, in the fifth century B.C.E., the First Commonwealth of Jewdom came to a tragic end. The people were torn from their homeland and from the rites and ceremonials that had unified them as a nation and served for centuries as a collective expression of their otherwise eclectic worship. The people took it upon themselves to mourn this event, which their spiritual leaders did not blame wholly on the conquering Babylonians but also on the people themselves, believing that the nation had invited this result by conduct unbecoming of a Godly people. The Books of Jeremiah, which include *Eichah*, or Lamentations, dramatize the sadness of the people and their sense of despair and brokenness. How this people, so rooted in its land and the myriad observances that were tied to it, managed to thrive leaderless, miles from their spiritual center and under the unrelenting thumb of one invading culture after another, is what Professor Ernest van den Haag called "The Jewish Mystique." But survive they did, flourishing for close to a thousand years in the land of their Babylonian conquerors. The House of Sacredness was rebuilt some seventy years later by a small group of exiles allowed to return by Darius the Second, but it would never be the same. Much of the original and essential sacred vestments and vessels were gone. The Ark of the Covenant, the very nucleus of the Temple, was gone. Little remained but a remnant of a temple that the people clung to tenaciously until the Romans destroyed it little more than four hundred years later, this time sending the people into an exile that would last not seventy but 1,900 years.

According to Jewish history, the destruction of the First Temple and that of the Second Temple four centuries later occurred on the same calendar day, the ninth day of the Hebraic moon of *Av*, usually corresponding to late July or early August. Traditionally, the Jewish people have been commemorating both events as one, fasting from sundown to sundown during the ninth of *Av*, which, like all Hebraic reckonings, begins the night before. As with the fast of Yom Kippur, the mourning of the ninth of *Av*, or Tisha B'Av, is observed with abstention from food, drink, sex, grooming, bathing, adornment, and so on. Yet, the rabbis reminded people that it was a day for *mourning*, not for getting depressed. If one got depressed and it was becoming clinically severe, one was supposed to break the fast immediately—not with bread and water, but with a feast of meat and wine, or the equivalent thereof (*Aruch HaShulchan, Orach Chayim* 554:7). Again, the day was not about getting depressed; it was about mourning a tragedy that, according to the ancient teachers, was invoked by conduct unbecoming. The lesson of the day is not depression but introspection, going inside ourselves to find the very traits and habits within us that contribute to the kinds of negativity that brought the house down (Babylonian Talmud, *Gitin* 57a).

Why was the first house destroyed? Because of three sins: idolatry, forbidden sex (i.e., adultery, incest), and bloodshed. If so, then why was the second house destroyed? Is it not fact that during the time of the second house the people were engaged in the study of Torah, the perfomance of *mitzvot* and deeds of charity? Alas! [the second house was destroyed] because of wanton animosity between people. This teaches that wanton animosity is tantamount to idolatry, forbidden sex, and bloodshed.

Babylonian Talmud, *Yoma* 9a

There were rabbis, like the second-century Rabbi Yehudah the Prince, who sought to abolish such periods of national mourning, even the heavy-duty commemoration of Tisha B'Av, but the practice prevailed anyway, and later sages rationalized that Rabbi Yehudah had meant only to abolish the observance of an alternate day of Tisha B'Av in times when Tisha B'Av fell on the Sabbath, on which day mourning is prohibited (Babylonian Talmud, *Megilah* 5b). It isn't clear what really happened, nor is it farfetched to assume that Rabbi Yehudah plainly meant that Tisha B'Av ought to be abolished altogether. After all, the Talmud reports that, instead of saving the Temple—both the First *and* the Second—the spiritual leaders of the people practically *welcomed* its demise. Regarding the First Temple, the Talmud recounts that the teachers went out to greet Nebuchadnezzar and declared: "The time has come for this house to be destroyed" (Jerusalem Talmud, *Sh'kalim* 6:2). Regarding the Second Temple, the Talmud recounts that Rabbi Yochanan ben Zakkai, when asked by the Roman general Vespasianus to ask for anything he wished, requested that the Romans spare not the Holy Temple, but Yavneh and its sages (Babylonian Talmud, *Avot D'Rebbe Natan* 4:6). Obviously, in both periods, the spiritual teachers knew when the religion of Temple rites was turning stale, and in both instances, their action sparked a major paradigm shift for Judaism and a significant shift in its practice and theology that each time weaned the people further and further from serving God through ritual sacrifice to serving God through deed and intention.

> Once, Rabbi Yochanan ben Zakkai was walking in Jerusalem with Rabbi Yehoshua when they passed the ruins of the Sacred House. Rabbi Yehoshua began to weep: "Woe unto us that this place has been destroyed, the very place where we performed rites of atonement for our wrongs!" Said Rabbi Yochanan ben Zakkai: "My son, do you not know that we have another means of atonement that is the same as [the sacrifices]? And what is that? It is the act of lovingkindness, as it is

written: 'Lovingkindness did I desire, not sacrifice' [Hosea 6:6]
. . . helping a bride prepare for her wedding and rejoicing with
her, accompanying the dead to their burial, giving money to
a poor person. . . .'

Babylonian Talmud, *Avot D'Rebbe Natan* 4:5

There are five national fast days: *Shiva Assar B'Tamuz*—
"the seventeenth day of the moon of *Tamuz*," which occurs
three weeks prior to Tisha B'Av and signifies the onset of the
siege around Jerusalem that preceded its destruction; Tisha
B'Av itself; *Tzom Gedaliah*—"the fast of Gedaliah," which
occurs the day after the festival of Rosh Hashanah and memo-
rializes the assassination of Gedaliah, a Babylonian-appointed
Jewish governor, at the hands of zealots. The assassination
brought down the wrath of the Babylonians and, ultimately,
the destruction of the Sacred House some 2,500 years ago.
The fourth fast day is *Asseret B'Teiveit*—"the tenth of the
moon of *Teiveit*," which occurs in mid-winter and commemorates the Babylonian king's advance upon Jerusalem and the
end of the First Commonwealth of the Jewish people. The fifth
is *Ta'anit Esther*—"the fast of Esther," which occurs the day
before the festival of Purim. Purim commemorates the near-
annihilation of world Jewry during the Persian era, some 2,400
years ago, thwarted by the interference of a Jewish woman,
Esther, who became queen of Persia at that time. Esther, together with the Jewish people across the world empire of the
time, fasted and prayed for three days before she approached
the king uninvited to plead on behalf of her people and to avert
the disastrous decree. It worked. The miracle is celebrated as
Purim, which, alongside Chanukah, is considered a postbiblical
holiday commemorating miraculous turnabouts of tragic events.
They are considered postbiblical not in the sense that their
occasions are absented from Jewish scriptures, but in the sense
that they are not part of the Mosaic tradition. And although
Purim and Chanukah are more about historic events than
spiritual practice, their observance has evolved over the cen-

turies to become an integral component of Jewish religious theology and observance, even picking up deep kabbalistic meanings along the way.

All of these national fast days are observed from sunrise to sundown except for Tisha B'Av, which lasts twenty-five hours, from twilight the previous night to after dark the following night.

How important these fast days are in our own time is subject to question, as all but the fast of Esther commemorate the same theme, the fall of the Jewish nation. The fast of Esther is a day commemorating how the people fasted and prayed to avert genocide. Tragedy, however, is not confined to what happened thousands of years ago. Numerous other catastrophes have plagued the Jewish people and other peoples across time long since the fall of Jerusalem. There is a gnawing need to reexamine how we can remember the distant past without losing sight of the significance of the more recent past. The relevance of recent history may feel more immediate and vivid to more people than that of ancient history. It's not about *mourning* the past; it's about *learning from* the past. Therefore did the ancient teachers throw as many lessons into the pot as they could drum up when they were wrestling with what it was that felled the House of Sacredness. According to some, it was wanton hatred; according to others, it was because some of the rabbis rendered excessively stringent halachic rulings that were more reflective of the letter of the law than the spirit of the law (Babylonian Talmud, *Bava Mezia* 86a). According to others, it was because of the excessive piety of Rabbi Zechariah ben Avkalus, who argued against the acceptance of Caesar's offering to the Jewish Temple because the animal had a slight, hardly visible blemish (Babylonian Talmud, *Gitin* 56a). The refusal was received by Rome as outright rebellion, and the Roman Empire did not take kindly to noncompliant subsidiaries. Other reasons included lack of respect between youth and elders; neglect of the Sabbath day; failure to educate young children; disrespect toward the wise; failure to admonish those who were doing not-nice things; and so on (Babylonian Talmud, *Shabat* 119b).

Whether it was this reason or that reason, clearly the sages didn't actually believe that it was, say, Rabbi Zechariah's excessive piety that destroyed Jerusalem. The point is not so much whodunnit as what are the lessons we can come away with from it. If we can use the drama of tragedy to drive home the danger of excessive piety, wanton hatred, religious stringency, disrespect, and child neglect, then so be it. A tragedy without a lesson is twice the tragedy. The irony of these commemorations, however, is that we have gotten stuck in remembering the lessons of *yesterday's* tragedies to the sore neglect of learning the lessons of *today's* tragedies.

CHANUKAH AND PURIM

Purim, which occurs in early spring, celebrates the botching of an attempt by a Persian prime minister, Haman, to annihilate the Jewish people worldwide some 2,400 years ago when the Jews lived throughout the Persian Empire. The story is recorded in the biblical Book of Esther and needs no repetition here. It is celebrated by levity, sacred partying, the exchange of food gifts between friends, and the liberal giving to the needy of ready-to-eat delicacies. Customarily, children and adults alike masquerade themselves since it is a day commemorating the fact that things are not always what they seem. On this day, tragedy was turned into joyfulness. It is a lesson for life: When things appear bleak, we need to transcend the face value and muster our faith in its turnabout.

The Book of Esther, read on Purim, is the story of how God intervened to prevent tragedy from occurring—but incognito, not through some major pomp-and-circumstance event as in the days of, say, Moses and Joshua. It is a reminder to us in our own times that miracles are with us every moment, and that they are—as the word *Esther* connotes—concealed. Only through constant appreciation for the gift of life can we hope to discover them both in major drama and in ordinary events of everyday situations.

Chanukah, too, is about how a seriously outnumbered Jewish people drove out Greek-Assyrian invaders some 2,200 years ago, after they had desecrated their Holy Temple, and how the priests discovered enough consecrated oil to keep the Eternal Lamp lit for only one night, but miraculously it burned for eight nights, long enough to procure and process fresh olive oils and consecrate them for the seven-branched sacred lamp, or *menorah* (Babylonian Talmud, *Shabat* 21a).

Chanukah is celebrated with the lighting of a makeshift *menorah*, a candelabra capable of eight separate lights, each symbolizing one of the eight days of the miraculous oil. *Menorah* means literally "That which gives light," and is an ancient and fundamental symbol of the Jewish people. Its shape is that of the *moriah*, a sage plant that grows in the desert of southern Israel. *Moriah* means: "The Creator will guide you." The ancient *menorah* in the House of Sacredness held seven lights, symbolic of the seven cycles of Creation described in the Book of Genesis. It was lit twenty-four hours a day throughout the year as a reminder to the people that the Creator's guidance is constant, and that the Creator lights our paths always.

Today, this ancient custom is remembered in the home by lighting the *menorah* around the time of the winter solstice during Chanukah. Using one candle (separate from the other candles of the *menorah*), we light one candle, and every night an additional candle, until all eight candles have been lit. The meaning of this is to remind us during the darkest time of the year that light will return.

Both Purim and Chanukah are commemorative of the miracles that happen in everyday life. Both holidays are sacred and festive. Both celebrate faith and the power of will.

TU B'SHVAT: CELEBRATING THE TREE

Ancient Jewish teachers taught that during the peak of winter, when the earth appears hard and lifeless, the first sap begins to flow in the trees, and the seeds of new life begin the dance of rebirth. It is during this time that the earth mother reaches out to us to remind us that life is eternal, always renewing itself, and that every moment of our lives, even when we feel petrified and lifeless, holds within it infinite potentials for fresh beginnings.

These mystics, many of whom were farmers and shepherds, saw trees as microcosmic representations of the proverbial Tree of Life. Each gift of the tree, then, each fruit, is like a fortune cookie: It has a message for us. As one second-century rabbi put it: "The trees speak to us and to all creatures" (*Midrash B'reishis Rabbah* 13:2). Some of us, like the date or the peach, for example, are soft and approachable on the outside, but hard and uncompromising on the inside. And some of us, like the pecan, are unpenetrable on the outside, but delicious on the inside. Every combination of fruit has a multitude of lessons for each of our life processes.

Trees, in other words, don't just feed us and shelter us—they teach us. In fact, the ancient rabbis felt it so important to celebrate the gifts of the earth that the first-century Rabbi Yochanan ben Zakkai went so far as to say: "If you are in the midst of planting a tree, and they tell you the Messiah has come, first complete the planting, then go and greet the Messiah" (Babylonian Talmud, *Avot D'Rebbe Natan* [version 2], Ch. 38).

Also known as the "new year" of the tree (Babylonian Talmud, *Rosh Hashanah*:), Tu B'Shvat is celebrated in a special feast featuring a variety of fruits, both dried and fresh, most notably figs, nuts, dates, and carob. Traditionally, Judaic festivals are celebrated around the different cycles of the seasons, but the mystics felt that it was important to thank the Creator for the gifts of the earth not only when they were most visible and ripe as in spring and summer, but even when they were virtually undetectable, like during the winter months.

Tu B'Shvat is abbreviated Hebrew for "the fifteenth day of the moon of *Shvat*," known in the ancient mystical tradition as "the Moon of Taste" (*Sefer Yetsirah* 5:42), as each month in the Hebraic lunar calendar corresponds with a physical sense or emotion.

The sacred seasons of the Jewish calendar year is then like an ongoing "show-and-tell." Each period has something to teach us, something to think about, to absorb through commemoration or feasting, special prayers or hands-on activity. Time is sacred in Judaism. Each moment and every experience is worthy of its very own holiday, or, unfortunately, its very own day of fasting. The talmudic tractate *Berachot*, for instance, is replete with blessings that one ought to say for virtually every occasion, from coming out of the bathroom after relieving oneself, to stretching one's limbs upon awakening, to seeing a rainbow, to encountering a beautiful person or an unusual animal. Judaism is about paying attention to the magic in every experience, and its sacred seasons are about training us several times a year to cherish every moment.

5

Women, Torah, and Feminiphobia

Let's not pull any punches. The fact is that Judaism as we have it, as it has come down to us through the ages, is about 85 percent female-free. There were as many women prophets as men prophets, the ancient teachers taught (*Shir Hashirim Rabbah* 4:22), and yet only a dozen were mentioned, and only two biblical books are named for any: the Book of Ruth and the Book of Esther. The prophetess Deborah gets two chapters in the Book of Judges (Chs. 4 and 5), and other prophetesses, like Sarah, Rebeccah, Hagar, Miriam, Abigail, and Chuldah, get token mention now and then. Prophetesses notwithstanding, the laws and traditions of Judaism were predominantly transmitted by men and interpreted by men. Resultingly, women were honored and held in high esteem among the Jewish people, but were generally less well-versed in the teachings of the tradition beyond what men chose to teach them, and generally less involved in religious function and participation beyond what men chose to allow them. Today this has changed and is still changing, and women are becoming rabbis and interpreters and innovators of ceremonials and liturgy and so on. Sadly, this has happened by the external influence of feminist consciousness, when it could just as easily have sprouted forth from the ancient Jewish spiritual tradition itself, which, upon close examination, knows little of the separatism that has been exercised toward women in Judaism for centuries.

It needs to be stated that the Judaic spirit path in itself is as much feminine as it is masculine, albeit evolving in a patriarchal paradigm; it adopted a male-oriented consciousness that eventually patronized women rather than held them as equals with men. So, while the five daughters of Tzelaphchad, for instance, were able to challenge Moses' laws of male-only land allotment in the Promised Land and get the law changed to include women (Numbers 27:7), they were also later instructed to marry only within their tribe (Numbers 36:6) so that, again, the land would eventually resume its patriarchal identity. Reading the account of these women, it is clear that what Moses had heard and what God had said were as different as male from female.

The compassion of men extends primarily to other men, whereas the compassion of God extends equally to men and to women, as it is written [Psalms 145:9]: "God is good to all, Whose compassion extends onto all creations."

Sifri on Numbers 27:1

The ancient rabbis admitted, therefore, that as a man Moses interpreted the God word from a male point of view, in a way that benefited the male members of the nation more so than the women. It took these sisters to compel Moses to reexamine what God had said, not what Moses had interpreted. To his credit, the great prophet did not react by admonishing the sisters for challenging the word of God. No doubt he, too, realized how subjective can be the interpretation of divine inspiration even by a prophet as profound as himself. Rather, Moses returns to the source of the revelatory instruction and brings the sisters' complaint to God, who responds: "They're right. If there are no men in the family, the land goes to the women" (Numbers 27:8). The ancient rabbinic interpreters went even further and quoted God as saying: "[What these sisters are claiming] is exactly the way I have it written in My book" (*Sifri* on Numbers 27:7). Who can know how many more divine instructions in the Torah got transmitted one-sided, as did the particular one that provoked the daughters of Tzelaphchad. Clearly, this incident is a teaching that sticks out and shouts aloud to us: "Speak up if something feels lopsided or unfair! Don't forget the meaning of your name: boundary crosser."

But we didn't speak up. And what continued snowballing was a virtually femini-free Judaism, where women were honored and patted on the back for their cooking skills and for rearing children, and for lending moral support to their husbands in *their* spiritual pursuits and in their performance of religious obligations that did not include women.

The bottom line is that men need women. Whereas women have been taught that they need men, men are actually the ones who need women.

> Rabbi Yehudah the Prince came upon the ghost of Elijah the Prophet. Said Rabbi Yehudah: "God is quoted in the Torah as saying, 'I shall make for the man a help-mate to complement him [i.e., woman]' [Genesis 2:18]. Pray tell, in what way is woman a help-mate for a man?" Said Elijah: "A man brings in wheat, but can he eat it? He brings in flax, but can he wear it? Is it then not so that she illuminates his eyes and puts him on his feet?"
>
> Babylonian Talmud, *Yevamot* 63a

The rabbis even went so far as to consider a man without a woman "an incomplete being" (Babylonian Talmud, *Yevamot* 63a; *Kohelet Rabbah* 9:9), or, in the kabbalistic tradition: *palga gufa*, or "half of a persona" (*Zohar*, Vol. 3, 7b, 296a). They also taught that a man without a woman in his life lives without the benefits of joy, blessing, goodness, Torah, shelter, peace, aliveness, forgiveness, motivation, wealth, and the like (Babylonian Talmud, *Yevamot* 62b; *Kohelet Rabbah* 9:9; *B'reishis Rabbah* 17:2; *Midrash Tehilim* 59:2; *Batei Midrashot* 2:6:5).

The wording in these teachings is not "A man who is not *married* to a woman," but rather refers to a man who goes through life without any involvement with a woman as a significant part of his life. The teachings are based on the scriptural description of the creation of woman and man as a single being that is called *adam* (Genesis 5:2), or, literally, "earth being," referring to the human who is described as being created from the *adamah*, or earth (Genesis 2:7). In other words, it isn't the act of *marriage* that promises a man joy and aliveness and blessing, and so on. Rather, it is the act of honoring woman for her power and mystique; for who she is as woman in *spite* of man, as opposed to *because* of man. Woman, in other words, is not an extension of man's definition of who and what she ought to be toward his personal agenda and betterment. Woman is a complete Other to man, deserving from him respect and awe rather than patronization and presumptuousness (Babylonian Talmud, *Bava Mezia* 59a). She is, in the words of the third-century Rabbi Ulla, "a separate nation" (Babylonian Talmud, *Shabat* 62a). She is neither an object created for man's muse nor a tool invented for man's use (Babylonian Talmud, *Kidushin* 70a). She is not man's "rib," but a complete and complementary half of what the two of them constitute in their meeting and complementation: *adam*. Man without woman, as well as woman without man, constitutes an incomplete human being, taught the rabbis (*B'reishis Rabbah* 17:2; *Kohelet Rabbah* 9:9). Or, as the third-century Rabbi Simlai put it: "Without woman, man is not; without man, woman is not; without the Divine Presence, neither are" (Jerusalem Talmud, *Berachot* 62:b; *B'reishis Rabbah* 8:9).

Today we are still pretty much stuck in a mindset that is male, that emanates from a "man's world," where women are becoming more and more welcome into roles previously the exclusive domain of men, yet still on terms and standards set by men. The ancient rabbis, however, cognizant of this lopsidedness to life in general and religion in particular, strove to impress upon Jewish men the importance of respecting women and seeing them as Other and as endowed with superior understanding and intuition (Babylonian Talmud, *Nidah* 45b) as well as with a greater intrinsic attunement to the spiritual and the sacred (Babylonian Talmud, *Berachot* 17a; *Pirkei D'Rebbe Eliezer,* Chs. 41 and 45; *Rabbeinu Bachai* on Leviticus 19:2). According to the sixteenth-century Rabbi Eliyahu Haltamri, men actually need women for their spiritual realization (*Shevat Musar* 2:1).

Of course, the question then arises around all the seeming restrictions in Judaism that kept—and, in some communities, continue to keep—women from functioning as rabbis and cantors, for instance, or from studying the Talmud, or from testifying in court, or from wearing prayer articles such as *tefilin* and *talit* (phylacteries and prayer shawl), or from being called up to recite blessings over the Torah reading during public worship, and so on. The list is certainly long and arduous; yet, unbeknownst to most Jewish women and men, just as there are sources in Jewish tradition that fence women out of these experiences, there are also sources that welcome them to these experiences. Everyone, the ancient teachers ruled, is called up to recite blessings over the Torah during public worship and even to read to the congregation from the Torah scroll, including women (Babylonian Talmud, *Megilah* 23a). The discontinuation of this practice was due not to anything theological or halachic, but to a communal mindset that was growing increasingly patriarchal.

Women were not disqualified from testifying in court because they were considered untrustworthy (for that matter, kings, also were disqualified). The functions of king and woman were held so essential that neither one could be diverted from his or her tasks to answer a court summons. Yet, concerning questions of *kashrut,* for instance, matters having to do whether food is kosher or not, and with matters of ritual balance and imbal-

ance, women not only were believed, but also were acknowledged as experts. Therefore, women *were* called upon—and
therefore qualified as witnesses for—cases concerning questions of religious matters (Babylonian Talmud, *Sanhedrin*
24a; Maimonides' *Mishnah Torah, Hilchot Eidut* 5:2; Karo's
Shulchan Aruch, Even HaEzer 17:3 and *Choshen Mishpat*
35); such cases were not bound by specific schedules and dead-
lines, as were litigation and criminal cases, for example, which
would have required a woman with children to leave them and
rush over to testify, had she been rendered legally "qualified."
Qualification, in other words, meant "under obligation." It was
felt inappropriate to obligate a woman or a king to drop everything to make a court appearance. Likewise, since women were
for similar reasons exempt from praying during the three specific periods of the day designated for prayer in Jewish practice, she also was not qualified to make up the quorum of ten
needed for the recitation of special prayers during the service.
Even a *man* was disqualified from making up this quorum of
ten if he was an *onen*, a mourner who hadn't yet buried his
dead, and who was therefore exempt from ritual obligations
such as prayer (*Shulchan Aruch, Orach Chayim* 71:1). Since
he was exempt, he did not qualify for the quorum of those who
were required. Now, some women certainly could make it to
court to testify without so much as batting an eyelash, but the
laws were based on averages, and it follows that just as times
and circumstances can change, so can the laws of averages
and the *halachah* (*Rama* on *Shulchan Aruch, Even HaEzer*
156:4; *Tosefot* [*parah*] on Babylonian Talmud, *Avodah Zarah*
24b and *Hulin* 47a [*kol*]).

Since the prayer shawl and the phylacteries were articles
worn specifically for ritual purposes, women were exempt from
donning them so that they would be freed up to tend to what
it was that women on the *average* were devoted to, and in
many communities still are—children. This idea is not a put-
down of women. Taking care of the young is a sacred task
that far outweighs any synagogue attendance or other ritual

activity. The ancient rabbis declared a mother's "guarantee of a station in the World to Come" greater than that of men "because they prepare the children for sacred deed and study" (Babylonian Talmud, *Berachot* 17a). One could easily surmise that the sages were perhaps attempting to encourage women in the endeavor of childrearing, but, even so, contemporary psychology is reaching the same conclusions that kids need their mom present in their lives more than just at breakfast and bedtime, and that daycare tends to rob children of the emotional and intellectual nurturance that only a mother can provide. Fathers, too, are essential to the development of children across all phases of emotional growth, but are not nearly as vital as mothers are during the early years, which is why women, not men, are biologically self-equipped to conceive and to feed. "A husband, no matter how willingly he gives himself to the role of householder or parent, never approaches such triumphs [as those experienced in mothering]" (Phyllis McGinley, *Sixpence in Her Shoe* [Macmillan Co., 1964], p. 14).

> Having created the child as a living entity [the mother] now has the power to create it as a social being, a member of the community; and without her this creation will not take place, whatever ritual initiation the men like to indulge themselves in acting out . . . the kind of adult it grows into will depend on her . . . the process of nurturing is hers, and its rewards are hers.
>
> Elizabeth Janeway, *Man's World, Woman's Place*
> [William Morrow & Co., Inc., 1971], p. 53

Feminist voices against such notions come more from reaction to centuries of men *keeping* women barefoot and pregnant than from truth and fact. Certainly, it is no man's right to throw chains around a woman in any manner, to restrict her choices about mothering, cooking, and housekeeping. Certainly, women do have the choice—at least in Judaism—to bear children or not to bear children, and they are even permitted to sterilize themselves if they so choose (Babylonian Talmud, *Yevamot* 65b; *Mahar'shal* in *Yam Shel Shlomo* 1:8). The option of contraception for women is a very ancient one in Jewish law, borne out of a theology that does not take woman for granted and that does not perceive her as an object of men's desires and whims. Attitudes toward women that do not seem to reflect this honoring of woman are therefore to be attributed to communal and individual ignorance, as well as to the negative external influence of misogynal cultures and religions.

What a lot of men and women don't understand, however, is that although women are exempt from the performance of time-designated rites and from wearing prayer shawls, they are certainly allowed to perform those rites and to do them at the designated times, if they wish, and to don phylacteries and prayer shawls, and so on (Babylonian Talmud, *Eruvin* 96a): "Even though the scriptures exempted them, there is no prohibition against them doing it, and this ruling applies also to those rituals that have designated times of performance" (Rashi on Babylonian Talmud, *Rosh Hashanah* 33a [*B'nai Yisroel Som'chin*]). Wrote the nineteenth-century sage Rabbi Yosef Bavad:

> Nonetheless, if women wish to put on *tefilin*, we do not stand in their way, and moreover they are rewarded for it. After all, they did not stop Michal the daughter of King Saul from putting on *tefilin*, nor did they admonish the wife of the prophet Jonah for making the pilgrimages to the Temple during the three designated periods of the year [Babylonian Talmud, *Eruvin* 96a].
>
> *Minchat Chinuch*, No. 121

The rabbis also ruled that a woman who wishes to recite the *Kadish*, or mourner's prayer—which is recited only by men and requires a quorum of ten men—may do so, and the congregation should accommodate her (*Pitchei T'shuvah* on *Shulchan Aruch, Yoreh De'ah* 376:4 [No. 3]; *Be'er Hetev* on *Shulchan Aruch, Orach Chayim* 132:2 [No. 5]).

It is evident from the ancient Jewish tradition that Jewish women were highly learned (Babylonian Talmud, *Sanhedrin* 94b and *Pesachim* 62b), joined the men in celebrating public rites and festivals (1 Samuel 1:45; Job 1:4; Babylonian Talmud, *Mishnah, Pesachim* 7:13, 8:1 and *Kelim* 1:8), performed sacred songs and dances for the people (Exodus 15:20; Judges 11:34, 21:21; 1 Samuel 18:6–7; 2 Samuel 19:36; Ecclesiastes 2:8; Ezra 2:65; Psalms 68:26), and frequented rabbinic discourses, moving freely in and out of the houses of study where men gathered throughout the day and night to study the Torah (Numbers 27:1; Deuteronomy 31:12; 2 Kings 4:23; *Vayikra Rabbah* 9:9; Babylonian Talmud, *Sotah* 22a, *Sof'rim* 18:8; Jerusalem Talmud, *Yevamot* 3a). There are also instances recorded where women's opinions were voiced during such discourses and even upheld against those of the rabbis (*Tosefta Kelim* 11:3)! Rabbi Yosef Bavad notes that not only can a woman participate in halachic discussions, but her opinion determines majority rule no less than that of a man (*Minchat Chinuch*, No. 78). Even feminist scholars agree that "ancient Israelite women fared better than modern western women" (*Religion and Sexism* [Simon & Schuster, 1974], p. 70).

It is anything but clear that the Judaic tradition prohibits a woman from becoming a rabbi. Biblically, there is the example of Deborah the prophetess, who is described as "judge" in the context of the premonarchic judges of Israel who decided on all cases brought before them, whether litigation or halachic application (Judges, Chs. 4 and 5). There are, of course, those commentators who claim that she didn't mess with *halachah*, but that is pure speculation in what appears to be part of a centuries-old patriarchal conspiracy to keep women out of the realm of religious decision making. It is apparent that mortal men made up all that stuff about women not qualifying for the rabbinate. Nowhere does the Torah itself disqualify women from becoming rabbis. Male rabbis made it up.

A surface exploration of some of the original text sources yields surprising evidence that the sages of ancient and medieval times took it for granted that women were qualified to handle halachic decision making. The second-century Beruria, who was married to Rabbi Meir, has a halachic ruling recorded in the Babylonian Talmud. In fact, her ruling was accepted by the sages as superior to the rulings of the male rabbis involved in the discussion (Babylonian Talmud, *Tosefta Keilim Bava Kamma* 4:9). The fourteenth-century Rabbi Aharon HaLevi of Barcelona, in discussing the prohibition against making halachic decisions while intoxicated, applies it to women as well:

> And the proscription against entering the sanctuary while drunk during the time of the Holy Temple applies to both men and women alike. And refraining from making halachic rulings while intoxicated applies to all situations and to all times, for men as well as for a woman who is qualified to render halachic decisions.
>
> *Sefer HaChinuch*, No. 158 [end]

Rabbi Zalman Schachter-Shalomi comments that he hopes there will come a time when male rabbis will respond to a halachic query with: "I cannot give you an answer until I have also consulted a woman rabbi for the woman's side of this." This is not at all un-traditional. Ancient teachers, like the third-century Rabbi Chisda, were not oblivious to the fact that women hold the key to levels of life understanding and insight not as easily accessible to men (Babylonian Talmud, *Nidah* 45b). Rabbi Schachter-Shalomi continues:

> There are things which a male rabbi cannot teach to a woman. A man can certainly talk about *mikvah* to a woman, but a woman can hear it better from another woman. There need to be woman rabbis out there who will do those teachings that are better transmitted by women, for women and men alike. It is my sense that most women will find it hard to listen to a man tell them about traditional women stuff in Judaism with-

out feeling patronized, but would hear it differently from a woman teacher. . . .

If from the Orthodox perspective I may be taking some bold risks in giving *s'michah* [ordination] to women, then I say like the first-century Rabbi Yochanan ben Zakai—who took some far more revolutionary risks with the traditional status quo of his own time: "Before me lie two ways, one toward *Gan Eden* [Paradise] and one toward *Gehinom* [Hell], and I know not toward which of these I will be led" (Babylonian Talmud, *Berachot* 28b). And yet I feel I need to make the wager based on what I'm feeling inside. I cannot live with the assumption that "Women are light-headed" (Babylonian Talmud, *Shabat* 33b). It doesn't ring true with the idea of "[The ways of Torah] are ways of pleasantness" [Proverbs 3:17], and so I am willing to gamble with that. Maybe they will throw me into *Gehinom* for this. Or maybe they will say: "Look indeed how that *schlepper* did some important stuff down there."

Conversation with the author, autumn 1993

The talmudic narrative informs us that in ancient times women, too, were welcome to recite blessings and read from the Torah (*aliyah*), except that the practice was discontinued "because of the honor of the congregation" (Babylonian Talmud, *Megilah* 23a), clearly a response to the growing aversion by men to feminine participation in religious function. We are now entering an era when most congregations would consider it an honor to be served by a woman rabbi. Whatever was at one time discontinued because of congregational unease needs to be reevaluated by each individual community. Women should be welcomed into the rabbinate precisely "because of the honor of the congregation." They belong in the rabbinate not by the reactive whims of social progress and political correctness, but by the blessings of the very tradition in whose name men—not God—have barred women from religious participation and decision making. In fact, referring to the banning of women from coming up to the *bimah*—the stand upon which the Torah is read during services—the eighteenth-century Rabbi Dovid Pardo wrote that if a woman nonetheless *did* go up to the *bimah* to read the blessings and even to read from the Torah, "we do not turn her away once she has come up, for by law she is permitted, and it is only a matter of 'the honor of the congregation,' not *halachah*" (*Chasdei Dovid* on Babylonian Talmud, *Tosefta Megilah* 3:4).

A common argument against inviting women up to the *bimah* at the synagogue, whether as a functionary or to recite the blessings over the Torah, is the erroneous assumption that a woman may not come in contact with the sacred articles during her menses. On the contrary, women *are* permitted by traditional Jewish law to touch the Torah scroll even when they are menstruating. Wrote *Rambam*: "All those who are in a state of ritual impurity, including menstruating women, are permitted to hold a Torah scroll and to read from it, for the Torah does not absorb any state of ritual impurity" (*Mishnah Torah, Hilchot Sefer Torah* 10:8, and Karo's *Shulchan Aruch, Yorah De'ah* 282:9). The sixteenth-century Rabbi Moshe Isserles (*Rama*) notes the following: "There are those who write that a menstruating woman, or a woman who has not ritually immersed herself following menstruation, may not enter a synagogue or pray or pronounce the Name [of God] or touch a Torah scroll—and there are those who say that all of these are permitted to her, *and that is the rule*" (gloss on Karo's *Shulchan Aruch, Orach Chaim* 88:1). The seventeenth-century Rabbi Zechariah Mendel of Cracow (*B'er Heitiv*) adds: "There are those who claim that a woman who has just given birth may not attend synagogue until she has waited forty days if she gave birth to a boy and eighty days if she gave birth to a girl. *This is an erroneous custom and should be stopped*" (on *Shulchan Aruch, Orach Chaim* 88:1, No. 2).

Clearly, many of the taboos aimed at women come not from the patriarchal *halachah*, but from the subjective attitudes of what has, over the centuries, become an exclusive men's club. In ancient times, evidence has it that women participated freely and regularly in the religious leadership and affairs of the community. The prophetess Miriam led the Israelites through the wilderness following their Exodus from Egyptian bondage (Micah 6:4). During the forty-year trek, the women refused to participate in any of the rebellious acts, including the Golden Calf incident (*Vayikra Rabbah* 2; *Bamidbar Rabbah* 21; *Pirkei D'Rebbe Eliezer*, Ch. 45). As a result, taught the fourth-century Rabbi Acha: "Each era is redeemed only in the merit of the righteous women who live in that era" and "It is in the merit of the women that the people were redeemed from Egypt, and in the time to come it will be in the merit of the women that redemption shall come again" (*Yalkot Shim'oni* on Ruth 606:4). According to the sixteenth-century kabbalist Rabbi Chayim Vital of Calabrese, "The reason the wives of the sages of our time are domineering of them, is because these men are reincarnated souls of the very men who rebelled during the ancient wilderness journey, and their wives are reincarnations of the souls of the women of that period, and, as we know, the women were not involved in any of these acts of dissention" (*Sefer Sha'ar HaGilgulim*, Ch. 20). It was in the merit of the prophetess Miriam, the ancient rabbis taught, that the people had water during their desert walkabout (Babylonian Talmud, *Ta'anit* 98 and *Bava Mezia* 86b). The twelfth-century B.C.E. Deborah the prophetess was both judge and teacher of her people (Judges, Chs. 4 and 5). Hagar, the Egyptian sister-companion of the Matriarch Sarah, is the only person recorded in the Jewish scriptures to have actually *named* God ("the God who sees me" [Genesis 16:13]).

Yet, over the ages, there arose a taboo against women studying Talmud. It was argued that women didn't have the intellectual faculties required for its proper study and understanding, that they would end up taking the teachings of the Talmud out of context, and so on. Ironically, this same argument is the basis for rabbis withholding from *even male* members of the Jewish community those opinions and rulings of the tradition that are more lenient than the ones composing the standard party-line customs and practices of Jewish orthodoxy. The fear is, and has been, that were the general public made aware of alternative opinions, they might choose them, or they might misconstrue their implications and end up violating the precepts of the Torah. The general rule, therefore, was that women were restricted solely to the study of those matters related to women (*Rama* on *Shulchan Aruch, Yoreh De'ah* 246:6). The tradition was based flimsily on the teaching of the second-century Rabbi Eliezer ben Azariah that "a man who teaches his daughter Torah, it is as if he is teaching her trivia."

What is rarely highlighted, however, is the context of this teaching. The discussion has nothing to do with women studying Torah. It has to do with the laws of *sotah*, the sacred water that was administered to a married woman suspected of committing adultery. If she was guilty, the sacred water would injure her womb; if she was innocent, she would become even more fertile than before (Numbers 5:12–27). Ben Azai then comments that "A man is obligated to teach his daughter Torah, so that in the event she is ever summoned to drink the potion of the *sotah* water, she could rest assured that the Torah will stand by her" (Babylonian Talmud, *Sotah* 20a). It is to this statement that Rabbi Eliezer ben Azariah reacts by saying, in effect, that "Anyone who teaches his daughter Torah with the intention of it serving for her as some kind of protective amulet in the event she is administered the *sotah* potion, it is as if he is teaching her in vain, because Torah study is for personal and spiritual ennoblement, not for occult protection." Ben Azai should not be faulted for his teaching, however, because he may have felt that the *sotah* ritual was wrong and ought not to be done altogether, that it smacked too much of a severe double standard. So he was perhaps punning more than rendering a ruling when he said that men ought to make sure that their daughters study Torah, a sacred deed, so that if they were ever called to the *sotah* rite by a jealous, possessive, paranoid husband, they could feel at peace with the knowledge that the Torah would protect them.

Actually, there is no record that any woman was ever adversely affected or proven guilty by this sacred water rite. It was obviously a placebo ritual. If she was guilty of having had an affair, she would possibly break down and confess before taking the water to her lips in order to avoid the promised consequences. Primarily, however, the waters of *sotah* were intended to allay the suspicions of the husband, and thereby to preserve peace in the marriage. To dramatize the importance of peace in the home, and the seriousness of the rite, a parchment containing the tetragrammaton, the ineffable God name *yhvh*, was placed in the basin, thus becoming erased by the water. The message was this: "See how important to God is harmony between husband and wife, that God even allows the Great Name to be erased in its cause."

> The real purpose of the ordeal is not to convict adulterous women who have been skillful enough to hide their transgression, but primarily to afford a way for women to clear themselves of suspicion. Suspicion of adultery in a close-knit community would be almost impossible to dispel, and could easily lead to ostracism and perhaps violent revenge. The ordeal of the "bitter water" allows a fairly simple, safe way for a woman to clear her name with divine approval, sanctioned by the priest and the Temple ritual. If this is the case we have a kind of inverted institution here: the trial by ordeal is transformed from a formidable test weighted toward guilt to an easy one, strongly biased in favor of demonstrating innocence. The ordeal is changed from a measure threatening women to a mechanism for their protection.
>
> Rachel Biale: *Women and Jewish Law*
> [Schocken, 1984], p. 187

If it was so important that women not study or be taught Torah, the Torah would have said so. An extracontextual discussion about the question hardly lends clarity to it, and is certainly too weak to stand as actual legislation. The fact is that Jewish women studied Torah since the time the Torah first came down to Moses atop Mount Sinai (Deuteronomy 31:12). So exactly what sort of Torah are women not to be taught? The practice has been not to teach them Talmud. But if it is Talmud they weren't allowed to study, how can Eliezer ben Azariah's teaching be employed as the proofsource, when there was no such thing as Talmud in his time? What we call Talmud wasn't compiled until the fifth century. The teachings of earlier sages like Ben Azai and Eliezer ben Azariah only later became part of the Talmud, but the form of it never existed before then. It is no wonder, then, that some rabbinic authorities, when asked by individual women for permission to study the Talmud, were puzzled by the question. They knew very well that nothing in Judaism forbids women from any form of Torah study, Talmud or otherwise. They were also conscious of the talmudic dictum that the fact that a "rule" exists does not automatically mean that it becomes universally applicable, let alone acceptable (Babylonian Talmud, *Kidushin* 34a). So when a sixteenth-century woman came to the saintly Rabbi Shmuel ben Elchanan Halkavi and expressed her burning desire to study the Talmud, the sage said to her: "Then do so, and from heaven shall you be aided." Moreover, he wrote, women desiring to study the Talmud are not only permitted to do so, "but it is incumbent upon the sages of their generation to assist them and to organize them, encourage them and strengthen them, and to reinforce their endeavors" (*M'eyn Ganim*, quoted in *Torah Temimah* on Deuteronomy 11:19, end of note 48).

Torah study is as much the responsibility of Jewish women as it is of Jewish men. The erroneous assumption that women are not to be taught Torah defies a history recorded in both scriptural and talmudic narratives that describe women as studying and teaching Torah. In Jewish history, it appears that much of the discrepancy between the education of men versus that of women resulted from the influence of host cultures to which the Jews were rigidly subjected for centuries, cultures and religions that kept their women subjugated and ignorant in order to secure male dominance and power.

The attitude of the Jewish religion toward women obviously went through some radical changes, most notably during the periods of Jewish history when the Church came down on independent thinking and sensuality, particularly as expressed by women. Millions of women of the Christian faith were burned at the stake or otherwise slaughtered at the hands of the Inquisition from the Middle Ages well into the seventeenth century, and even in what later became the United States. It therefore became clearly a matter of survival for Judaism and other earth-based, femini-active religions living under the strictures of the Church to squelch their creativity and certainly to squelch their women. While in the second century a woman like Beruria could go around freely declaring her innovations and opinions regarding Jewish law, in the medieval period such activity would have placed her in danger, as it did Joan of Arc, who was a faithful *Christian* woman. One can easily trace how much of Jewish law around women and sensuality became increasingly rigidified as the Church power overtook more and more of the world over the last eighteen centuries. It was safer to keep women from learning too much or from teaching or from becoming public figures, just as it had proved safer for Jewish *men* to avoid being too much in their bodies or dabbling too much in kabbalistic shamanism. The once vibrant and richly unfolding tradition of this ancient people—not unlike that of Native America and other earthy, dynamic spirit paths around the world—suffered greatly during these many centuries. Yet it must be admitted that women did suffer more than men, especially since over time it was forgotten that it was circumstances of history, not Jewish theology, that had absented woman from religious study and participation.

While it is true that the halachic process, for instance, has been regulated and controlled exclusively by men for many centuries, it is also true from the evidence in our sacred texts that women, too, can and ought to participate. Otherwise, *halachah*, even Judaism itself, will continue to hop on one leg, taught and understood solely from a single perspective, a solitary dimension that is exclusively or primarily masculine. Torah is a feminine word, and the Torah is referred to throughout the Jewish Bible and the Talmud as "she," and yet she lacks a feminine identity.

Yet by far the worst crime that has been committed against Jewish women by Jewish tradition is not their exclusion from public religious function or leadership, but their subjection to a body of patriarchic laws governing marriage and divorce that has trapped a great many of them in a marital prison. Specifically, I am referring to the tragedy of *agunot*, Jewish women who are unable to remarry because their husbands refuse to grant them a *get* (religious divorce).

What is most heinous is the inexcusable helplessness alleged by rabbinic authorities. The rabbi is obligated to be there for the people, to wrestle with the law, bend it, abrogate it if necessary, when it stands in the way of personal aliveness and spiritual growth. Any rabbi who is helpless should find another line of work. The standard party-line contention that *halachah* (Jewish religious law) "does not change" is absolutely shocking. No rabbi of the second century, for instance, would feel at home with twentieth-century *halachah* (Babylonian Talmud, *Bava Batra* 120a), because *halachah* does change, has changed, and will continue to change. Often, the argument goes something like this: "The idea that the *halachah* is available to us to modify is false. The problem here is not the *halachah*, but the evil in men's hearts. Do we have the authority to prevent evil from being perpetrated in our communities? Yes. But not by changing God's law."

Ironically, the late Rav Moshe Feinstein, a world-renowned Orthodox halachic authority, went out of his way several times to annul marriages outright in situations where the woman would otherwise become an *agunah*. Unfortunately, old-school rabbis like Moshe Feinstein are fast becoming extinct, replaced by overzealous, albeit impotent "halachic authorities" who shy away from taking the daring risks their predecessors took. The difference between the old school of Orthodox rabbis and the latter-day school is that the old guys considered in their halachic rulings the *spirit* of the law, whereas the newcomers are tragically stuck on the *letter* of the law, to the detriment of these hapless women. The rabbis of yesteryear changed "God's law" regularly, and their rulings are recorded in half the books that adorn the shelves of today's velveteen rabbis. The genuine rabbis of yesteryear did not consider their halachic innovations as "changing God's law," but as preserving it. God's law is not etched in stone. This is the fundamental difference between Judaism and Christianity: that we Jews do not have a black-and-white, nonnegotiable relationship with God or Torah. We never took the word literally, but interpreted it and reinterpreted it throughout the ages, a process that is responsible for keeping Judaism alive all these centuries. For rabbis to claim that they are helpless, that there is nothing they can do, is tantamount to holding the *halachah* as some kind of deity; it is pure idolatry.

It is bad enough that the Orthodox rabbinate cries "heresy" at the notion of innovative solutions to the problem of *agunot*, but even worse is its refusal even to employ *ancient* solutions! The word "annulment" frightens them to no end, especially since the laws of marriage and divorce are among those so-called "immutable" ones (immutable according to what sources, please?). "Immutable" is a label employed often by rabbis in order to exempt themselves from having to wrestle an issue and risk losing their share in the World to Come.

Enough emoting. Let us examine the sources of our tradition, which is more compassionate than many of those who purport to be its propagators.

Since the ceremonial agenda for a marriage in Judaism was formulated by the rabbis, anyone who marries by Jewish religious ceremony becomes married by rabbinically ordained conditions. If those conditions are not met, then the same authority that instituted the marriage by that particular rite may, in turn, dissolve it. Wrote Rashi: "The rabbis can thus annul the marriage because during the ceremony, [the couple's] intentions were to become married by the customs established by the sages of Israel" (on Babylonian Talmud, *Gitin* 33a).

Certainly, the sages did not design within their ritual requisites for marriage that the institution be in any way misused for the purpose of extortion or creating *agunot*. For example, the ancient rabbis ordained that a man who has not fulfilled the *mitzvah* of bringing children into the world should remarry if his present wife is unable to conceive—which implies divorce where polygamy is proscribed (Babylonian Talmud, *Yevamot* 64a), and he certainly may not marry a barren woman to begin with. Yet throughout the centuries rabbis permitted—even obligated—husbands of infertile women to remain married to them, and those wanting to marry barren women to go ahead and marry them in situations where either the couple were deeply in love or the woman in question might otherwise never find a mate and thus join the ranks of the *agunot*-by-marriage.

How did these devout rabbis dare to overturn the ordinances of their predecessors? How dared they tamper with "God's law" and say that it is acceptable to be in a situation where the fulfillment of the commandment to have children is impossible? "Because," wrote the nineteenth-century Rabbi Aryeh Zunt of Plotzk, "on the contrary! The sages would never have approved of such a thing [to force the separation of two persons who are in love with each other], nor would such an action be pleasing to the Creator, to whom peacefulness is sacred" (*M'shivat Nefesh* [Warsaw, 1849], No. 18). Another rabbi wrote: "Our sages have instructed us to seek remedies for the prevention of *igun*" (responsa of *Hemdat Shlomo* [Warsaw, 1836], No. 46; see also *Torat Chessed* [Lublin, 1890], 42:35). Rabbi Moshe Feinstein, when confronted with a similar case, prefaced his lenient ruling with these words: "Who am I to enter into the discussion of this matter [when great sages have already ruled on it]? But since there is a danger of her becoming an *agunah*, and the sages require us to make a great effort to help her, and preserving harmony between husband and wife is so important that the Torah allows the Divine Name to be erased for it, I will therefore not be deterred by respect for these great men" (*Igrot Moshe, Even Ha-Ezer*, Vol. 1, No. 63; see also No. 67, and a touching yet amusing related tale in *Shir Ha-Shirim Rabbah* 1:31).

According to rabbinic tradition, the Torah (God's "immutable" law) requires two male eyewitnesses for testimonies. Women were disqualified. Slaves were disqualified. However, if it was a case concerning *agunah*, where a woman was in danger of spending the rest of her life unable to remarry because it was not known for certain whether her missing husband was dead or alive, then the ancient rabbis "changed God's law" and not only allowed for a single witness if one came forward, but decreed that it mattered not whether this witness was a slave or free person, a man or a woman "because of the danger of her becoming an *agunah*" (Babylonian Talmud, *Yevamot* 87b, 88a). In general, whenever a woman was in danger of becoming an *agunah*, the ancient teachers ruled with great leniency (Babylonian Talmud, *Yevamot* 88a and *Gitin* 3a).

Clearly, then, there was a time when the rabbis had no scruples about retroactively annulling a marriage (Babylonian Talmud, *Gitin* 33a), such as in cases where the woman might have found herself legally powerless to dissolve her marriage. The same applies to marriages that had been contracted on false assumptions, on promises or conditions by one of the couple that were not or could not be fulfilled (Babylonian Talmud, *Kidushin* 48b, 49b, 50a). A more recent example of this can be found in the timely responsa of Rabbi Moshe Feinstein, where in several cases he permitted the annulment of marriages retroactively—without requiring a *get*—because the husband either refused to grant a *get* or was mentally incompetent to implement one. In one case, the marriage was annulled when it was discovered that a clinically impotent man had failed to inform his wife of his sexual dysfunction prior to their marriage (*Igrot Moshe, Even HaEzer*, Vol. 1, No. 79). In another case, it was determined that the husband was psychotic, unbeknownst to his recent bride, though Rabbi Feinstein ruled similarly in a case where the woman had been aware of her husband's psychotic history previous to the marriage but had been told that he was cured (*Igrot Moshe, Even Haezer*, Vol. 1, No. 80, and Vol. 3, No. 46). As the ancient teachers put it: "No one should be expected to dwell in the same den with a serpent" (Babylonian Talmud, *Yevamot* 112b).

The ancient teachers also remind us that the first woman was called "mother of all life" (Genesis 3:20), which they applied to women suffering from painful marital situations; that in marriage, a woman's life was supposed to improve, not get worse: "[Woman] was thus given unto life, and not unto suffering" (Babylonian Talmud, *Ketuvot* 61a).

It is obvious from these traditional halachic sources that today's *agunot* are imprisoned not by *halachah*, but by rabbis who fear *halachah* and who worship it like some kind of unbending deity. (While other false gods ate virgins for breakfast, this one feeds on married women.) It is ironic that rabbis who would uphold the halachic precedence that permits us to violate the holy Sabbath to alleviate the discomfort of a milking cow will not uphold the halachic precedence for alleviating years of agony that is the lot of thousands of *agunot*. Something is seriously amiss here. (Re milking a cow on the Sabbath, see *Magen Avraham* on *Shulchan Aruch, Orach Chayim* 305:19.)

The tragic irony of our *agunot* is that these women are suffering because of their staunch loyalty to a male-controlled halachic system that is slowly killing them. Yet, the prophets have repeatedly taught about the divine precepts: "And you shall live by them" (Leviticus 18:5, Ezekiel 20:11, Nehemiah 9:29), and—add the ancient teachers—"not die by them" (Babylonian Talmud, *Yoma* 85b and *Sanhedrin* 74a). Woe unto us so-called rabbis, then, if we continue for another millisecond to withhold the cures and life-giving potions of our living Torah from those whose lives have become suspended in a living hell of physical and psychological limbo. What kind of God do we envision that would want us to offer living sacrifices to the divine word while so totally oblivious to the divine will? Certainly not a God of compassion, but more probably a false god we have created in the image of our own personal insecurities. If there is indeed "a time to do for God even if it means overturning the Torah in the process" (Psalms 119:126 as interpreted in the Babylonian Talmud, *Berachot* 54a), then this is it: Free the *agunot*; annul the marriages of women held captive by their husbands' refusal to grant them a *get*. To refuse to do so is antithetical to our Torah, "whose ways are ways of pleasantness" (Proverbs 3:17).

What a sad disgrace that we have to be dealing with this issue altogether. What a blatant *chilul Hashem*—profanation of God's name—to issue such outright inhumane rulings against these women in the name of God! What an outrage to hold our disadvantaged sisters emotionally hostage in the name of the One Who gave us the Torah as a blessing and not as a curse. How many more hours, days, months, years of physical and mental hell will have been meted out to these women in the name of a Torah that teaches compassion?

We should indeed honor *halachah*, but we should not be intimidated by it, and certainly not when it comes to the urgent issue of *agunot*, when it has gotten so misused so as to cause such tragic and inexcusable human misery. As it stands, rabbis are permitting recalcitrant husbands to misuse *halachah* to desecrate Torah. Worse yet, they are permitting men to misuse *halachah* to abuse other human beings! They permit all this when they feign helplessness in freeing the *agunah*.

Again, *kidushin*—the Jewish wedding rite—is an institution formulated by mortal male rabbis to begin with, not God, and therefore there is no excuse for rabbis not to exercise their authority to pull the rug from under the extortion schemes of recalcitrant husbands. Even biblical God-ordained precepts are suspended when they stand in the way of so much as human *economic* needs, let alone human physical and emotional needs. You eat on Yom Kippur if you are ill and you feel that fasting will only worsen your illness, even if a hundred physicians have diagnosed otherwise (Babylonian Talmud, *Yoma* 82a and 83a). You violate the Sabbath to extinguish a flame for someone who is ill or frightened (Babylonian Talmud, *Shabos* 29b and *Yoma* 84b; *Shulchan Aruch, Orach Chayim* 276:1), and—of course—to milk a cow if her udder is painfully full. But it is unfair to do nothing for a woman whose husband refuses to give her a *get* and who is therefore sentenced to a life of social stigma and physical and emotional agony.

In the first century B.C.E., Hillel the Elder instituted the *prusbol* contract that enabled people to bypass the biblical law that canceled debts every seven years (Deuteronomy 15:1–2), "because he saw that people were unwilling to lend money to one another" (Babylonian Talmud, *Gitin* 36). As recently as 1888, noted sages followed suit and ordained the bypass of yet another "seventh year" law of the Torah that forbade the working of the land for an entire year. The people then were in dire economic straits and could not afford to suspend farming for a whole year (E. Shimoff's "Rabbi Elkhanan Spector" [Yeshiva University Press, 1959], p. 134). The contention that we have no authority to modify *halachah* is therefore contrary to historical and theological fact. We have wrestled with, reinterpreted, modified, altered, and changed God's law as long as we have been a people. Without this right, the quality of our relationship with God is no different from that between an *agunah* and her unbending husband.

According to the ancients' understanding of Torah law, it was the man who initiated marriage, and therefore the man who dissolved it. The woman could not sue for divorce. In the tenth century, however, Rabbeinu Gershom decreed that women, too, could initiate *get* proceedings, although it was still up to the man to grant it to her and the rabbinic court to compel him to do so if he refused. What is standing in our way of decreeing, in our own time, that a woman may not only sue for divorce, but also give the man a *get*? The most common reply is: Who are *we*? Rabbeinu Gershom and the others who modified *halachah* when it stood in the way of aliveness were giants, celestial angels, whereas we in our many sins are but worms and nothings. This is the attitude. This is the impotence of the contemporary rabbinate.

The argument that the laws of marriage and divorce are too complex and are immutable, that we cannot be radical when messing with these issues because of the immense sanctity of marriage and family life, is an argument worthy of the Hittites and Yevusites and those other ancient cults who sacrificed human life upon the altars of home-brewed, self-serving standards of "sanctity." Is keeping a human being's aliveness painfully on hold "sanctity"? Is stomping up and down on the dignity of a woman held prisoner by a *get*-refuser "sanctity"? Is forcing a young heterosexual woman to spend the rest of her life without a mate "sanctity"?

Moreover, we claim the need to act zealously in protecting this "sanctity" because the Jewish people depend on it for its survival. "Jewish people?" I ask. If we truly wish to preserve the *Jewish* peoplehood, we need to stop this blind obeisance to double-standard "sanctity" and do something that would indeed be Jewish, like freeing up all those *agunot*, and like changing the *halachah* that gives men the power and wherewithal to abuse women. Judaism has no room for this kind of insensitivity.

If we can remain so callous toward a woman's devious suffering and, by omission, be so supportive of a man's "halachic supremacy" even while it is whittling away painfully at another human being, there is something essentially wrong, and we need to do some heavy *tikun*—repair. All the noise from both secular and religious feminists about "patriarchy this" and "patriarchy that" should not be dismissed lightly as New Age rhetoric. Clearly, there is a lot of truth to the unfair control that men wield over women in religious life, sometimes to their detriment. As our ancient teachers put it: "Men are more compassionate to other men than toward women. But God's compassion extends equally to men and to women alike . . . as it is written, 'God is good to all, Whose compassion is upon all creations' (Psalms 145:9). . . . For all are equal before God" (*Tankhuma, Netzavim*, par. 2).

Some well-meaning rabbis have tried to tackle the *agunah* issue with the formulation of a prenuptial agreement that would render the marriage null and void if one of the parties refuses *gitin* (ritual divorce proceedings). Unfortunately, this contract will not be recognized by most Orthodox rabbis, even though some of the rabbis behind its authorship are Orthodox themselves. And women who remarry by the authority of this agreement will therefore be considered by many as adulterers, and any subsequent children as *mamzerim*—illegitimate. Moreover, even if this document were to be accepted unanimously by the rabbinates, it would not benefit the thousands of *agunot* whose marriages took effect years ago and who therefore did not have access to such recently introduced innovations. This is not the solution. The solution involves the more daring process that our rabbinic predecessors engaged toward alleviating anguish and preventing people from prostituting Torah principles for their own exploits. That process is about decreeing actual modifications in the *halachah*, such as shifting the right to effect *gitin* from its heretofore exclusive male domain to include women as well, so that if a man refuses to grant his wife a *get*, she may give him one, and if he refuses to accept it, the next step is to allow her to remarry anyway by declaring the marriage null and void retroactively, since it is no longer a marriage in the spirit and intention of the sages who instituted it to begin with. The sanctity of marriage and divorce will return only when it is no longer vulnerable to abuse. The prenuptial agreement does not address the cancer that is thriving at the core of this tragedy. We need radical surgery, not first aid. Simply put, we need to rid our tradition of the proverbial double standard.

A fitting *Chelm* story is this one: Once upon a time, the Chelm village council called a meeting to discuss the problem of a treacherous road that led up and around a steep hill to the neighboring villages. Travelers would frequently lose their balance along the edges of the curvy, uneven road and fall off the cliff. After a long night of weighing and assessing, of pondering and proposing, of debating and berating, of arguing and vetoing, the council finally reached a solution: They would build a hospital at the bottom of the hill!

Rabbinic authorities can either continue building more and more hospitals at the bottom of the hill, or take preventive measures at the top. Rabbis have a long tradition of building fences, but it's time they started building some where they are really needed.

Appendix:
Tumah and Taharah Reexamined

LAKME BATYA ELIOR

If we read many parts of the Torah that relate directly to women, the rituals prescribed for menstruation and birth seem to us to be lumped into the same categories as those for corpses, running sores, worms, and sin. In fact, this has been enough to make some people, especially non-Orthodox women, decide that the Torah is hostile to women and demeans experiences that women can otherwise find exalting. They decide that the Torah is not a source of self-worth or healthy body-image for women and girls. Or they decide that the Torah is not teaching things that are relevant, because if a whole treatment of one theme is so vividly discriminatory and tough to swallow, the rest may be suspect also. For many disillusioned Jews, therefore, the only experiential relationship to their heritage is self-identity and Eastern European cuisine.

But what if—in the tradition of talmudic interpretation and midrashic explorations of stories and texts, so richly carried on to this day in responsic writings—we examine the assumptions and the definitions that are the basis of wrong-feeling interpretations? And, then, what if we try out totally different, brand-new assumptions and definitions on the text?

In the Torah are two words that are set in contrast to each other. These words, universally translated into English as "pure" and "impure," have been used for centuries in Hebrew with these same usages and connotations. The words are *taharah*, translated as "pure," and *tumah*, translated as "impure."

What if *tumah* does not mean impure—*treif* (non-kosher)—unclean? What if, rather than speaking of "purity" and "impurity," the words *taharah* and *tumah* are both speaking of sacredness? What if *tumah* and *taharah* really are two kinds of purity?

There is precedence for this concept in Judaism. *Fleishig* (meat), *meilkhig* (dairy), and *pareve* (neutral) foods are all kosher. The Sabbath and the workaday week are both holy. Different people have different ritual obligations: priests, High Priests, men, women, children, single people, married people, parents, farmers, soldiers, and so on. Days differ also: High Holy Days, Passover, minor fast days, major fast days, Rosh Chodesh, and ordinary days. Each of the roles and relationships people are in, each of the days, have different needs and purposes. None of the examples just listed are bad, dirty, *treif*, unholy, or inherently wrong. Yet each one has laws, customs, and practices that distinguish one from the other. While there are things that are inherently *treif*, there is a vast category of *treif* that comes from mixing two or more kosher things or from using something that is kosher in one context within a second context where it is not kosher, or performing an act that is perfectly kosher at one time during a time when it is not. Some examples are: kosher meat with cream sauce; *challah* during Passover; any food on Yom Kippur; building a synagogue on *Shabbat*; or getting married on Tisha B'Av.

When we reread each of the passages in the *Chumash* (Five Books of Moses) that deal with the concept of *tumah* and *taharah*, reading *tumah* as its own kind of holiness and *taharah* as its own kind of holiness—and looking for when and how they are to be kept distinct from each other—what unfolds for us is rich and beautiful ways of looking at daily life, lifecycle events, and even the history of the Jews in biblical times.

Taharah becomes the state of divine grace of everyday life, uninterrupted in flow, in which it is particularly difficult to feel the God-presence without a lot of external spiritual practices. This is the state that Temple service was meant to teach us is holy.

Tumah, on the other hand, becomes a set of experiences of divine grace that come upon us when we are brought into contact with the physical manifestations of the God-presence at the boundaries between this world and the next. *Tumah* comprises those states in which it is nearly impossible to forget that the life of human hopes and intentions is fundamentally subject to being acted upon by the universe. People who normally have an antagonistic or noninvolved relationship with religion often seem to want God and need religion when faced with a serious illness or death—their own, or that of a family member or friend. Finding the God-presence in a *tumah* state is still much easier for a human being than it is to truly experience the God-presence in a *taharah* state.

Many who have attended a birth in a home or a birthing room, or indeed in a hospital or taxicab, can attest to the joy and being "blown away" inherent in birth-*tumah*. And a few who have had the honor of washing and arranging the body of someone who has died peacefully, as I have, may also attest to the other-worldliness, the deep peace, the supreme sacredness of this act. Indeed, it is considered one of the highest of all the *mitzvot* (good deeds) to bury the corpse of even a stranger (Babylonian Talmud: *Sotah* 14a, *Berachot* 18a, *Megilah* 23b).

But if *tumah* is the result of such a holy occurrence as God touching a human life, then why is *tumah* forbidden in the Torah? *It is not!* It is only the seeking out of certain sorts of *tumah* that is advised against; and one is not to go to Temple services when in a *tumah* state. At other times, *tumah* is, in fact, to be sought out. Although burying a dead person makes one biblically *tumah* for a week (Numbers 19:11), it is still a *mitzvah*. It has been considered a *mitzvah* for a married couple to make love as a celebration of *Shabbat* (Babylonian Talmud, *Ketuvot* 62b; Nachmonides, *Iggeret HaKodesh*, Ch. 3), although this makes them both *tumah* for the duration of the Sabbath (Leviticus 15:18). And having children is a great *mitzvah* for the parents. How can a great *mitzvah*, and such a great joy, create an "unclean" or "unholy" state in mother and baby?

> And *yhvh* spoke to Moshe saying: Speak to the children of Israel saying: [when] a woman has matured a human seed and gives birth to a male child, she shall be *tumah* for seven days, just as in the days of her *niddah* [menstruation] shall she be *tumah*. And on the eighth day the flesh of his foreskin shall be circumcised. And she shall remain in the blood of *taharah* for thirty-three days. . . . And if she gives birth to a female child, she shall be *tumah* for two weeks just as at her time of *niddah* and remain upon the blood of *taharah* for sixty-six days (Leviticus 12:1–5).

Of course, if *tumah* is thought to mean "impure," then it is disgusting to give birth to a boy and twice as disgusting to give birth to a girl. And yet, if *tumah* means "holy," then it is holy to give birth to any child and twice as holy to give birth to a girl, and why not? The child will one day, it is to be hoped, be capable of giving birth herself!

And Leviticus 12:4 continues thus: "She shall touch no sanctified thing and not come into the Sanctuary until the days of her *taharah* are complete."

Why not? Why not go to the Temple when experiencing God so directly (in *tumah*)? Because, since you have so vividly encountered the God-presence at the door between life and death, it would be nonsensical to run to the Temple to ask the Priest to open a window to the God-presence for you. It would be like declaring at a laden holiday table: "There is no food here!" and then going off to a restaurant. Very insulting to your host!

It is quite clear that the point between conception and birth is when we are each crossing from the "next world" to "this world," the realm of human endeavor. And death is leaving "this world for the next." The explanation and advice given about being around corpses and diseased flows teach that the human spirit and mind touch the veil between the worlds by even approaching death. Physically our bodies do also, by way of contagion.

But eventually the time comes when it is, indeed, appropriate to go to the Temple and cross back to the *taharah* way of being in life:

> And when the days of her *taharah* are completed, for a son or for a daughter, she shall bring . . . an ascent offering, and a . . . *khatas* ["bring-close" offering], to the entrance of the tent of appointed meeting, to the priest. He shall bring it near before the presence of God and effect an at-one-ment for her, and so she will be *taharah*, away from the source of her [birth] blood.
>
> Leviticus 12:6–7

Why does the woman need at-one-ment?

The rabbis in the Talmud debate Leviticus 12:6 with some difficulty. A "bring-close" offering has been thought of and translated as a "sin" offering, and the ancient rabbis could not quite figure out what the woman's "sin" might be, although they proposed a few possibilities—like vowing during labor never to have sex again, which the woman does not mean, therefore making a false vow that requires a "sin offering."

But other rabbis declined to find any sin in the birthing experience. The fourteenth-century Rabbeinu Bachai, in his commentary on Leviticus 12:6, said that there was another circumstance where thinking of the *khatas* as a sin offering is also inappropriate. For they were brought after a person had successfully fulfilled a vow of a period of asceticism. Such a person, he wrote, surely was bringing not a sin offering, but rather an offering to effect a change of spiritual states from his (her) asceticism back to everyday life. Likewise, the pregnant woman is finishing her changeover from a very powerful and sacred *tumah* state to a *taharah* state.

The nineteenth-century Rabbi Yisroel Horowitz, commenting on Leviticus 12:6, writes that the purpose of the *khatas* was to console the woman who, after having participated so fully in the miracle of bringing forth life, and after living in the immediate experience of the Presence of the Beloved, might easily feel let down during the thirty-three or sixty-six days of her "*taharah* blood"; she might miss the immediacy of the God-presence (part of "postpartum blues"?). And the offering was to restore her to the experience that God exists always and everywhere, even in so-called mundane life (*Madregat HaAdam*).

Why such an elaborate need for separating *tumah*-holiness from *taharah*-holiness? Perhaps it was because learning *taharah* was so hard. *Tumah* is engrossing, and much spiritual practice among neighboring peoples in biblical times sought to extend *tumah* states as much as possible, to worship them and the images of them. There was, initially, so much concentration on *tumah* that there was no room for *taharah*-consciousness to enter. The distinction was not made in order to promote one over the other; rather, it was to teach the sacredness of both: that God is accessible not only at the doorways of life and death, but also just as much in-between, in the everyday flow of everyday life.

And that is the essential teaching of the Holy Temple: that the Divine Beloved wants us to also find the God-self walking beside us when we are not overwhelmed by the supernal drama of life and death. We were not meant to turn away from these miracles, to call them "unclean" and "ungodly." Rather, we were to broaden our view to include a close, relevant God who is available even when we are not in the midst of need, but are happily being our own powerful little selves.

6

Judaism and the Non-Jew

He said to me: "Rabbi, it happened that I sold to a star-worshipper four *kurs* [the equivalent of twenty-eight bushels] of dates, and I measured them out to him inside a dark dwelling . . . and because it was dark I measured out three *sa'in* [the equivalent of about half a bushel] less than what he paid for. I then took the money and bought a pouch of oil for myself and put it in the same place where I had sold the dates to that star-worshiper. But the pouch burst open and the oil spilled out and vanished." I said to him: "My son, it is written in the Torah, 'You shall not swindle your fellow' [Leviticus 19:13]. Your fellow human is like your own brother or sister [Jewish or not]."

Tana D'Bei Eliyahu, Ch. 15

Judaism does not believe that Judaism is the only legitimate path to God. In fact, the Torah's concluding statement is that there never again arose among the Israelites a prophet as great as Moses (Deuteronomy 34:10), to which the ancient teachers add: "Among the *Israelites* there never arose one like Moses, but among the nations of the world it is possible that such a one could arise" (*Bamidbar Rabbah* 14:19). Judaism also does not see itself as the sole embodiment of wisdom (*Eichah*

Rabbah 2:13) or the only avenue to Paradise in the hereafter. Rather, everyone—Jewish or not—can earn a portion of the World to Come (Babylonian Talmud, *Sanhedrin* 105a and *Tosefta Sanhedrin* 13:1), because we are judged not by our religious affiliation, but by our actions in the world: "I call heaven and earth as witnesses that anyone, Jew or gentile, man or woman, slave or maidservant, can bring the Divine Presence upon oneself, all in accordance with one's deeds" (*Tana D'Bei Eliyahu Rabbah* 10:1). Some sages even went so far as to extend the name *yehudi* (Jew) to anyone who denied belief in idolatrous worship (Babylonian Talmud, *Megilah* 13a). The fourth-century Rabbi Yirmiyahu held that a non-Jew who endeavored in the study and practice of Torah was equivalent to a *kohein gadol*, the Jewish High Priest (*Sifra Acharei Mot* 13:12). Even the ancient Holy Temple of the Jews was built by King Solomon with the prayer that God accept from it not only the prayers and offerings of Jews, but those of other peoples as well:

> And also regarding the stranger who is not from among your people Israel, but who comes from a distant land for your name's sake, for he has heard of your great name and of your mighty hand and outstretched arm, and he wishes to come and pray in this house—you shall listen to him from the heavens, the place of your dwelling, and you shall do for the stranger whatever it is he prays for, so that all the peoples of the earth will become aware of you in the same manner as your people Israel, and come to know that your name is called upon this house that I have built.
>
> 1 Kings 8:41–43

A great many of the misconceptions that evolved regarding Jewish relations with non-Jews are the result of erroneous conclusions drawn from certain talmudic principles and terminology. For example, the Talmud teaches that if the ox of a Jew injures the ox of an *akum* (acronym for *Avodat Kochavim*

U'Mazalot—worshiper of stars and constellations), the Jew is not liable for the *akum*'s loss. The misconception lies in the blanket application of *akum* to imply all non-Jews, an interpretation that probably grew out of centuries of being persecuted by non-Jewish peoples. Wrote the nineteenth-century Rabbi Baruch HaLevi Epstein: "It is certain that the Talmud's specific use of the term *akum* clearly excludes those non-Jews who observe the seven Noahide laws. And such is the case with the majority of the non-Jewish peoples of our time. And thus do all the laws apply to our relations with them as they would to our relations with other Jews, meaning that damaging their property must be judged in the same way as the judgment of damages caused to Jewish property. And there is not the slightest degree of doubt about this" (*Tosefet B'rachah, B'har*; see also Maharal of Prague in *B'er HaGolah*, p. 144; *Baruch Sh'amar* on *Avot* 3:14). Contrary to what many people think, these same principles apply to the laws of the Sabbath: A Jew is obligated to violate the Sabbath to rescue the life of a non-Jew (13th-century Rabbi Menacham Me'iri on Babylonian Talmud, *Yoma* 84a). The injunction to "Love your fellow as yourself" was understood by many of the teachers to include love of non-Jews as well, not just fellow Jews (*Tana D'Bei Eliyahu Rabbah* 15; *Baruch Sh'amar* on *Avot* 3:14; *Sheylot Ya'avetz*, Vol. 1, No. 41; *Sefer HaB'rit HaShalem* 2:13:1). And for those who interpret the verse to imply Jews alone, the Torah repeats the instruction a few paragraphs later specifying the "stranger who lives among you" (Leviticus 19:34). Writes the eighteenth-century Rabbi Pinchos Eliyahu of Vilna:

> The essence of loving one's fellow human being is that one should love one's fellow regardless of peoplehood, language, race, and so on, because everyone is created in the image of the Creator. The only exemption to this rule is that we are not obliged to love barbarians and murderers. . . . And if we wish to know if this is a self-made nicety [for a Jew to love non-Jews] or an outright directive of the Torah, we need only

investigate the verse "And you shall love your fellow as yourself" [Leviticus 19:18]. There, the passage is not referring to
Jews, for it reads *rey'acha*, your fellow, and when referring
specifically to other Jews the term *achi'cha*, "your brother,"
is used [Leviticus 25:35], or *b'nei ameh'cha*, "children of your
people" [Leviticus 19:18]. . . . And of course all the negative
connotations in the Torah referring to non-Jews concerns only
those who are barbaric in their actions and go about destroying their fellow human, even their own blood relatives. But
certainly does the Torah not imply anything negative toward
those non-Jews who observe the Seven Noahide Laws [requir-
ing the pursuit of justice; forbidding murder, stealing, incest,
idolatry, eating an animal while it is yet alive, and cursing the
God Name (Babylonian Talmud, *Sanhedrin* 56a)], or those
who contribute constructively to humanity even if they do
worship idols.

Sefer HaB'rit HaShalem 2:13:1

Nonetheless, viewing the principle of the rabbis in its broader
perspective, even idol-worshipers must be dealt with honestly
and constructively by those walking the Judaic spirit-path. The
bottom-line criterion, as delineated by Rabbi Pinchos Eliyahu,
is that we owe our respect to anyone who lives a reasonably
moral life, meaning that they promote rather than destroy
humanity and its welfare. The term *rey'ah*, or fellow human,
therefore extends beyond those who observe the seven Noahide
laws, to include all who uphold rightness in their personal relationships and in their relationship with the planet. Taught
the fourth-century Rabbi Abbaya: "One should always promote
peacefulness with every person, even with the idolator in the
marketplace. It was said of Rabbi Yochanan ben Zakai that he
was always the first to initiate greetings to people in the street,
even to idol-worshipers" (Babylonian Talmud, *Berachot* 17a).

It is prohibited to fool fellow humans, even idol-worshipers.

Babylonian Talmud, *Hulin* 92

We are obliged to feed the non-Jewish poor exactly in the same manner as we feed the Jewish poor, and to visit their sick and bury their dead.

Babylonian Talmud, *Gitin* 61a

Wrote the sixteenth-century Rabbi Shmuel Edels (*Mahar'sha*): "There are those who gather for themselves riches dishonestly and by profaning the name of God [by swindling non-Jews], and then they contribute this money to charity. And this is a matter of a good deed achieved through an evil deed, and is thus pointless and without any merit" (on Babylonian Talmud, *Ketuvot* 67a).

A Jew may not behave wrongly toward anyone of the other peoples, as he would not toward a fellow Jew.

12th-century Rabbi Yehudah HaChasid
in *Sefer Hasidim*, No. 1094

One of the most lucid examples of the Jewish attitude toward non-Jews appears in the Torah text itself, concerning the case of a Jew who became a slave to a non-Jew by selling himself into servitude in order to repay a debt, for example (Leviticus 25:47). According to the scriptural context, the non-Jew is living in a Jewish-governed Israel as "a stranger who lives among you." The Torah then instructs the Jewish community to take immediate action toward redeeming its member from servitude to the "stranger." At this point, one would speculate that the sovereign Jewish nation can then simply coerce the non-Jewish sojourner into accepting some minimal token payment for the freedom of this Jewish slave, or it can simply compel the alien to free the Jewish slave. After all, this is a sovereign Jewish nation, and the gentile master is only a guest and wields no power against the host nation. But that is antithetical to the way of Torah, which preaches equal rights for all in the Jewish homeland, "for the citizen and the stranger alike" (Leviticus 24:22), and accordingly the Torah directs the redeemers to be meticulous about making certain that the non-Jewish slaveowner is properly compensated (Leviticus 25:50): "And [the redeemer] shall reckon with [the gentile slaveowner] from the year that [the Jewish slave had] sold himself to him unto the year of the Jubilee [when he would have gone free anyhow, as did all slaves]; and the price of his sale shall be according to the number of years, according to the time of a hired laborer [had he continued] with him. . . ."

> Said Rabbi Shimon (first century): "Perhaps you would think that we can simply snatch the Jewish slave by force, but then the Torah says 'a redemption shall it be for him.' Perhaps you would think that you can redeem him with an arbitrary sum, but then the Torah says 'you must reckon with him that bought him.' Perhaps you might presume that this particular case involves a gentile who is not under Jewish jurisdiction; after all, what else can you then do but compensate him meticulously? But when the Torah informs us that if the Jewish slave is not redeemed 'he goes free in the Jubilee year' [applicable only in Israel], it is obvious that the Torah is referring to a non-Jew living in the Jewish commonwealth."
>
> *Sifra* on Leviticus 25:54

Judaism, then, is not about thoroughbreeding—neither racially, culturally, nor religiously. In fact, many Jewish customs, even down to the music that cloaks Jewish liturgy, are pretty much borrowed or adapted from the melodies of other peoples. If a non-Jew had something positive that we could learn from, grow from, become nourished by, then we had no problem with incorporating it into our spiritual practice—even if that someone was an enemy like Bil'am, the Midianite prophet who was hired by Balak, king of the Moabites, to curse the Israelites during their walkabout in the wilderness in the fourteenth century B.C.E. In the course of carrying out his instructions to curse the Jews, Bil'am was so inspired by what he saw that he was instead moved to declare: "How wonderful are your tents, O Jacob; your dwelling places, O Israel!" (Numbers 24:5) This declaration was incorporated in the Jewish prayerbook as a recital (known as the *Mah Tovu* prayer) upon entering the synagogue! Thus did the utterances of an enemy Midianite sorcerer become an official Jewish prayer.

If learning and adapting from other spiritual traditions is heresy, as some people argue, then Judaism has always been a heretical religion. Any such student of Jewish history will then find it surprising that such great luminaries as the twelfth-century Rabbi Yosef ibn Aknin and Rabbi Bachya ibn Pakuda were so "blasphemous" as to spike their Judaic teachings with heavy dosages of Sufism, or that their contemporary Maimonides was so "brazen" as to write his classical Jewish philosophy while holding the Torah in one hand and Aristotle in the other. In fact, Maimonides' son, Rabbi Avraham, went so far as to introduce Sufi practices into the synagogue (*Encyclopedia Judaica*, "Sufism")! Even more amazing is the behavior of Judaism's greatest prophet, Moses, in relationship to his non-Jewish father-in-law Jethro (Yitro), who is a Midianite priest. When Jethro approaches Moses with instructions on how to provide spiritual guidance for the Israelites, Moses does not grit his teeth and shrug him off; on the contrary, Moses humbles himself before the non-Jewish teacher, listens to him intently, absorbs every word, and then applies his teachings (Exodus 18:14–24). Long before the existence of Moses the teacher of the Jewish people, Abraham the *father* of the Jewish people learned from the non-Jewish spiritual master Malkizedek (*Pirkei D'Rebbe Eliezer*, Ch. 8). Abraham himself dabbled in astrology (Babylonian Talmud, *Bava Batra* 16b).

The irony is that many Jews are averse to the adaptation of spiritual teachings and practices that originate outside of Judaism, all the while zealously guarding traditions of Jewish dress and cuisine that are anything but Jewish. Many Jewish values and customs, dress, and food, if traced to their roots, emanate surprisingly from religions and cultures that persecuted the Jews relentlessly. The Cossacks and Polish lords and peasants of the seventeenth through the twentieth centuries raped, pillaged, and massacred Jews *en masse*, and yet many Jews continue to wear the traditional garb of these marauders on the Sabbath and festivals. Even more, Jews relish the foods that these people ate—it is, in fact, considered widely as "Jewish food"! Well-meaning *mavens* ("experts"), however, don't realize that potato *kugel*, blintzes, and *latkes* with sour cream are but throwbacks to dishes and customs of peoples who hated our guts and whose favorite pastime consisted of burning down our homes and depriving us of our livelihood.

There is nothing terribly wrong with emulating the dress of an era that graced us with spiritual giants, or eating the foods our people ate while living in lands where they were hated. *Hasidim* do not wear long black coats and knickers and fur hats to memorialize the Cossacks and Polish lords and peasants who pillaged us across three centuries; the *Hasidim* dress as they do to memorialize the great masters of their tradition who sprang up during an age and in a culture that dressed that way. The dress is to honor their teachers who flourished in eighteenth-century Eastern Europe, and who dressed like the people of the land. Likewise, *latke* and *kugel* devotees consider Eastern European delicacies as traditional Jewish cuisine because their parents fed it to them and they came from Eastern Europe, where this kind of food was eaten by all, not just by Jews. Why, then, consider it "un-Jewish" for a Jew in America to wear jeans or an Apache necklace? Neither cowboys nor Indians as a group ever entertained the notion of harming Jews. Why protest or become repulsed when Jews borrow from the customs and teachings of the Navajos or the Hindus or the Buddhists, peoples who have never laid a finger on Jews or so much as entertained a negative thought about them? This is the irony.

Many rabbis lead their synagogue worship services with a potent dosage of church decorum and protocol, and much of cantorial chant sounds little different from Christian Gregorian song. Yet it is often these same rabbis or their congregants who are the most outspoken critics of those who conduct their services with a pinch of Sufism, Buddhism, or Lakota Sioux. Certainly, Judaism has its right to boundary, to self-immunity; and there is nothing wrong in hyphenating with aspects of other spirit paths unless it is allowed to *supplant* rather than augment. Rabbi Zalman Schachter-Shalomi says that he doesn't want to see Judaism "contract AIDS," or to see Christianity or any other religion "get AIDS"—that each path needs to honor its immune system, its distinctiveness, its unique contribution to the planetary mind. At the same time, says Reb Zalman, neither ought religions to avoid intercourse with one another altogether. Like AIDS, it is an issue of responsibility, not abstinence (conversation with the author, spring 1987).

Again, Judaism is not about purity—racial, religious, or otherwise. We have borrowed and adapted from the ways of others since our inception. This is because Judaism is about being in relationship with the world around us, and about acknowledging and appreciating that which is positive and wholesome, whether it comes from the Baal Shem Tov or from Swami Satchidinanda. "If they will tell you there is Torah amongst the nations," the ancient rabbis taught, "don't believe it." Torah is the distinct body of wisdom of the Jews. It is their identity and contribution to the world. No one else can bring Torah alive like we can. It's ours; it's personal. However, the rabbis continued, "If they will tell you that there is wisdom amongst the nations, believe it" (*Eichah Rabbah* 2:13). Judaism does not hold a monopoly on universal wisdom and truth. Wisdom and truth is not the exclusive domain of any one religion or peoplehood; Judaism proclaims this loud and clear, and therefore it has always been open to learning from other paths. "Who is the wise one?" asked the second-century Rabbi Ben Zoma. "The one who learns from everyone" (Babylonian Talmud, *Avot* 3:1)—not just from rabbis, but also from Choctaw medicine women and imans and swamis and kids and trees and peddlers in the park and fiddlers on the roof. Any roof.

When Rabbi Akiva sought a prime example of how to honor one's parents, he did not hesitate to bring the example of a non-Jew in Ashkelon (Babylonian Talmud, *Kidushin* 31a).

Matzoh-ball soup is Jewish food only when Jews are eating it. If the Jicarilla Apache were to adopt it, it would become Jicarilla Apache food, even though it's got Hebrew lettering on the box. God is not Jewish, and does not discriminate between peoples and traditions (*Sh'mot Rabbah* 19:4) Judaism is but one of many paths, of many varieties of ways of experiencing life, of being spiritual. It is not the only path, nor is it the best path for everyone. The very Torah of the Jews demonstrates this, not only in the story of Moses bowing to and learning from the priest of Midian, but also in the story of the ancestral father Abraham, who learns from the non-Jewish Malkizedek (Genesis 14:18), and who does not take over "the promised land" by force even though God has told him it will be his. Rather, Abraham negotiates squatting rights, purchases land, and honors the people already living there, allowing them the right to not buy into his vision of God promising the land to him (Genesis 17:8).

> And Abraham rose from mourning his dead wife Sarah and he spoke to the children of Chet saying: "I am a stranger and guest-dweller in your land. Give to me a burial place among you so that I can bury my dead who lies before me." And the children of Chet answered him, saying: "Listen to us, our master, among us you are known as a prince of the all-powerful God, so therefore choose from the choicest of our burial spaces and bury your dead. None of us will withhold from you any burial space or stand in your way from burying your dead wherever you choose." And Abraham spoke to them, saying: "If your souls truly are open to my burying my dead from before my face, then please listen to me and bring me to a meeting with Efron the son of Tzochar, so that he might give to me the cave of Machpelah that he owns, which is in the midst of his field, and that I would want to acquire with a great sum of silver so that he may give to me a burial space among you."

And it was that Efron was sitting amongst the children of Chet, and Efron the Hitite answered Abraham before the ears of the children of Chet and before all who were coming and going through the gate of his village, saying: "Please, my master, listen to me. I have hereby given this field to you, and the cave that is on it I give to you. In front of the eyes of all who the children of my people do I give this to you, so go and bury your dead." And Abraham bowed to the people of the land, and he spoke to Efron in front of the people of the land, saying: "Please hear me out as well. I hereby give to you silver for the field. Take it from me and I shall bury my dead there." And Efron answered Abraham, saying: "My master, please hear me. Between you and I, what is four hundred silver *shekels* for this land, and then you can bury your dead." And Abraham heard Efron and doled out the silver that was spoken of before the ears of the children of Chet, four hundred silver *shekel* in accordance with the value that was common amongst merchants. And so, the field of Efron that was in Machpelah near Mamre, the field and the cave that was on it, and all the trees that were in the field and that were around all the surrounding borders, were given to Abraham as his possession before the eyes of the children of Chet and all the people going in and out of the gate of the village.

Genesis 23: 3–18

The first Jew teaches us not only about how to live with those not of our faith, but also about how to honor the beliefs of others and to not assume that our beliefs override theirs (Genesis 21:22–34, 23:4–20). The narrative of the Torah also makes it clear that as God is with the Jewish people, so is God with all peoples. While God is raising Isaac, the progenitor of the Jewish people, God is simultaneously raising Ishmael, the progenitor of the Arabian people (Genesis 21:20). Jonah the Jewish prophet is chastised by God for his refusal to go on a mission to the non-Jewish kingdom of Ninveh (Jonah 1:3), and learns in the end that the Creator is concerned for all peoples, not only Jonah's (Jonah 4:10–11).

Appendix: Ancient and Medieval Teachings about Conversion to Judaism

Why was the Torah given to us in the wilderness? Because just as the wilderness is accessible to anyone, so is the Torah accessible to anyone.

Tanchuma, V'yakhel, No. 8

God says to us, "As I welcomed Jethro the Midianite in the wilderness of Sinai, so must you welcome anyone who comes to you to join your people."

Yalkot Shim'oni, Yitro, No. 268

The Holy Blessed One does not favor any one person over another, but receives all; the gates are always open, and anyone who wishes to enter may do so.

Sh'mot Rabbah 19:4

1. If someone who is not Jewish comes before us and requests to become Jewish, we must welcome them with open arms (*Mechilta* on Exodus 18:6). We must neither dissuade them nor encourage them (*Midrash Rut Rabati* 2:17), but ask them: "What did you see to make such a choice? Do you not know we are a people that has been brutalized and downtrodden and unpopular, and our ways

are very different from the ways of the rest of the world?"
We do this in order to try their conviction (Babylonian
Talmud, *Gerim* 1:5), for a person must convert only by
personal choice, not under duress or for an ulterior
motive (Babylonian Talmud, *Gerim* 1:1 and 7; *Yevamot*
47a).

2. In cases where the convert is romantically involved with a
Jew, distinction needs to be made between someone who
is asking to convert to please his or her partner and someone who is asking to convert because it is something he
or she wants to do, the relationship notwithstanding. In
the second instance, although the convert is romantically
involved with a Jew, we accept the convert (Babylonian
Talmud, *Menachot* 44a). However, according to the
Jerusalem Talmud, even if someone requests conversion
because of romantic involvement with a Jew or for any
other motif of personal advantage, we must not repel the
convert, but must welcome him or her openly and warmly
(*Kidushin* 36a).

3. If after the tribunal's attempt at "dissuasion" the convert
says: "Even so, I am not worthy," we accept the convert
without further ado and immerse him or her partially in
living waters (Babylonian Talmud, *Gerim* 1:3). We then
share with the convert several key concepts of Judaism,
a few heavy ones and a few light ones, primarily about
the oneness of God, the wrongness of idolatry, and the
importance of charity to the poor (Babylonian Talmud,
Gerim 1:3 and *Yevamot* 47b). But we do not overwhelm
the convert with too many teachings or burden him or her
with too many lessons (Babylonian Talmud, *Yevamot*
47b). The convert then immerses, and the tribunal welcomes him or her into the Jewish people with words
of praise and encouragement (Babylonian Talmud, *Gerim*
1:5).

4. If the convert is a woman, we immerse her in living waters;
and if the convert a man, we circumcise him first, and

then—after he has completely healed—immerse him in living waters. However, if there is fear of infection by doing it in this order, the order may be reversed and immersion may take place first and then circumcision (Isserles [*Rama*] on Karo's *Shulchan Aruch, Yorah De'ah* 268:1).

5. If the male convert was already circumcised prior to his conversion, according to the ruling of Shammai (first century B.C.E.), a ritual "letting of blood" is performed with a tiny incision on the penis, and, according to Hillel, no blood-letting is necessary (Babylonian Talmud, *Shabat* 135a and *Gerim* 2:2). If he has a damaged or severed penis, the requirement of circumcision for a male convert is waived altogether, and he requires only immersion (Karo's *Shulchan Aruch, Yorah De'ah* 268:1).

6. A male convert who has been immersed but not circumcised, or circumcised but not immersed, is a convert (Babylonian Talmud, *Yevamot* 46a and *Gerim* 1:6; see *Nachalat Yaakov* commentary).

7. The tribunal of acceptance should be composed of three Jews learned in the laws of conversion (Babylonian Talmud, *Yevamot* 46b). If there were only two, the conversion is still valid (Babylonian Talmud, *Yevamot* 47b). After the fact, however, even a single witness is acceptable (Babylonian Talmud, *Yevamot* 47a—*Tosefot* [*yesh*]).

8. In the case of immersion for a female convert, a female tribunal observes the immersion (Babylonian Talmud, *Yevamot* 47b), and a male tribunal performs the ceremony from behind a partition (Karo's *Shulchan Aruch, Yoreh De'ah* 268:2). In either case, the woman enters the water until it covers her shoulders while the tribunal addresses her; and in the case of a male tribunal, the men turn away when she is done with her immersion and about to emerge (Karo's *Shulchan Aruch, Yoreh De'ah* 268:2).

9. If need be, immersion may take place in loose clothing (Karo's *Shulchan Aruch, Yoreh De'ah* 198:46).

10. The tribunal then repeats the question as to why the convert wants to convert. Again, the tribunal shares several teachings of the Torah that reflect the essence of Judaism, such as the belief in one God, and the Judaic ways of benevolence (Babylonian Talmud, *Yevamot* 47b). Again, we do not overwhelm the convert with too many teachings. When the convert feels ready to immerse, the tribunal recites the following: "Source of blessing are You, Wellspring of the Universe. In performing Your will we bring more sanctity into the world, and it is Your will that we immerse those not of our people who wish to become as we" (Karo's *Shulchan Aruch, Yoreh De'ah* 268:5). [It is customary for the convert to then proclaim the oneness of God: the *Shema*.]

11. [The convert then immerses at least once. Custom is to immerse thrice: the first time as a shifting from his or her previous spiritual path as his or her primary path; the second time as creating for himself or herself a neutral space, from which newness can develop; the third time as a rebirth into his or her new primary path.] The convert is then welcomed and received with joy and celebration by those present (Babylonian Talmud, *Gerim* 1:5).

12. Someone who comes to a Jewish community and declares: "I was not converted properly"—if they have children, we say: "You can disqualify yourself, but you cannot disqualify your children." The children are then considered Jewish, but the parent must undergo immersion (Babylonian Talmud, *Yevamot* 47a).

13. Someone who comes to a Jewish community and declares: "I was once not Jewish and then I converted"— they are believed (Maimonides in *Mishnah Torah, Hilchot Isurei Bi'ah* 13:10; Karo's *Shulchan Aruch, Yoreh De'ah* 268:10).

14. Someone who comes to a Jewish community and de-

clares: "I am a Jew"—they are believed (Babylonian Talmud, *Pesachim* 3b).

15. If someone without proof or declaration of his or her conversion is seen observing Jewish practice and living a full
Jewish life, he or she is to be considered as an authentic
convert to Judaism, the lack of proof or witnesses notwithstanding (*Tur, Yoreh De'ah*, No. 268; Maimonides
in *Mishnah Torah, Hilchot Isurei Bi'ah* 13:9; Karo's
Shulchan Aruch, Yoreh De'ah 268:10).

16. If someone not of the Jewish faith performs the ritual of
immersion in living waters with the intent to do so for
Jewish religious purposes, and there were Jewish witnesses to the fact, then, if he or she decides to convert,
that immersion can be considered retroactively as immersion for the sake of conversion and the conversion is valid,
even though the immersion was not performed with the
intent to convert (Babylonian Talmud, *Yevamot* 45b;
Shulchan Aruch, Yoreh De'ah 268:3).

17. A minor may be converted by a tribunal (Babylonian Talmud, *Ketuvot* 11a) at the request of the minor (*Shulchan
Aruch, Yoreh De'ah* 268:7) or along with the conversion
of the child's parents. However, once the child reaches
an age of maturity of reason and independent choice
making—on the average, around what would be the bat
or bar mitzvah period (twelve for a girl and thirteen for a
boy [Babylonian Talmud, *Kidushin* 16b])—the child must
be asked by a tribunal whether he or she still wishes to
remain Jewish. If the answer is no, the conversion is void
retroactively (Babylonian Talmud, *Ketuvot* 11a). This
procedure is not necessary if the child lives a fully active
Jewish life (*Shulchan Aruch, Yoreh De'ah* 268:8).

18. If a woman converts while she is pregnant, the child is
automatically Jewish (Babylonian Talmud, *Yevamot* 78a).

19. If someone converts before a tribunal of Jews who are not
qualified to perform conversion, after the fact, the conversion is still valid. The same applies to someone who

was not questioned about his or her convictions or motives by the tribunal and it turns out that the convert converted for ulterior motives, or to someone who was not taught the essentials of Judaism (Tur, *Yoreh De'ah*, No. 268, and Maimonides in *Mishnah Torah, Hilchot Isurei Bi'ah* 13:17).

7

The Judeo-Christian Myth

The term "Judeo-Christian" is both theologically and histori-cally an oxymoron. And the lumping together of Judaism, Christianity, and Islam as "the three major world religions" is disrespectful to the numerous other religions, many of which are older and no less "major," and with which Judaism has more in common than it has with Christianity or Islam. The concept "Judeo-Christian" is purely a Christian myth that is based on the fact that Jesus was of Jewish lineage and that his teachings emanated from the Judaic tradition. While this is true, it was not the Jewishness of Jesus' teachings that fashioned Christendom or Christian morality, but the venomous anti-Jewish diatribes and self-righteous theological absoluteness that make up the bulk of the New Testament *after* Jesus' time. How can Christendom embrace Judaism and call it a partner of any kind when it has, for over 1,500 years, encouraged the ran-dom persecution and slaughter of Jews and inspired the geno-cide of millions of others for their refusal to convert? Judaism, on the other hand, never demanded of others that they con-vert, nor did it consider non-Jews as second-class citizens to be exploited, persecuted, and raped. On the contrary, at its core, shamanically and philosophically, Judaism enjoys more in common with the Choctaw and the Dervishes of Shisti Sufism than with either Christianity or Islam. While it may share some scriptural writ with Islam and Christianity, it shares the concept of a compassionate, imminent, non-discriminatory Creator with the first two faiths mentioned. The fact that two or more religions claim their roots in common scriptural literature is a weak foundation for theological synonymity. Ironically, Judaism has been persecuted most predominantly by those very religions that trace their roots to the Jewish scriptures, while nonbiblical religions have left Jews to flourish in peace.

The terms "Judeo-Christian tradition" and "Judeo-Christian morality" are therefore wrong and misleading. They are a slap in the face of all the great Jewish teachers throughout history, whose responses to today's moral questions would in no way resemble those of the Vatican or of the Christian Right, and whose attitudes toward sin, physical pleasure, human dignity, and the earth differ vastly from those of Christianity. The Christian faith is entitled to its doctrines and world outlook, but it is not entitled to its claim of kinship with Judaism, neither theologically nor cosmologically. At least during its centuries of barbarism and savagery against Jews and other non-Christians, Christianity was authentic enough not to associate its theology with that of Judaism. In our current age of openness and ecumenism, it ought to remain at least as authentic and not attempt to heal its wrongs against Jewdom by claiming retroactive fellowship with Judaic theology and cosmology. This is only a further wronging of the Jewish heritage and its way of life by a religion that has already wronged it enough.

When Esau, who had compelled his brother Jacob into exile, ultimately matured and made peace with his brother, he offered to call them a team, to declare their two very different lifestyles a combined Esau-Jacobian ethic. Jacob, however, declined the offer—not of peace and restored brotherhood, but of Esau's attempt to lump their two conflicting mindsets into a single hyphenated blend (Genesis 34:12, 16, 17). Likewise, Jews welcome wholeheartedly Christianity's gesture of restoring fellowship and peacefulness between the two religions after centuries of hatred and tragedy. But, in the process, the theologically ignorant Jewish establishment has also allowed this reconciliation to create a superficial merger of these two very different spirit-paths into a single umbrella of religious and moral values that somehow got labeled Judeo-Christian. What is it about Christianity that Jews owe it any special kinship? Making peace even with old enemies is an essential ideal of ancient Judaic teachings, but going beyond that and artificially merging beliefs and ethics systems that bear no resemblance is no longer appeasement, but outright sycophantic. More than that, it is bootlicking a mindset that holds itself as superior to the indigenous peoples of the numerous countries it has conquered and whose cultures it has subdued in favor of its own. This mindset is about as un-Jewish as you can get. Judaism honors the sovereignty and culture and spirit-path of other peoples, and does not have room in its belief system for changing the way other peoples live unless there is violation of human rights.

Judaism is unrelated to any religion that claims that it is the one and only true religion and the sole ticket to heaven, and that if you don't join, you're damned. Judaism can have no degree of theological kinship with such a religion. Rather, it finds kinship only with spiritual paths that see themselves as among many possible ways to the Creator, and that honor the dignity and welfare of the human being regardless of religious persuasion or lack thereof; regardless of whether or not one is a potential candidate for conversion. You will not find a single Jewish missionary on a Navajo reservation, but you will find Jews working on the reservation as physicians and agricultural advisors.

It is a further misnomer to perceive of Judaism and Christianity as "having a lot in common" when they actually have very little in common. The teachings in the Christian gospels that "sound Jewish" *are* Jewish, not Christian. They were uttered by a man who was reared in the Judaic tradition, and who, like every other rabbi of his time, employed parables and exegetical interpretations of the Hebrew scriptures to support his teachings and inspire his followers. He died as did many Jewish teachers in his time, though the martyrdom of other rabbis of his era are recorded as having been far more gruesome and painful than his. Many of the greatest masters of Judaism were killed for empowering the people with their spiritual teachings, which the paranoid Roman empire feared would lead to rebellion. Rabbi Akiva's flesh was scraped slowly from his body, his final words being: "I have served God with all of my heart and with all of my being. But finally an opportunity has come for me to serve God with all of my soul, too" (Jerusalem Talmud, *Berachot* 9:7). Rabbi Hananiah ben Teradyon was rolled up inside a Torah scroll and slowly burned to death while a Roman soldier held a wet cloth to his heart to further slow his demise, and Rabbi Yehudah was dragged by his tongue through the streets of Jerusalem (Babylonian Talmud, *Avodah Zarah* 17b-18a). Rabbi Yosee was sawed and then crucified (*B'reishis Rabbah* 65:22). Rabbi Shimon ben Gamliel and Rabbi Yishmael were beheaded, each one pleading to the executioner that he be first "so that he not witness the death of his friend" (Babylonian Talmud, *Avot D'Rebbe Natan*, Ch. 38:5). In Christian history, Jesus was the only rabbi who suffered a painful death for his love of the people; in Jewish history, he was *one* of many, most of whom suffered far more than he did.

After all is said and done, those tens of thouands crucified in Judea were Jews. *In concentrating on the suffering of Jesus, with no regard to how widespread crucifixion was, the Gospels convey the impression that he was a rare victim of this brutal form of Roman execution.*
Lillian C. Freudmann in *Antisemitism in the New Testament*
(University Press of America, 1994), p. 26

Judaism has known all too well the tragedy of martyrdom, even into the twentieth century, when millions of Jewish children, men, and women encountered torture and death in the Holocaust that was far more heinous than how Jesus is reported to have suffered. Indeed, in Jesus' name, millions of people of many religions have died more tragic deaths than he did.

Jesus was a great man, one of many powerful rabbis who shook the almighty Roman government and challenged the politics of religion during the turbulent period the Middle East experienced some two thousand years ago. But, to Jewdom, he taught and accomplished nothing different from the teachings and accomplishments of other rabbis of that momentous period. Had it not been for Paul, who never met Jesus, Christianity would have gotten no further than any of the other Jewish sects of the time. Had it not been for Emperor Constantine of Rome, it never would have become as widespread as it did through forced conversions and military conquests.

For the most part, the first followers of Jesus were practicing Jews belonging primarily to the very sect that the New Testament writers so venomously vilified: the Pharisees. Theologically, however, the Pharisees could not have possibly sought his demise; historically, it could have been only the Romans, whose power-hold on Israel was at stake, and the Sadducean priests, whose power-hold on the Holy Temple was at stake. The Pharisees, however, were followers of the rabbis, whose sentiments on life and whose love of the people are clearly echoed in the teachings of Jesus. Not unlike Jesus, the Pharisaic rabbis, too, criticized those who called themselves Pharisees but who were hypocritical. Those unfamiliar with talmudic literature, however, read every mention of "Pharisee" in the New Testament as a blanket allusion to all the Jews in general and to all the Pharisees in particular.

Ironically, it was not the *life* of Jesus that forged Christianity, but his death. His life and teaching were purely Jewish in every dimension. In order to bring to fruition a *new* religion, a theology had to evolve *after* his life. Christianity, then, is founded not so much upon Jesus the man as upon Jesus the concept, and the resulting theology that was invented to support it. Christianity is, therefore, to be honored as the distinct religion that it is in its own right, not as a "daughter religion" of Judaism, or as the "next phase" of Judaism. The term "New Testament" was born out of the assumption that the Hebrew scriptures had become antiquated and obsolete and, therefore, the "Old" Testament. This is, and has always been, a slap in the face to Jews, for whom the so-called Old Testament is as alive now as it was three thousand years ago. The New Testament's Hebrew title, *B'rit Chadashah*, translates as "New Covenant," again a blatant dismissal of Judaism by a new religion that felt a dire need to justify itself by declaring itself to be a divinely ordained replacement of an already well- established older religion. This attitude that constituted the very seeding of Christianity is clearly apparent in Christian evangelism, which thrives on exalting itself by putting down everyone else; that thrives on deprecating the Jews and all other non-Christians, and sometimes *even Christians* who are of a different denomination.

It would be more earnest and authentic for Christianity to rip its Gospels out of the combined "Old Testament" and "New Testament" bibles that it has published for centuries and to instead call its Gospels "the Christian Scriptures" and claim its right to be what it is on its own merits. It would be more truthful for Christianity to simply declare that whereas its initial inspiration was Judaic, its prevailing creed is not; is uniquely and independently Christian, not *Judeo*-Christian, not the "next phase" of Judaism. Judaism's next phase is its own business. Judaism's scriptures, too, are for *Jews* to interpret, not bible-babbling evangelicals.

The mystery of another lies deep within him, and it cannot be observed from without. No man outside of Israel knows the mystery of Israel. And no man outside of Christianity knows the mystery of Christianity. But in their ignorance they can acknowledge each other in the mystery.

Martin Buber, *Die Stunde und die Erkenntnis*, p. 155

All the ecumenism of this age notwithstanding, Jews and Christians know very little about one another. Each presumes to know the other because they marry one another, share podiums at interfaith dialogues, and hold hands in solidarity marches and at peace demonstrations, causes whose promotion is not unique to either spirit-path, but is shared universally. The two are so caught up in the Judeo-Christian myth that they neglect to invite representatives of the Bah'ai faith or the Navajos, Hindus, and Australian Aborigines.

To most Jews, even those who attend the interfaith weddings of their children, the mention of "Jesus" remains an uncomfortable taboo, even though Jesus the persona is less Christian and more Jewish than anything else associated with the Church and its rites. It is ironic that the mention of "Jesus" is so revolting to many Jews, because of the centuries of atrocities committed in his name against the Jewish people, and that the mention of "Church" is not. It was, after all, not Jesus but the *Church* that has perpetuated anti-Jewish sentiment and violence over the past 1,700 years. But that is just an example of the ignorance that fills the moat between these two religious institutions. On the contrary, Jews ought to consider reclaiming Jesus the *Jew*, Jesus the *Pharisee*, Jesus the *Rabbi*, and realize—as should Christians realize—that Christianity did not begin *with* Jesus, but *after* Jesus.

Would it be Jewishly blasphemous to posit that leaving Jesus the man out of the Jewish tradition is tantamount to leaving out Rabbi Akiva or Rabbi Tarfon or any of the other great Jewish teachers of that age? It is my contention that Jesus the rabbi got torn away from the very heritage he loved, supported, and died for only because of the centuries of slaughter and persecution perpetrated against his own people in his name.

But that has nothing to do with Jesus the man; it has rather to do with Jesus the religion, a religion that evolved long after his tragic death, a religion that he would have found completely unfamiliar.

This is not much different from how the teachings of the revered Rabbi Antigonos of Socho inspired the far more "heretical" sect of the Sadducees. Christianity evolved out of what Paul did with the teachings of Jesus, and Sadduceeism evolved out of what Zadok and Boetus did with the teachings of Antigonos. And just as Antigonos was not deleted from Jewish religious history on account of the theology of his disciples, likewise ought Jesus not have been left out on account of the theology of *his* disciples. If Jesus actually lived, he lived and died as a Jew. No less than the ten rabbis of his era who were tortured and martyred by the Romans for defying their authority and teaching publicly the word of God, Jesus, too, belongs among our spirit-heroes, those who gave their lives rather than deprive the people of the spiritual nourishment they so desperately needed during those tumultous times.

Unlike Christianity, Judaism does not hold up the Bible as *the* beacon of light that shows us how to live morally and nicely: Indeed, believing in biblical writ never stopped anyone from murdering, raping, or abusing their kids and spouses. In fact, historically, more people have been slaughtered in the name of the "word" than by any other circumstance. The Jewish religion, which is based on the "Old Testament," challenged its scriptures when something in it felt wrong, felt contradictory to its conviction that God is compassionate and nondemanding and personal. The ancient rabbis struggled constantly with the discrepancy between God and religion (see *The Place Where You Are Standing Is Holy* by G. Winkler and L. Elior). To them, the most important will of a compassionate God would, in turn, have to be harmony and goodwill between people. "If we were to worship idols but exercise harmony between ourselves, God would not judge us for violating the commandment against idolatry" (*B'reishis Rabbah* 38.6).

The rabbis recognized that even "nonbelievers" can do the God will since the God will is more about benevolence than about religious worship. The Creator, Judaism believes, is not so insecure that the Creator will fall apart because someone down here doesn't believe in or glorify the Creator. Throughout Isaiah and the books of other prophets of the Jewish people, the teachers were constantly reminding the people that what is important to God is not so much the rituals as reaching out to the orphans and the hungry, and living in peacefulness.

Rightness is not a biblical invention. It resides deep within each of us, believers and nonbelievers alike. The Bible works only when we wrestle the word until it speaks to us, too, not only to the particular mortal prophets who shared what was uniquely *their* experience of the God word. Judaism does not believe that the Bible is the word of God; rather, as Rabbi Abraham Joshua Heschel put it, it believes that "the Bible is the Word of God AND man; a record of both revelation and response; the drama of covenant between God and man." This may be alien to a lot of Bible fans outside the Jewish faith because most non-Jews presume a knowledge of Jews and Judaism by way of the Bible, not realizing that the Bible is but the bones of what Judaism is all about. Its flesh, however, is composed of 3,500 years of wrestling with and processing the ever-continuing revelation into downhome earthly application. Therefore, when learned Jews read the sayings of Jesus as recorded in the Synoptic Gospels, they read nothing different from that with which they have been raised in their studies of the Talmud, the recorded teachings of the rabbis who lived before, during, and after the historic period of Jesus. From a Jewish perspective, then, Jesus was not rejecting or outmoding the Mosaic teachings (and he even says just that), but rather was doing what rabbis had been doing for centuries and would continue to do for centuries afterward: lending fresh interpretations to the scriptural text in ways that would continue to address the new age and circumstance of his own time; in ways that would stir the people to reexamine the form in which they were exercising their spiritual practice when that practice was becoming stoic and stale.

There isn't an iota of what Jesus is recorded as teaching that would in any way represent blasphemy or heresy to the Jewish tradition—not one iota. The Pharisees who challenged him represented but a single school among several other Pharisaic schools. They did not represent all of the rabbis of that time. The Talmud quotes various opinions on issues held by different rabbinic schools of thought. Unfortunately, the New-Testament writers chose to include only one of these schools, the one reflecting his opponents.

Once, when I conducted a Passover seder for a Catholic church in a small Colorado city, the local press quoted a participant's disappointment over the fact that the seder included no mention of Jesus. (Sort of like reading a book on golf and getting disappointed over the absence of any mention of soccer.) There is a real need for people of different faiths to learn how to "Other," how to truly honor someone and their beliefs for what they are, and to stop defining everything solely against the backdrop of their own belief system. Every December I am asked by well-meaning people whether I had a nice Christmas. When our daughter was born, we were asked when we were going to baptize her. They know I'm a rabbi. They know we're Jewish. The lady who was disappointed that I didn't mention Jesus knew I was Jewish and should then also have known that Jesus is no more or less a part of my belief system than any other first-century rabbi. Obviously, it wasn't a question of whether she knew this or not but more a question of whether she could separate my religion from her own and "Other" me. I honor that Jesus is the sum total of all that she believes, and I ask in turn that she and other Christians honor that I have a whole different belief system than theirs. And for Pete's sake, I tell people, stop calling our Bible "the old testament." Maybe it's old for some, but for my people it has for thousands of years remained a vibrant, dynamic and ever-youthful scripture.

Bible-believing Christians may go into shock at the suggestion that the Bible is not the absolute determinant of how to live in the world, and that God's word as recorded by the prophets can be challenged when it seems wrongly received or transmitted. As a rabbi, however, I am speaking from the 3,500–year-old theology that grew out of my people's unique relationship with its own revelations. Judaism honors that there are many paths to engaging the Creator in relationship. We believe that Black Elk's revelation for the Oglala Sioux atop Harney Peak is no less sacred than Moses' revelation atop Mount Sinai for the Hebrews. As one first-century rabbi put it: "Greater is the giving of rain than the revelation to Moses at Sinai. For the revelation on Mount Sinai was sent but to a single people, whereas rain is sent to all creatures, to all peoples and to the birds of the sky and the animals of the fields" (*Midrash Tehilim*, Ch. 117).

What follows, then, is but a sampling of the parallels of the ancient Judaic teachings and those attributed to Jesus in the Synoptic Gospels of the "New Testament." We shall refer to the Hebrew Scriptures, the so-called "Old Testament," as *Tenach*, a Hebrew acronym for *Torah* (Genesis through Deuteronomy), *Nevi'im* (Joshua through Malachi), and *Ketuvim* (Psalms through Chronicles, Esther, Song of Songs, and so on). These examples are presented to demonstrate that teachings in so-called Judeo-Christian theology parallel one another not because they are "similar," but because they were taken straight out of the Jewish tradition. Jesus was Jewish. What he taught was Jewish. To take his teachings and call them anything but Jewish is plagiarism, not parallelism. The fact that Christianity emerged *because* of Jesus does not render his teachings any less Jewish or any more Christian.

A BRIEF SAMPLING OF PARALLELS

Synoptic Gospels	Jewish Sources
Do not be called Rabbi. [Matthew 23:8]	Despise the position of Rabbi. [Babylonian Talmud, *Avot* 1:10]
If someone smites you on the cheek, turn to him the other also. [Matthew 5:39]	Let him give his cheek to him who smites him. [*Tenach*, Lamentations 3:30] I gave my back to the smiters and my cheeks to them that plucked off the hair. [*Tenach*, Isaiah 50:6]
Love your enemy. [Matthew 5:43]	Help your enemy with his load. [*Tenach*, Exodus 23:45] If your enemy is hungry, give him bread; if he be thirsty, give him water [*Tenach*, Proverbs 25:21], and God shall bring harmony between you. [*Kohelet Rabbah* 25:21] Forgive the insults of others. [Babylonian Talmud, *Derech Eretz Zutta* 6:3] He who hears himself cursed and is silent, is a partner with God Who is silent though His holy name is blasphemed. [*Midrash Tehilim* on Psalms 86:1] Forgive those who insult you. [Babylonian Talmud, *Avot D'Rebbe Natan* 67a]

Mar Zutra used to say: "If anyone hurt me, he is forgiven."

[Babylonian Talmud, *Megilah* 28a]

They who are insulted but insult not back; who hear themselves reproached but answer not; who serve out of love and rejoice in their affliction—of them is it written in Scripture: "They that love God are as the going forth of the sun in its might" [*Tenach*, Judges 6:31]

[Babylonian Talmud, *Yoma* 23a, *Gitin* 36b, *Shabat* 88b]

The Son of Man is coming at an hour when you do not expect him.

[Matthew 24:44]

Three things come upon a man when he does not expect them: a lost item, the sting of a scorpion, and the Messiah.

[Babylonian Talmud, *Sanhedrin* 97a]

For to everyone who has, even more shall be given.

[Matthew 25:29]

Give to a wise man, and he will be yet wiser.

[*Tenach*, Proverbs 9:9]

A filled vessel can contain; an empty vessel cannot contain.

[Babylonian Talmud, *Berachot* 40a]

Parable in which the king [God] expresses to the people that they can please the king by pleasing one another.

[Matthew 25:40]

One who is pleasing unto other people is pleasing unto God.

[Babylonian Talmud, *Avot* 3:3]

By not doing for others, you betray God.

[Matthew 25:45]

One who neglects deeds of lovingkindness betrays God.

[*Kohelet Rabbah* 7:4]

One who betrays his fellow, it is as if be has betrayed God.

[Babylonian Talmud, *Tosefta Sh'vuot*, Ch. 3]

Insulting someone is like murder.

[Matthew 5:21–22]

One who shames the face of his fellow, it is as if he has murdered him.

[Babylonian Talmud, *Bava Mezia* 58b]

The sin of causeless hatred is akin to the sins of idolatry, adultery, and murder.

[Babylonian Talmud, *Yoma* 9b]

Gazing lustfully upon a married woman is akin to adultery.

[Matthew 5:28]

One who gazes lustfully upon the small finger of a married woman, it is as if he has committed adultery with her.

[Babylonian Talmud, *Kallah*, Ch. 1]

One can commit adultery not only with one's body, but even with one's eyes.

[*Vayikra Rabbah*, Ch. 23]

God causes it to rain for the wicked as well as for the righteous.

[Matthew 5:45]

God causes it to rain for the wicked as well as for the righteous.

[Babylonian Talmud, *Taanit* 7a]

Don't do good deeds to be noticed.

[Matthew 6:1]

Don't do good deeds to be noticed.

[Babylonian Talmud, *Berachot* 17b]

Give alms to the poor in
secret; let your left hand not
know what your right hand
does.

[Matthew 6:3]

He who gives alms in secret is
greater than Moses.

[Babylonian Talmud,
Bava Batra 9b]

The greatest form of charity is
when you give and do not
know to whom you give, and
the recipient takes and does
not know from whom he
takes.

[Babylonian Talmud,
Bava Batra 10b]

Do not lay up for yourselves
treasures upon the earth,
where moths and rust destroy,
and thieves break in and steal.
But lay up your treasures in
heaven, where neither moth
nor rust destroy, and where
thieves do not break in or
steal.

[Matthew 6:19–20]

It happened that Manobaz had
squandered his father's wealth
to charity. His brothers ad-
monished him: "Your father
gathered treasure, and you
wasted it all!" He replied: "My
father laid up treasure where
human hands control it; I laid
it up where no hands control
it. My father laid up a treasure
of money; I laid up a treasure
of souls. My father laid up
treasure for this world; I laid
up treasure for the heavenly
world."

[Jerusalem Talmud, *Pe'ah* 15b]

Do not elongate your prayers.

[Matthew 6:7]

For God is in heaven and you
are upon the Earth; therefore
let your words be few.

[*Tenach*, Ecclesiastes 5:2]

One who prays too intensely
and too lengthily brings on
himself heartache.

[Babylonian Talmud, *Berachot* 55a]

The prayers of the righteous are brief.

[*Mechilta, B'shalakh*]

God knows of your needs even before you pray for them.

[Matthew 6:8]

And it shall be that even before they call, that I [God] will answer.

[*Tenach*, Isaiah 65:24]

If any part of your body causes you to sin, cut it off, for it is much better to lose a limb than for your whole body to go to Hell.

[Matthew 5:29–30]

Rabbi Tarfon said, "Better that one's belly burst than one should go down into the pit of destruction."

[Babylonian Talmud, *Niddah* 13b]

Nahum of Gamzu was delivering a gift to his father-in-law's house when he was stopped by a man who was covered with boils, who said, "Give me something to eat." He replied, "I will give you something when I return." When he came back, the man was dead. He said, "May my eyes that saw you when you were in need, be blinded; may my hands which did not reach out to give to you, be broken; may my feet which did not hasten to your care, be broken." And thus it happened accordingly.

[Jerusalem Talmud, *Pe'ah* 21b]

Be perfect as is your Father in heaven.

[Matthew 5:48]

As God is, so shall you be: As God is merciful, so shall you, too, be merciful.

[*Sifri, Ekev* No. 49]

Do not worry about where your food will come from tomorrow, or your drink.
[Matthew 6:25–31]

He who has what to eat today, and says, "What shall I eat on the morrow?" has little faith.
[Babylonian Talmud, *Sotah* 48b]

Each day has enough of its own troubles.
[Matthew 6:34]

Each day has enough of its own troubles.
[Babylonian Talmud, *Berachot* 9b]

Do not judge, lest you be judged. . . . By your standard of measure are you measured.
[Matthew 7:1–2]

By a person's standard of measure, is he, too, measured.
[Babylonian Talmud, *Mishnah Sotah* 1:7]

Do not judge your fellow until you have been in his place.
[Babylonian Talmud, *Avot* 2:14]

Do not be a judge of others, for there is no judge but the One [God].
[Babylonian Talmud, *Avot* 4:10]

How you judge others, does God judge you.
[Babylonian Talmud, *Shabat* 127b]

Make no vows at all . . . but let your Yes be Yes, and your No be No.
[Matthew 5:34–37]

He who makes a vow, even if he fulfills it, is called sinner.
[Babylonian Talmud, *Nedarim* 77a]

A righteous yes is Yes; a righteous no is No.
[Babylonian Talmud, *Bava Batra* 49b]

Yes is like an oath; No is like an oath.

> [Babylonian Talmud, *Sh'vuot* 36a]

Everyone who asks shall receive.

> [Matthew 7:8]

Open your mouth and I shall fill it.

> [*Tenach*, Psalms 81:11]

. . . Who seeks shall find.

> [Matthew 7:8]

Seek and you shall find.

> [*Tenach*, Proverbs 8:17; Jeremiah 29:13]

One who says to you, "I have searched and I have found," believe him.

> [Babylonian Talmud, *Megilah* 6b]

Relate to others as you would have others relate to you—is the meaning of the Torah and the Books of the Prophets.

> [Matthew 7:12]

What is hateful to you, do it not unto others—this is the entire Torah, and the rest is commentary.

> [Babylonian Talmud, *Shabat* 31a]

The harvest is plentiful, the workers are few.

> [Matthew 9:37]

The day is short, the work is great, and the workers are lazy, and the reward is great.

> [Babylonian Talmud, *Avot* 2:2]

Wisdom was given to the babes.

> [Matthew 11:25]

Prophecy has been taken from the wise and given to the babes.

> [Babylonian Talmud, *Baba Batra* 12b]

The Sabbath was made for man, not man for the Sabbath.

> [Mark 2:27]

The Sabbath was given into your hands, and you were not given into her hands.

> [Babylonian Talmud, *Yoma* 85b]

One may trespass one Sabbath in order to observe many more Sabbaths.

[Babylonian Talmud, *Yoma* 85b]

Jesus is challenged for "faith healing" on the Sabbath.

[Mark 3:2–4]

The rabbinic school of Shammai forbade faith healing on the Sabbath. The school of Rabbi Hillel permitted it.

[Babylonian Talmud, *Tosefta Shabat* 7:14]

Jesus is challenged for permitting a formerly paralyzed man, whom he had just healed on the Sabbath, to carry his bed in the streets. The issue was not carrying—since carrying is permitted on the Sabbath in a walled city—but handling something on the Sabbath that was not needed, like the bed, for which the healed man no longer had an immediate need.

[John, Ch. 5]

The school of Rabbi Shammai forbade the handling of an item on the Sabbath for which there was no need, and might have challenged the action of Jesus. The school of Rabbi Hillel permitted the handling of an item for which there was no need on the Sabbath, if the item became not needed after the Sabbath had already begun; and would have agreed with Jesus.

[Babylonian Talmud, *Betzah* 26b]

There will be no marital union in the world to come.

[Matthew 22:30]

There will be no marital union in the world to come.

[Babylonian Talmud, *Berachot* 17a]

Jesus opposes rabbis who insist on tithing even of plants grown only for their seeds.

[Matthew 23:23]

Tithing from plants grown only for their seeds was a ruling held exclusively by the school of Rabbi Shammai, but not by that of Rabbi Hillel.

[Babylonian Talmud, *Ma'asrot* 4:5–6]

One who blasphemes against God is not forgiven.
[Mark 3:29]

One who profanes the heavenly name has no forgiveness but through death.
[Babylonian Talmud, *Avot D'Rebbe Natan* 29:8]

{There is however, another teaching that when one blasphemes the name of God, God follows that person through the streets, waiting patiently for him to repent—return.
[*P'sikta D'Rav Kahana* 17:25]}

Jesus opposes rabbis who permit people to pledge all they own to the Temple.
[Matthew 15:5–6]

Only the school of Rabbi Shammai permitted this and also ruled that one could not be released from such vows. The school of Rabbi Hillel was in opposition to this ruling and would have agreed with Jesus.
[Babylonian Talmud, *Shabat* 127b, and *Nazir* 9a]

Whoever wishes to save his life [in this world], shall lose it [in the world to come], and whoever wishes to lose his life [in this world], shall save it [in the world to come].
[Mark 8:35]

Alexander the Great asked of the rabbis, "If one wishes to live [in the world to come], what should he do?" They replied, "He should die [in this world]." He asked, "And if one wishes to die [in the world to come], what should he do?" They replied, "He should live [in this world]."
[Babylonian Talmud, *Tamid* 32a]

Forgive others and God shall forgive you. If you do not forgive others, then shall God not forgive you.

[Matthew 6:14–15]

Only if you forgive others will God forgive you.

[Babylonian Talmud, *Rosh Hashanah* 17a]

Forgive your fellow's sin against you, and your sins against God shall be forgiven when you pray.

[Apocrypha, Ben Sira in Ecclesiasticus 28:25]

One who is merciful toward others, God will be merciful toward him.

[Babylonian Talmud, *Shabat* 151b]

If you bring an offering to the altar and there is conflict between you and your friend, then first make peace with your friend, and then bring your offering.

[Matthew 5:23–24]

Yom Kippur atones for all sins, but first you must reconcile your conflict with others.

[Babylonian Talmud, *Yoma* 85b]

Of the greatest command-ments is "Love your fellow as yourself [Leviticus 19:18]"

[Mark 12:31]

Said Rabbi Akiva, "And you shall love your fellow as your-self [*Tenach*, Leviticus 19:18]—this is the greatest principle in the Torah."

[*Torat Kohanim* on *Tenach*, Leviticus 19:18, and Jerusalem Talmud, *Nedarim* 9:4]

A widow who gave one cent to the treasury of the Temple, because it was all she had, was considered to have given more than all of the other contributors.

[Mark 12:42–43]

A woman bought a handful of flour for an offering, and the priest rejected it, admonishing her: "What kind of an offering is that!" In a dream that night, the priest was told: "Despise

her not, but consider it as if
she had brought herself as an
offering!"

[*Vayikra Rabbah* 3:5]

And if one cannot afford to
bring a bullock as an offering
one can bring two turtledoves,
and if one cannot afford two
turtledoves, one can bring an
ephah [the smallest measure]
of flour.

[*Tenach*, Leviticus 5:6–11]

[It matters not] whether one
does a lot, or a little, as long as
one's intention is directed
toward heaven.

[Babylonian Talmud,
Berachot 5b]

And why do you notice the
splinter that is in your
brother's eye, but consider not
the beam that is in your own
eye? . . . Hypocrite! First cast
out the beam that is in your
eye and then shall you see
clearly to cast out the splinter
that is in your brother's eye.

[Matthew 7:3–5]

He who condemns others,
sees in them his own faults.

[Babylonian Talmud,
Kidushin 70a]

Do not rebuke your fellow with
your own blemish.

[Babylonian Talmud,
Bava Mezia 59a]

[On the other hand . . .] Rabbi
Tarfon said, "I wonder if there
be anyone in this era who will
allow himself to be reproved. If
someone says to another,
'Cast out the speck that is in
your eye!' he will retort, 'Cast
first out the beam that is in
your own eye!'"

[Babylonian Talmud,
Er'chin 16b]

One who hears but does not do is likened to a building with no foundation, and when the stream hit it, it was destroyed.
[Luke 6:49]

One whose knowledge exceeds his actions, is likened to a tree with many branches but few roots, and when a wind comes along, it is destroyed.
[Babylonian Talmud, *Avot* 3:17]

One who studies Torah but does not do good deeds is likened to one who builds with a foundation of straw, so that even a minor flow of water will destroy it.
[Babylonian Talmud, *Avot D'Rebbe Natan* 24:1]

Those who know not God's will are less liable.
[Luke 12:48]

Those raised without knowledge of God's will are not held accountable for trespassing the commandmends.
[Babylonian Talmud, *Shabat* 68b]

One who transgresses owing to circumstances beyond his control is not liable.
[Babylonian Talmud, *Nedarim* 26a]

He who exalts himself shall be humbled; he who humbles himself shall be exalted.
[Luke 14:11]

One who pursues greatness, it shall flee from him; one who flees from greatness, it shall pursue him.
[*Tanchuma, Vayikra,* par. 3]

Jesus is criticized for reaching out to sinners, and responds with a parable and teaching about the importance of doing so.

[Luke, Chapter 15]

The critics were probably of the school of Shammai, which taught, "One should not teach but those who are wise, humble, and of good parentage," while the school of Hillel held as did Jesus.

[Babylonian Talmud, *Avot D'Rebbe Natan* 3:1]

When I say unto the wicked, "O wicked man, you shall surely die," and you do not speak to warn the wicked from his ways, then that wicked man shall die in his iniquity, but his blood will I require of your hand."

[*Tenach*, Ezekiel 33:7]

There is joy in heaven when one repents.

[Luke 15:10]

In the place where penitents stand, even those who are flawless cannot stand.

[Babylonian Talmud, *Berachot* 34b]

The gates of prayer are sometimes open, and sometimes shut, but the gates of repentance are always open.

[*Devarim Rabbah* 2:7]

Rabbi Yaakov taught, "More endearing [to God] is one moment of sincere penance in this world than an eternity in the world to come."

[Babylonian Talmud, *Avot* 4:17]

So great is repentance that if a man so much as contemplates it in his heart, his intention rises above and beyond all the spheres of the universe unto the very throne of God.

[Babylonian Talmud,
Avot 4:17]

The Holy Blessed One waits more eagerly for sinners to repent than does a woman for her husband, or a father for his son.

[*Tanna D'bei Eliyahu
Rabbah* 31:5]

Parable of the father who went out to meet his recalcitrant son.

[Luke 15:11–20]

A king had a son who sinned against his father and fled as far as a hundred days' distance. His friends begged him to return to his father. He replied, "I cannot, for my shame is too great." When his father heard about this he sent to him a message: "Take but one step toward me, and I shall meet you the rest of the way."

[*Pesikta Rabbati* 184b]

Says the Holy Blessed One, "If you are too ashamed to return unto Me, then I will take the first step and return unto you."

(*Pesikta Rabbati*, 184a)

It is easier for a camel to go through the eye of a needle than for a rich man to enter the kingdom of God.

[Matthew 19:24]

Says God, "Open one door for penance as small as the eye of a needle, and I shall open for you doors wide enough for caravans of coaches and wagons."

[*Shir Hashirim Rabbah* 5:3]

He who is free of sin cast the first stone.

[John 8:7]

Says God, "I will not punish your adulterous daughters, for you, too, commit harlotry."

[*Tenach*, Hosea 4:14]

Rabbi Shimon ben Shetakh said, "If I have sinned, then those who testify against me had better be free of sin themselves."

[*Midrash Asseret HaDibrot*, No. 9]

Let every judge see himself as standing at the gates of Hell [on account of his own sins] before judging others.

[Babylonian Talmud, *Yevamot* 109b]

If the husband is not free of sin, then his accusations of adultery against his wife are rendered inconsequential.

[Babylonian Talmud, *Sotah* 47b]

Before you chastise others, first chastise yourself.

[Babylonian Talmud, *Baba Batra* 60b]

Jesus calls his opponents "children of Satan."
[John 8:44]

Some rabbis called the disciples of Shammai "firstborn of Satan."
[Babylonian Talmud, *Yevamot* 16a]

Jesus scolds the Pharisees throughout the Gospels, especially in Matthew 23.

The rabbis recognized that not all "Pharisees" were kosher. "There are seven types of Pharisee, the Pharisee who looks over his shoulder to see whether anyone is observing the good deed he is about to perform; the Pharisee who keeps a record of every good deed he does; the Pharisee who adds a good deed to his day to compensate for the lack of good deeds for the previous days; the Pharisee who constantly asks 'What is my duty now?'; the Pharisee who [is so cautious about not looking at women that he squints his eyes and] bumps into walls until his head bleeds; the Pharisee who serves God out of fear; and the Pharisee who serves God out of love. Which is the preferred type? The one who serves God out of love."
[Babylonian Talmud, *Sotah* 22b (bracketed portion is Rashi's commentary)]

Do what [the Pharisees] bid you, but not what they themselves do, for they say and do not.

[Matthew 23:3]

Pleasant are the words of those who practice them; disgraceful are those who require what is good but do not themselves practice it.

[Babylonian Talmud, *Hagigah* 14a, and *Yevamot* 63b]

They [the Pharisees] take advantage of widows and rob them of their homes.

[Mark 12:40]

What is the "plague Pharisee"? He who gives advice to orphans in order to benefit from the widow.

[Jerusalem Talmud, *Sotah* 3:4]

Said King Yannai to his wife: "Fear not the Pharisees or they that are not Pharisees, but fear rather the hypocrites who imitate the Pharisees."

[Babylonian Talmud, *Sotah* 22b]

The meek shall inherit the earth.

[Matthew 5:5]

The meek shall inherit the earth.

[*Tenach*, Psalms 37:11]

Jesus said, "Who sins against me, sins against God."

[John 5:23]

Whoever sins against the faithful shepherd sins against God.

[*Midrash Mekhilta*, *B'shalakh*, No. 6]

Our Father Who art in heaven, hallowed be Thy name. . . .

[Matthew 6:9]

My Father Who art in heaven, be Thy great name blessed.

[*Tanna D'bei Eliyahi*, pp. 83 and 89 of Friedmann/ Vienna edition]

"Our Father Who art in heaven"
is used throughout the Talmud.
[Babylonian Talmud, *Yoma*
85b, *Sotah* 49b, *Avot* 5:20;
Midrash Sifri, *Kedoshim* [end];
Vayikra Rabbah, Ch. 32;
Midrash Tehilim on Psalms 12:5]

Thy kingdom come . . .
         [Matthew 6:10]

May God's Kingdom be established during the days of your
life. . . .
    [second line of the *Kaddish*
prayer]

Thy will be done, on Earth as
it is in heaven. Give us this day
our daily bread. . . .
       [Matthew 6:10–11]

Do Thy will above and give
comfort to those below, and to
everyone his need.
    [Babylonian Talmud, *Berachot*
29b, and *Tosefta Berachot* 3:11]

And forgive us our trespasses
as we forgive those who
trespass against us. . . .
        [Matthew 6:12]

One who is merciful toward
others, God will be merciful
toward them.
    [Babylonian Talmud,
Shabat 151b]

Only if you forgive others will
God forgive you.
    [Babylonian Talmud,
Rosh Hashanah 17a]

And lead us not into temptation, but deliver us from the
evil one. . . .
        [Matthew 6:13]

Bring me not into temptation,
and lead me away from iniquity . . . and save me from the
evil one. . . .
    [Babylonian Talmud,
Berachot 80b]

For Thine is the kingdom and
the power, and the glory,
forever and ever.
        [Matthew 6:13]

For Thine, O Lord, is the
greatness and the power and
the glory and the victory and
the majesty. . . .
    [*Tenach*, 1 Chronicles 29:10]

The Jewish scriptures, as well as the sacred literature of the rabbis who lived before, during, and after Jesus, are full of accounts of people performing miracles. Judaism does not discount the miracles that Jesus performed, but neither does it consider them any different from those performed by so many others who were recorded as healing by faith (e.g., 1 Kings 13:6, Babylonian Talmud, *Berachot* 5a); miraculously duplicating food supplies (e.g., 2 Kings 4:1–7 and 42–44); ascending to the heavens alive (e.g., Genesis 5:24, 2 Kings 2:11; *Midrash Heichalot Rabati*, Babylonian Talmud, *Kalah* [end]); resurrection (1 Kings 17:21–22 and 2 Kings 4:34; Babylonian Talmud, *Shabat* 152b; Jerusalem Talmud, *D'mai* 1:3 [3b]); and so on. Such miracles and unearthly feats were experienced long before the advent of Christianity in the sacred traditions not only of Judaism but also of the Choctaw, the Buddhists, and so on. The following two examples from the Talmud represent but a single teacher of the second century, Rabbi Pinchas ben Ya'ir:

[In the second century] there was a pious man who busied himself digging wells and cisterns on behalf of passing travelers. One day, his daughter, who was about to be married, drowned in a river. Everyone came to console the man but he would not be soothed. Then came Rabbi Pinchas ben Ya'ir, but the man refused to receive his consolation, too. When the attendants explained to Rabbi Pinchas the piety of the man and the tragedy of what had befallen him, the rabbi said: "Is it so that he who has honored his Creator with water should become afflicted through water?" Soon thereafter, a tumult erupted in the village and word spread that the man's daughter was seen emerging from the river. . . . Some say that an angel appeared to her in the water and resurrected her, and that the appearance of the angel was like that of Rabbi Pinchas ben Ya'ir.

Jerusalem Talmud, *D'mai* 1:3 [3b]

Once Rabbi Pinchas ben Ya'ir was journeying with his disciples when they came to the G'nai River, which had become too swollen to cross. Said he: "O river, why do you keep me from going to the house of study?" The waters instantly divided and he crossed to the other side. His disciples observed in amazement and then called to him, saying: "May we, too, pass over?" Said he: "Any among you who has never insulted another may cross over unharmed."

Jerusalem Talmud, D'mai 1:3 [3b]

Judeo-Christianity is a myth. We are separate religions with separate theologies and cosmologies. What Jesus taught is distinctly Jewish. The miraculous feats he performed were commonplace. How he lived and how he died was not much different from how other Jewish teachers of his era lived and died. What later disciples did with his life and teachings is distinctly Christian. It is, therefore, important that when a Jewish person speaks Bible talk, the speaker be heard as a Jewish person speaking from the Jewish understanding of the Jewish Bible; that the speaker not be judged by how Christians understand the Bible.

If we are going to do the healing that is so needed between Christians and Jews, we are going to have to do some serious homework on this issue. Jews are going to have to start examining the Synoptic Gospels of the Christian scriptures to realize how Jewish Jesus really was, and Christians are going to have to start looking at both the Hebrew scriptures and the Talmud to realize the same.

8

Capital Punishment

A court that has executed someone as infrequently as once in seven years is a murderous court; others say, even once in seventy years.

Babylonian Talmud, *Makot* 7a

In the ancient Judaic teachings about life, emphasis is placed primarily on the sanctity of life. Therefore, it was permitted to withhold life-sustaining medicines or equipment from a patient who was dying in immense anguish. Life for the sake of life itself does not hold as much respect in Judaism as does the sacredness of life, the quality of life. Therefore, abortion laws in the Judaic tradition, especially in ancient times, were quite liberal in situations where the woman's emotional or physical health was in danger. Contraception laws were even more liberal and required no qualifications. No woman was obligated to bear children, since childbearing may endanger one's life, and any woman who so chose could drink the *kos ikrin*, an ancient potion of herbs that caused sterilization (Babylonian Talmud, *Yevamot* 65b). On the other extreme, sanctity of life also means that "if the enemies of Israel come and say: 'Surrender one of you to us to be killed and we will spare all of you,' we surrender no one, for no one can say 'My blood is more red than yours'" (Babylonian Talmud, *Pesachim* 25b). Unfortunately, during the Holocaust, many Jewish communal leaders violated this principle and surrendered hundreds in return for the promise that thousands would be spared. In the end, they traded thousands for tens of thousands, and ultimately no one was spared as the Nazi death machine overran all "deals" and agreements.

The principle of "sanctity of life" extends deeply into the severe restrictions governing ancient Judaic laws concerning capital punishment. It took a minimum consensus of twenty-three judges and a maximum of seventy-one to actually send someone to death. Jewish jurisprudence did not have room for lawyers, only uninvolved judges whose job it was to interrogate witnesses individually, both those who claimed to have witnessed the crime and those in defense of the accused. If the witnesses presented contradicting or differing stories, or if one claimed to have witnessed the crime at a time when the sun was situated significantly distant from its position during the time claimed by the other, they both were disqualified (Babylonian Talmud, *Sanhedrin* 5:3). A minimum of two witnesses was required for capital cases (Deuteronomy 17:6 and 19:15), and those witnesses who were deemed by the court as living dishonestly or immorally were also disqualified (Babylonian Talmud, *Sanhedrin* 3:3).

The proceedings for a capital crime would begin in a semicircle with a minimum of twenty-three judges, and if they could not all agree on a verdict, two more judges were added, and then another two, and another, up to seventy-one (Babylonian Talmud, *Sanhedrin* 5:5). Each time the court was in conflict about the guilt of the accused, the judges would split into pairs to discuss the case, "and they would abstain from eating excessively and from drinking wine, and they would deliberate all night, rise early in the morning, and return to the court to present their opinions." If the decision of "guilty" was reached, they would suspend the verdict yet another day and deliberate during the entire period until then, again abstaining from excessive eating and from intoxicating beverages while they reexamined their decision (Babylonian Talmud, *Sanhedrin* 5:5). Three scribes were assigned to the proceedings—one to record the arguments of those in favor of conviction, one to record the arguments of those in favor of acquittal, and a third to record both arguments, pro and con (Babylonian Talmud, *Sanhedrin* 4:3).

> If twelve of the judges are in favor of acquittal and eleven are in favor of conviction, we acquit. Twelve find guilty and eleven find not guilty, and even if eleven favor conviction and eleven favor acquittal and the twenty-third is indecisive, or even if twenty-two favor acquittal or conviction, and one is indecisive, we add two more judges to the case up to seventy-one. If thirty-six favor acquittal and thirty-five favor conviction, not guilty. If thirty-five favor acquittal and thirty-six favor conviction, they discuss one with the other until those in favor of acquittal can sway those in favor of conviction [or until there is at least a majority of one in favor of acquittal].
>
> Babylonian Talmud, *Sanhedrin* 5:5

Once an individual judge had decided on acquittal, he could not rule differently even if he changed his mind. However, a judge who had decided on a conviction could change his opinion in favor of acquittal, and it would count. This rule applied solely in cases involving capital offenses, further demonstrating how the ancient rabbis bent over backward to prevent execution and to make certain of the guilt of the accused in situations calling for capital punishment. "Cases involving monetary matters are opened with arguments for both nonliability and liability; cases involving capital offenses are opened only with arguments for acquittal. In monetary cases, those who argue nonliability may change their stance and argue liability; in capital-offense cases, those who argue acquittal cannot change their stance and argue conviction. No cases are argued on the eve of either the Sabbath or a festival" (Babylonian Talmud, *Sanhedrin* 4:1). Rabbi Akiva ruled that once a court has sentenced someone to death, the judges involved must taste neither food nor drink on the day of the execution, basing his ruling on the scriptural law forbidding Jews to eat anything mixed with blood (*Sifra* on Leviticus 19:26). The taking of life was not perceived as a light matter in the eyes of these masters of the Judaic spirit-path.

Even upon conviction, the execution procedure was set up in such a way that allowed for last-minute testimonies or evidence or change of heart on the part of the judges or the witnesses. The accused was led to the house of execution, which was situated a significant walking-distance from the courthouse, so that in the event new evidence arose, there would be time to halt the execution. The court also would assign someone to walk the streets, announcing the pending execution, so that anyone who had favorable testimony to offer could step forward and prevent the judgment from being carried out.

> One man was assigned to stand outside the house of judgment holding a scarf in his hand. Another was assigned to ride a horse at some distance within a range that allowed him to see the man with the scarf. Should a new witness come forward with favorable testimony on behalf of the accused, the man with the scarf waves to the man on the horse who then rides speedily to stop the execution. And even if the accused himself claims to have thought of some new evidence in his favor, they halt the procession and return him to the house of judgment. And this they do even if it happens four or five times. . . . And criers are sent out before him, announcing: "So-and-so the son of so-and-so has been convicted of such-and-such capital offense and is being led to the house of execution! So-and-so and so-and-so are the witnesses against him! All who have testimony in his favor, step forward now and testify!"
>
> Babylonian Talmud, *Sanhedrin* 6:1

These teachings certainly did not rule out capital punishment, but they certainly made it close to impossible to sentence someone to death, did everything possible to delay execution, and leaned toward every possibility of acquittal rather than conviction. In our own time, these rules would appear politically incorrect, albeit reasonably compassionate; two thousand years ago, however, they were extraordinarily compassionate, and reflect an attempt at wrestling a balance between respect for the sanctity of life and respect for the needs of society. On the one hand, someone was murdered, and the culprit who did it deserved to die for it, for deliberately taking the life of another and thereby also destroying all who could have generated from the victim. With all of our hype about the cruelty of capital punishment, we take life lightly these days. We have no right to take lightly the life of the victim or to take lightly the lives of potential future victims should the murderer succeed at escaping from prison or earning early release, situations we read about in the papers regularly. On the other hand, we have no right to take lightly the life of someone who may be innocent and who cannot afford attorneys as proficient as those from the D.A.'s office. And even if the accused is proven guilty beyond the shadow of a doubt, are we still allowed to take a life? On the one hand, who are we to take the life of a convicted murderer? On the other hand, can we endanger the lives of others by letting a murderer live?

The sixth saying of what is erroneously translated as the Ten Commandments—"Ten Sayings," in the Hebrew—does not state "Thou shalt not kill," but "*lo tirtzach*"—"Thou shalt not murder." Judaic law clearly allows you to kill someone who is bent on killing you. Your life counts, too, and you have a right to defend it even at the cost of taking the life of another, as long as that "other" is not an innocent bystander, but the very person who is trying to snuff you out. If I have moral license to kill someone who is trying to kill me, do I also have moral license to kill someone who has murdered before and would murder again, whether I would become the potential victim or someone else would? Judaism allows me the same moral license to kill someone who is trying to murder someone else as to kill someone who is trying to murder me. On the other hand, I am not allowed to kill someone if someone else has threatened to shoot me if I don't.

> A man appeared before Rabbi Abba Arecha (4th-century) and said: "The governor of my province has threatened to kill me if I do not assassinate so-and-so." Said Rabbi Abba Arecha: "Rather let him kill you than commit murder, for why presume your own blood to be any redder than that of the other?"
> Babylonian Talmud, *Pesachim* 25b

As mentioned in earlier chapters, virtually nothing about Jewish law is absolute. Every rule has its qualifications. While the detailed and situational qualifications for capital punishment are absent from the writ of the Jewish scriptures, they constitute the bulk of the text of the Talmud, which, in essence, represents the oral tradition that accompanied the written tradition side-by-side ever since the genesis of the written tradition in the Mosaic Code. Even the written tradition of the Torah takes pains to differentiate between premeditated murder and involuntarily manslaughter, carefully doing so in order to preserve the life of an accidental killer while also respecting the pain of the victim's survivors. In fact, the community was responsible for rescuing the accidental killer from any bloodthirsty members of the victim's family. And after it had been determined that the killing had occurred unintentionally, the killer was then sent to any one of several *ahrei miklat*—cities of refuge—designated for the purpose of shielding unintentional killers from possible blood vengeance at the hands of the victim's family (Numbers 35:11–26).

All these sources clearly describe a system of jurisprudence that raises serious questions about the contention of the Christian tradition surrounding the death of Jesus. First, no rabbinic court could have condemned him for anything he did or said, since even a cursory examination of the Talmud yields narratives about rabbinic acts and teachings that virtually parallel those of Jesus. Second, even if he had been indicted for crimes deserving of capital punishment, there was no rabbinic court in Jerusalem to try him. The rabbis had relocated their Sanhedrin court from the grounds of the Holy Temple in Jerusalem to the settlement of Yavneh as early as 23 A.D. since, like Jesus, they considered the Temple corrupt (Babylonian Talmud, *Shabat* 15a). Third, even if they had tried him in Yavneh, which would contradict the story in the Gospels, his trial would have been anything but the undignified mockery of justice described in the New Testament. The rabbinic court and the traditional Jewish community could have had nothing to do with his execution, which was clearly political and exacted by the Roman government through the hands of the collaborating Sadduccean priests at the Temple who held no power or station in the eyes of the rabbis or their pharisaic followers. According to Josephus Flavius, the historian of the first century, the majority of the Jewish population of that period followed the ways of the rabbis, placing many of the rabbis—not only Jesus—at risk of death by torture for the crime of insolence. "Whereas the Sadduccees are able to persuade none but the rich," wrote Josephus, "and have not succeeded in winning the hearts of the populace, the Pharisees have the multitudes on their side" (*Antiquities of the Jews* 10:6). The Pharisees, the sect to which the rabbis belonged—vilified en tote in the Gospels—are also described as being the most lenient among the sects of that period, *most notably concerning punishment*: "Indeed, the Pharisees do not practice severity in punishment, not even on occasion" (*Antiquities of the Jews* 10:6).

This chapter is not about Judaism in the first century, but it is about capital punishment in Judaism, and as such beckons to address the centuries-old accusation of deicide lodged against an entire people by a body of literature composed mostly by people who never met the man who they claimed was tried and condemned by "the Jews." Millions of Jews have died over a period of close to two thousand years because of the venomous libel that has, to this day, fostered hatred and suspicion of Jews among Christians worldwide. Easter continues, in most churches, to be a time to repeat this lie and inject fresh potions of poison into an unknowing populace, a strategic move by the early Church fathers in their campaign to wrest the new faith from the bosom of its mother religion, Judaism. Certainly the Romans could not be blamed, because the Church was then taking its universal root in what was evolving into the Holy Roman Empire.

> The writings that have been incorporated into the New Testament neither directly opposed nor found fault with the Roman regime except possibly the Book of Revelation in its cryptograms. Instead Christians indulged and pacified the Romans by projecting all of the latter's guilt and evil onto their vanquished foe. In one stroke the early founders of the Church attacked their rivals and made common cause with the Romans by identifying the Jews as a mutual enemy.
> Lillian C. Freudmann, *Antisemitism in the New Testament*
> (University Press of America, 1994), p. 26

Anyone who examines the teachings of the rabbis in Jesus' time will discover, to their amazement, a Judaism that would never have tolerated crucifixion, let alone a trial that would have taken place on the eve of a festival, let alone a trial for a capital offense that would have lasted less than thirty minutes! Most importantly, they would discover a Judaism that paralleled rather than contradicted anything Jesus said or did.

> It is a cruel irony that Jews, who were the victims of crucifixion, have been associated with the guilt of the cross in the New Testament and subsequent Christian writings. Crucifixion is forbidden by Jewish law. It was no more a Jewish method of capital punishment than were the gas chambers and Cyclon-B gas used by the Germans. To blame Jews for crucifixion instead of the Romans is comparable to later generations condemning Jews for the death camps and crematoria in which

they perished instead of the Germans who killed them there. In both cases—crucifixion and asphyxiation in gas chambers— Jews were the victims.

Lillian C. Freudmann, *Antisemitism in the New Testament* (University Press of America, 1994), p. 28

The Gospels' account of the trial and execution of Jesus contradicts everything ever written about ancient Judaic jurispudence.

Even though everything associated with Jesus' trial and execution was contrary to Jewish custom and law and consistent with Roman practice, blame was transferred from the powerful offenders to the vulnerable victims themselves.

Lillian C. Freudmann, *Antisemitism in the New Testament* (University Press of America, 1994), p. 26

Nobody was ever executed without trial, and trials for capital punishment, as the sources from that era clearly indicate, were extremely arduous—to the point that very few courts ever actually got to execute anyone, and those few courts who did manage a consensus for conviction that resulted in execution were called "murderous courts."

Where, then, does today's Judaism stand on capital punishment? It is no more cut-and-dried than it was thousands of years ago. Judaism does not seek absolute, one-size-fits-all solutions—not in its jurisprudence and not in its spiritual teachings. Life is dynamic, and each situation needs to be wrestled with, assessed, and examined independent of any other situation, regardless of similarity. This principle applies even more stringently to the question of capital punishment, as the ancient sources demonstrate.

There are valid arguments both for and against capital punishment, especially in a society such as the United States, for instance, where more people have been murdered cold-bloodedly on the homefront than on any battlefield. A country that is up in arms when women are being raped in a war across the Atlantic and offers little or no reaction to the daily rapes of its own women is a country that needs to look at its soul before deciding its stance on crime and punishment. A country that is up in arms at the news of four of its soldiers being shot by an enemy thousands of miles away and offers little or no reaction to the hundreds of its own citizens who are brutally murdered every day on the homefront needs to reexamine carefully its position on capital punishment for capital crimes such as murder. Before we draw any conclusions about whether or not it is moral to execute a convicted murderer, we need to look at some far deeper moral issues that are burning us alive as we stumble haphazardly at the doorstep of the twenty-first century. When we reconsider the morality of sentencing a murderer, we need to include also the victim who has died and the potential victim who may die at the hands of an escaped or paroled killer.

> Said Rabbi Tarfon and Rabbi Akiva: "If we were among the judges who sat on the Sanhedrin, no one would ever have been executed." Said Rabbi Shimon ben Gamliel: "Indeed, and you would have thereby also caused murders to increase in Israel."
> Babylonian Talmud, *Makot* 7a

The question of the morality of capital punishment is anything but black-and-white. It will tear us apart in our guts if we execute, and also if we don't. The issue is a double-edged sword, and all we can do is dance our best two-step upon it.

9

Ritual Implements

The religious artifacts described here represent only some of the many objects and symbols used by the Jewish people to this day, primarily in the home, so that the household maintains the consciousness of the teachings behind these articles, which are about harmony with self, other, God, and the planet, and awareness of the sacredness of everything and everyone. It cannot be sufficiently emphasized how important it is for Jewish households to possess all, or at least most, of these objects. They are powerful reminders to us of our distinct Jewish heritage and spirit-path, and a resonating experience for our children, most of whom grow up these days with minimal exposure to Jewish learning and experience.

MEZUZAH

This container has inside it a scroll made of sheepskin upon which are written, by hand and in natural black ink, ancient teachings about the unity of our diversity. Because the ancient Jewish people were primarily shepherds, the scroll is made of sheepskin. The writ begins with the declaration of the oneness of the Creator. The *mezuzah* is placed on doorways and gateways so that when you move from one situation to another, from one room to another, from indoors to outdoors and vice versa, your experience of transition does not splinter you psychologically because you see the *mezuzah* and are reminded about how diversity and separateness are but illusions because there is only one reality, and that is the one Creator.

In our day-to-day life experience we sometimes feel split, and we go from one emotion to another. The *mezuzah* stops us dead in our tracks and brings us back to our center. It is generally affixed on doorways throughout the home so that members of the family are always reminded of the Great Parent of all. In moments of anger or frustration, the *mezuzah* is a vivid visual wake-up call to the fact that "there is nothing real but God, so get it together."

TEFILIN

These objects are bound on the left arm (or on the right arm, for lefties) and around the head, so that the two boxes are on the muscle—the center of physical strength—and on the forehead between the eyes—the center of spiritual awareness, or the "mind's eye." In each box are scrolls on which are written the ancient instructions concerning the importance of binding together your physical actions and your spiritual thoughts in the service of the Creator. Judaism teaches that body and spirit are equal partners in this life, not that one is holier than the other. All the material used in making the *tefilin* are of the skin and leather of sheep, since the ancient Jewish people were primarily shepherds. Even the scrolls inside are made of sheepskin. The *tefilin* are worn after the onset of puberty, usually at age twelve for a girl and age thirteen for a boy; the first wearing of *tefilin* is part of a rite of passage for children into adulthood. Traditionally, they have been worn exclusively by men, with rare exceptions by women.

Translation of the Text
for the *Mezuzah* and the *Tefilin*
(from Deuteronomy 6:4–8):

Listen, O God Warrior!
The One Who is, was, will be, and Ises is the source of our powers!
The One Who is, was, will be, and Ises is one.
And you should love your Creator, the source of your powers,
with all the parts of your heart, and with all of your spirit,
and with all of your physical might.
And these words that I instruct you today should be upon your heart.
And you should teach them to your children.
And you should speak of them when you sit in your home,
when you walk on the road,
and when you lie down, and when you get up.
And you should bind them as a sign upon your hands
and they shall be as symbols between your eyes,
and you shall write them upon the entrance ways
of your homes and of your gates.

TALLIT

The *tallit*, or sacred blanket, is used mostly for prayer. It is wrapped around the worshiper completely, even sometimes over the head, so that the worshiper can pray with the sense of being enwrapped in the wings of the Creator. The fringes hanging from the corners were required on all garments that had four corners, so that all such garments became prayer shawls as well as regular clothing that the people wore. The four corners are highlighted by the fringes to remind us of the four winds that come from the four directions, and the teaching of each wind (Isaiah 11:2): the wind of the Creator to the north, the wind of awareness of the Creator to the south, the wind of counsel and balance to the east, the wind of knowledge and understanding to the west. The fringes of the four directions wave in our peripheral vision as we sway in prayer or walk about, reminding us of how life is so much bigger than our narrow view of it in the moment.

MENORAH

Menorah literally means "that which gives light," and is an
ancient and fundamental symbol of the Jewish people. Its shape
is that of the *moriah*, a sage plant that grows in the desert of
southern Israel. *Moriah* literally means "The Creator will guide
you." The ancient seven-branched *menorah* was lit twenty-
four hours a day throughout the year, as a symbol to the people
that the Creator's guidance is constant, and that the Creator
lights up our paths always.

Today, this ancient custom is remembered in the home by
lighting the Sabbath candles and by lighting the eight-branched
menorah, which is used around the time of the winter solstice
during the eight-day holiday of Chanukah. The basic meaning
of this rite is to remind us during the darkest time of the year,
or of our lives, that light will return. It is a ceremony about faith.

SHOFAR

The *shofar* is usually the horn of a ram, but may also be the
horn of an antelope. It is a sacred object of great shamanic
power that is still used today during the season of the harvest,
which is the new year for the Jewish people and a period of
introspection and forgiveness. The sounding of the *shofar*
evokes the parts of us deep inside our hearts that have no
words, yearnings and dreams that we are barely aware of and
that the spirit voice of the *shofar* calls to the surface of our
awareness. In ancient times, the *shofar* was sounded not only
during the harvest prayer, but also during battle, and also to
announce joyful celebrations.

HAVDALAH *CANDLE*

This sacred object is made up of several individual candles that
are intertwined in a single candle. It symbolizes the sacredness

of individuality and togetherness as separate states of holiness. Traditionally, the candle is lit at the end of a holy day, such as the Sabbath (Saturday) or a festival, as an acknowledgment that the sacredness of the back-to-normal routine is no less holy than that of the holy festival or Sabbath day; that all of life is sacred, not just the religious occasions and practices. Literally, *havdalah* means "separation," for it is the ceremony of acknowledging the uniqueness, the separateness, of different states of holiness, of different ways of being in sacredness, both in religious practice and in everyday routine living. The holy and the so-called mundane are bound together in this candle under a single flame. In this manner, the candle also symbolizes the Jewish belief that all peoples and all religions are special in their own ways, yet all are bound together as coming from and returning to the same Creator.

MEGILAH

Megilah is a scroll of sacred Hebrew scripture believed to be inspired during a spirit quest that usually took place over a period of many days and nights of solitude in the wilderness. The writings contained in these scrolls date anywhere from 2,400 years ago to 3,500 years ago. The people who went out on these quests were called *navi'im*, customarily translated as "prophets," but literally meaning "those who bring," since they brought the Creator's message to the people. Jewish tradition teaches that there were just as many female *navi'im* as there were male *navi'im*, and that all peoples are blessed by the Creator with their own *navi'im*. Some of the *navi'im* were also called "seers." These scrolls are, to this day, written by hand on sheepskin with plant dye and with the feather quill of a nonpredatory bird. The folios are woven together with sheep ligaments. The scroll can be any Jewish scriptural text from the Five Books of Moses, or the Torah, to the various Books of the Prophets such as the Book of Isaiah, or the Book of Esther.

KETUBAH

The *ketubah* is an ancient Judaic marriage contract instituted by the rabbis more than 1,900 years ago for the economic protection of women. The original text contains solely the voice of the groom promising security and support to his bride, and also promising her financial security from his estate in the event the marriage is dissolved owing to death, divorce, or abandonment.

Loose Translation
of the Original Aramaic Text
of the *Ketubah*

On the _____ day of the week, the _____ day of the month _____ the moon of _____ in the year _____, in accordance with the calendar reckoning with which we are accustomed, here in _____, be it witnessed how the groom _____ son of _____ of the family _____ declared to the bride _____ daughter of _____ of the family _____:
    "Be for me a wife in accordance with the customs of Moses and Israel, and I will in turn cherish and honor you, support you and sustain you, in fulfillment of the laws concerning the conduct of Jewish husbands toward their wives, to cherish, honor, support, and sustain you with sincerity and honesty. And in good faith of my commitment to you I hereby pledge onto you of my estate and of all that I own, plus food, clothing and other life necessities, in quantities rendered universally comfortable and sufficient toward your security should anything happen to me or to this marriage that would jeopardize your economic welfare. And I order herewith that you receive of my estate only of the best of what I own under the skies, both general and personal property, even the shirt off my back. And it is with this quality of commitment that I undertake to live with you as husband with wife."
    And the bride _____ daughter of _____ volunteered her consent.

Be it noted that the bridegroom has taken upon himself the responsibilities indicated in this marriage contract in addition to the required declarations instituted by the ancient sages of blessed memory in protection of the welfare of the daughters of Israel. As such, this contract is not to be regarded as symbolic, stereotypic, or inconsequential. Rather, we the undersigned have effected the legal formality of binding agreement between _____ son of _____ of the family of _____, and _____ daughter of _____ of the family of _____, by an instrument that is legally appropriate for establishing a transaction.

And everything is valid and confirmed.

Says: _____, witness

Says: _____, witness

THE YARMULKA

The *yarmulka*, or skullcap, is probably the most misunderstood of the religious implements in Judaism. It may come as a shock to many that wearing a *yarmulka* has no foundation in either the Torah or the Talmud, and not even the codes of Jewish law. It evolved over the centuries as a custom, which many unassuming practitioners later considered law, but a custom that arises out of misinformation or ignorance is invalid (Babylonian Talmud, *Sofrim* 14). In essence the practice was to cover one's head during prayer only, and some of the teachers would do so even in their daily routine as a conduct of piety. But it never became a law, and even as a custom it varies to this day from place to place. In some communities it is worn only during worship and sacred study while in other communities it is worn at all times. The entire question is best summed up in a responsum on the issue by the sixteenth-century Rabbi Shlomo Luria in his halachic treatise *Sheylot V'Tshuvot MaHaRSHaL* (No. 72), which translation into English now follows:

I do not know of any prohibition against reciting a prayer or blessing without a head covering. Moreover, the questioner insists that of course one would need to cover their head for sure when pronouncing the name of God, but I do not know from whence comes even *this* notion. And I found in the Babylonian Talmud that there is this dispute around how clothed one needs to be in order to recite the *sh'ma* prayer: "One whose knees are exposed, or his clothing torn, or his head is uncovered may nonetheless recite the *sh'ma*. Others say that with exposed limbs or torn clothes may one recite the *sh'ma* but not with the uncovered head, for with an uncovered head is one not fit to pronounce the name of God" (*Sof'rim* 14:15). And our master Rabbi Yerucham (14th century) ruled that "it is forbidden to recite a blessing with an uncovered head" (end of Treatise 16 of his halachic work *meisharim*). And if it were not for the fact that I am not accustomed to dispute the early masters, and if a great sage would side with me, I would be inclined to rule leniently and permit the recitation of a blessing or prayer without a head covering, even to recite the *sh'ma* without a head covering would be appropriate. For after all, there is the *midrash* of Rabbi B'rechyah (4th century), who taught:

> When a king of flesh and blood dispatches a royal proclamation, what do all the people of the kingdom do? They bare their heads and stand in great awe and fear, trembling and perspiring as they read the king's proclamation. But the Holy Blessed One says to Israel: "Recite the *sh'ma* for it is My proclamation. But I do not wish to burden you with having to read it standing up or with your heads bared" (*Vayikra Rabbah* 27:6).

We see from this teaching that there exists no prohibition against praying with an uncovered head, but that keeping the head covered in prayer is only because God, unlike a mortal king, does not wish to burden us with *baring* our heads. And what am I to do when rabbis over the centuries have already ruled that praying with an uncovered head is forbidden? But I am puzzled mostly by the fact that they have also ruled it a prohibition for us to walk around without a head covering even when we are not engaged in prayer. And I have no idea where they get the basis for such a prohibition, because the only source of any kind forbidding uncovered heads is the statement in the Talmud that includes bareheadedness as a violation of Women's Religious Customs (Babylonian Talmud, *Ketubot* 72a), but for men it is mentioned solely as a matter of pious conduct and only in regard to not walking more than four cubits with their heads uncovered (Babylonian Talmud, *Shabat* 118b). And even there it is discussed not as a law but as a conduct of piety as is borne out elsewhere: "Said Rabbi Yehoshua ben Leyvi, It is forbidden for a man to walk four cubits with an upright [proud] posture, for it is written 'The whole earth is filled with God's glory' (Isaiah 6:3). Rabbi Hunna the son of Rabbi Yehoshua never walked more than four cubits with an uncovered head, for he would say 'The *shechinah* [divine presence] is above my head'" (Babylonian Talmud, *Kidushin* 31a). We see from this talmudic passage that the only outright prohibition mentioned was against walking around with an upright [proud] posture, and that walking around with an uncovered head is not forbidden, only that Rabbi Hunna adopted the personal practice of not walking bareheaded more than four cubits solely as a conduct of piety (see also *Shulchan Aruch, Orach Chayyim* 3:6, where the wording distinguishes between proud striding [it is forbidden to . . .] and bareheadedness [and one ought to not . . .]). But these days it is totally the opposite: we are neglectful about walking pridefully—for on the contrary, the proud and the have-it-alls walk about with outstretched necks—but we are meticulous around the issue of bareheadedness! Moreover, our concern about keeping our heads covered has nothing to do with pious conduct but with our erroneous assumption that it is Jewish law and custom! . . . And I also found it written in the name of Rabbi Meir of Rothenburg (13th century) that all of this is solely a matter of piety, not law (Tash'batz No. 549). Nonetheless, the Rif (11th-century Rabbi Yitzchak of Fazi [Morocco]) wrote that we ought to discourage bareheadedness in the synagogue. Also, the Tur (14th-century Rabbi Yaakov ben Asher) did not require a head covering except for prayer, albeit not for the recitation of the sh'ma. Yet, what can I do when the people consider bareheadedness as forbidden. It is inappropriate that I then exercise leniency on the matter in front of them.

And I heard about a sage who would study Torah without a head covering, claiming it felt too weighty for him to wear something on his head. Nevertheless, even though there is no prohibition against bareheadedness, and it is not even a matter of piety when you are not pronouncing God's name, nevertheless a scholar ought to wear a head covering since the fact of the matter is that the masses perceive bareheadedness as licentious and as tantamount to a violation of established Jewish law and custom. And even to study bareheaded in the privacy of his own chamber is not recommended since one of the ignorant might see him and judge him as a transgressor. Not in vain did they teach that "everything that the sages forbade because it might lead people to think ill of you, is also forbidden in the most private chamber within chambers" (Babylonian Talmud, *Shabat* 64b).

And now I will reveal the abuse of the *Ashkenazim* (Jews of Western Europe). One of them who drinks the sacramental wine of non-Jews and eats fish cooked in non-kosher utensils—and the strict among them will not do this but will trust the cook to have cooked the fish in a kosher pot—is not suspected of transgressing anything, and he is given all honors due if he is a rich man. But one who is strict about eating kosher food cooked in utensils known for certain to be kosher, is vilified and treated as a transgressor if he walks around bareheaded!

Therefore, the eyes of the wise one is in his head, and he knows how to be careful that he will not be misjudged by the ignorant. And if it is too weighty for him to wear a head covering then he should cover his head with a covering made of light materials such as flax. Nevertheless, it appears that if someone wanted to recite a blessing over some food, and it is in the middle of the night when he is not wearing a head covering, or if he is in the bath, for instance, then it is sufficient for him to employ any kind of head covering whatsoever, even his hands. And even though a great sage ruled that using your hand as a head covering is invalid . . . according to everything I have written it is certainly alright, especially since we have established that bareheadedness is not forbidden, and that covering the head is merely a practice of piety, not law, so covering your head with your hand is sufficient, especially when it is done irregularly.

Index

ABOUT THE AUTHOR

Gershon Winkler is the rabbi of the San Juan Valley Hebrew Congregation in Durango, Colorado, and of Har Shalom in Missoula, Montana. He has authored ten books, including four works on Jewish mysticism, philosophy, and folklore, and was ordained by the late Rabbi Bentseon Bruk of Jerusalem and by Rabbi Zalman Schachter-Shalomi. His own journey of spiritual dissolution and re-emergence has brought him to a gleaning of the rich teachings from Judaism's lesser promulgated, non-mainstream ancient Hebraic and Aramaic texts. Rabbi Winkler is married with Lakme Batya Elior, and the couple reside in the Nacimiento Mountains of northwestern New Mexico, where they conduct wilderness spirituality retreats together with Native American shamans.